THE FONTAINEBLEAU

Based on a true story.

Paul S. Bradley
Robert H. Edwards

COPYRIGHT

Paul S. Bradley is a pen name for Paul Bradley.
© 2024 Paul Bradley of Nerja, Málaga, Spain.
© 2024 Robert H Edwards of Torrox, Málaga, Spain.
The moral right of Paul Bradley and Robert H Edwards to be identified as the authors of this work has been asserted in accordance with the Copyright, Design, and Patents Act, 1988.
All rights reserved.
No part of this publication may be reproduced or transmitted in any form or by any means, electronic or mechanical, including photocopy, recording, or any information storage and retrieval system, without permission in writing from the authors.
This is a fictional account based on a true story. Some names and identifying details have been changed to protect individuals' privacy.
Editor: Gary Smailes; www.bubblecow.com
Front Cover Design and Illustration:
Simon Thompson; sthompson01@hotmail.co.uk
Publisher: Paul Bradley. Nerja. Spain.
First Edition: September 2024
Contact: info@paulbradley.eu
roberthedwards54@gmail.com
www.paulbradley.eu

Approximate Currency Conversion Rates in 1974
1 US Dollar = 60 pesetas
1 Pound Sterling = 141 pesetas

INTRODUCTION

As the nineteen-year-old son of a reasonably well-heeled London bookie, I'd lived a charmed life without lifting many fingers. A beautiful riverside house, plenty of pocket money, an annual cruise, regular holidays, and being driven around in a luxury car might have boosted my ego. But provided little toward my path through life.

Was I worried? No, Dad had it all worked out.

How could I question his plan or disagree with his opinions on how the world worked when the fruits of his hard work were laid bare before me daily? My route to happiness and personal growth must be to go with the flow.

With the Conservative Party in its death throes, Dad's suggestion to sell up and move to Nerja, Spain, seemed an ideal solution. Lower taxes and a warm climate sounded far more promising than a cold, grey island crowded with misery. After selling his chain of betting shops and our primary home, we loaded up the Rolls and headed south. With my father's successful track record in business, how could we fail?

My parents' principal objective was to retire and enjoy the sunshine. Dad invested in a hostel business to provide an income. He would show my brother and me the ropes before heading off with Mum to sharpen his gardening skills.

I harboured no doubts I would be equally successful as Dad, marry a lovely girl, buy a luxury car, and enjoy a fantastic life in my adopted country. Yet, this transition to the sun-drenched but unknown eastern Costa del Sol was not without perils. A new language and culture presented unforeseen challenges and potentially dangerous misunderstandings. I was naïve to think this wouldn't matter.

Regardless of my almost comical lack of preparation, circumstances beyond my control were swinging in my favour. What I lacked in business acumen, I made up for in luck, but would this be enough to see me through?

The Spanish miracle that had fuelled rapid annual growth of over six per cent between 1959 and 1974, particularly in the automotive industry, was fading rapidly. The reliance on imported oil had ramped up inflation, but while Franco, the brutal dictator, still lived, the rest of the world viewed Spain as a pariah state. With little to no inward investment, his government would have to look elsewhere for foreign currency or run out of fuel. In this respect, Franco was smart. Tourism had kicked off on the Costa Brava and Marbella in the 1960s. In the 1970s, it was encouraged to expand rapidly. New airlines emerged to transport North European package holidaymakers to hastily expanded airfields in Barcelona, Alicante, Almeria, and Málaga. Mass tourism had arrived. On the coasts, Spain appeared to be booming.

The timing for our venture in Nerja should be perfect.

Shouldn't it?

HODSON'S CHOICE

Cedric Hodson may have been eight years older than my tender twenty but was neither mentor nor boss. We ran a part-time mobile disco called 'Narixa' and performed at private parties, weddings, and rugby clubs across West London. We shared everything on a fifty-fifty basis, but 'business partners' was too strong a description for our relationship. It was just something we both loved doing.

Cedric lived in a four-bedroomed pebble-dashed house with three others on a road parallel to Hounslow High Street in West London, near Heathrow Airport. I parked my beloved, but not so new, silver Jaguar 420G in the driveway behind his bright orange BMW 2002 Coupe. I jumped out, rang the *Rule Britannia* doorbell, and waited for the usual tardy response.

The depressing front garden resembled a scrap heap. Wrecked bike frames and a rusting Lambretta scooter with smashed chrome wing mirrors squashed a carpet of rotting weeds interwoven with the remnants of a few daffodils. The dark grey sky threatened an imminent April shower.

"Hi Robert," said Harry, opening the squeaking door. Harry was a short, ginger-haired man in his mid-twenties. He was dressed in his BEA uniform. All four housemates were pilots working one week off and one week on for the iconic airline. They were never present simultaneously. "Cedric didn't mention you were coming."

"He rarely does. We are off to buy some new speakers," I said. "He's in his room, is he?"

"Er... yes," said Harry, grinning. "Go on up. He'll be delighted to see you."

A trim phone was ringing somewhere, and David Bowie's *Rebel Rebel* was blasting on the stereo record player in the lounge. I trotted up the linoleum-covered stairs, wondering why Harry was so effusive when he was usually as quiet as a church mouse. I paused outside Cedric's door to admire the Narixa advertising poster. The two of us stood behind the sound system, wearing our trademark bright red mock military jackets, surrounded by adoring teenage girls. I knocked and, as always, walked straight in.

The untidy room stank of body odour and sex.

Cedric, a tall, well-muscled, mousy-haired man in his mid-twenties, was under the bed covers, lying back against the headboard. His freckled hairy arm was wrapped around a naked young blond girl, who was snuggling into his manly chest. She glanced up.

"Robert," she said.

I could have been the cleaner for all her affection toward me. She was, after all, Tracy, who, until this moment, I could have sworn had been my faithful girlfriend for over a year.

"Is this a joke?" I said.

"Ah, er... Robert, sorry, I forgot you were coming," said Cedric.

"Distracted, were you?" I said, clenching my fists.

"It appears so," said Cedric, blushing.

"Anything to say, Tracy?" I said, stepping closer to the bed and glowering at both.

"You know how I am with uniforms," said Tracy. "Especially flyboys."

"Joysticks, Tracy," I said. "Have always been your priority. Well, Cedric, thanks for your loyalty, mate. You have shown your true colours at last. After this, we can't continue working together, and you owe me. Tell you what. Your choice. Narixa or the girl?"

Cedric glared back and forth between the two of us several times. Tracy gazed at him, ignoring me.

"Tell you what, old boy," said Cedric, turning and putting his other arm around Tracy. "I'll take the girl."

"Er… fine, I'll pack the gear and leave. Goodbye."

I walked down the stairs, pulse racing. Harry stood at the bottom, his astonished expression staring up at me.

"Expecting a punch-up, were you?" I asked.

"I was hoping," said Harry. "The arrogant arsehole deserves it. Little does Tracy know, but she's the third in three days."

"Then they are well suited."

"What will you do?"

"I gave him a choice. The girl or the business," I said.

"And he took the girl?" said Harry.

"Correct."

"Mad bastard. Listen, Barbados is calling, and I must leave for work; otherwise, I'd give you a hand with the gear. I'll leave the door on the latch; help yourself."

"Thanks, I will."

"Nice to have known you," said Harry, shaking hands.

"Likewise," I said, heading out the door.

Adrenalin surged around my body, causing my hands to shake. Was I angry, disappointed, or hurt? I was certainly confused by this turn of events, even though half of me had been expecting something. My relationship with Tracy had recently cooled. Was it because she and Cedric had been an item for a while? Although finding them together was a shock, I now had a clean field to decide my future without emotional entanglements.

I opened the vehicle doors and, piece by piece, transferred the valuable equipment from the cupboard under the stairs. The well-practised routine didn't take long. I knew exactly where everything went, so it fitted in and didn't rattle around.

The main console came in a solid wood cabinet with a removable lid comprising two turntables, a pre-amplifier, and a mixing console with a microphone. A separate external amplifier fed two-meter-high speakers. A sound-on-light, a unit that fed off the pre-amp music signals and transferred them to mobile light boxes, which reverberated off the bass, mid-range, and treble frequencies. A few bubble-light machines created mysterious shadow patterns via a projector onto walls or ceilings and various lamps for special effects.

I was about fourteen when introduced to the emerging concept of a disco. On one of our many trips to Spain, we were heading to Andalusia and paused overnight in Tossa del Mar. A delightful unspoiled village in north-eastern Spain, where an English couple ran a disco in the basement of a hotel on the beach. The dolly bird wait staff had a white line stitched around the bottom edge of their briefest miniskirts, which, when highlighted in the dark by the ultraviolet bulbs, were mesmerising to a teenage boy seriously distracted by increasing levels of testosterone.

As soon as I had an opportunity, I formed my disco. I met Cedric when performing at a local rugby club, and he expressed interest in joining me in my venture.

Significant events such as the Watergate scandal and the Beatles' breakup rocked the world, while the rise of feminism and environmental awareness provoked a revolution. Our audiences crossed the spectrum of Britain's progressively diverse population. As music is an expression of the times, our collection reflected these global upheavals with the continued growth of rock, emerging disco, and punk for youngsters. With old favourites for grandmas at weddings, such as Frank Sinatra and Nat King Cole.

Within a year, Cedric and I had amassed over a thousand singles and dozens of LPs, which we stacked into a custom-made timber cabinet. A removable lid revealed the discs, organised in rows and subdivided into Pop, R&B, Soul, Rock & Roll, and Oldies. The cabinet was heavy and needed two persons to lift it, but pumped up after the bedroom confrontation, I managed to heave it into the back seat alone.

I returned inside for a final check and heard them at it upstairs. Tracy's orgasmic shrieks reminded me of when it was me pleasuring her. My heart skipped a beat. She'd not been much of a girlfriend, rarely said anything meaningful, and I knew she didn't love me.

Notwithstanding, I was fond of her, had grown accustomed to her kooky foibles, and tolerated her frequent demands for money. I'd given up counting how many hours I'd waited to pay for another pair of shoes. I don't know why I had been so generous with her. Maybe it was because she reminded me of Spain, where we had met. But why had she gone off me? Was I too tall or skinny, did my full beard tickle her neck, or was my long hair too effeminate? Perhaps Cedric had a bigger wallet?

I gave them two fingers, left their front door open, climbed into the Jag, and pondered the future while departing Hounslow forever. Then the heavens opened. I selected a cassette from my favourites in the glove compartment and inserted it into the player. I set the volume to max and sang along to; *I Can't Stand the Rain* by Ann Peebles at the top of my discordant voice. Breakup and lousy weather were appropriate themes for the mood, I thought as I put the car into gear.

I drove aimlessly westward, needing a diversion to rid my mind of its churning confusion. My ego was bruised, and my confidence dented. Sunbury should do it.

The windscreen wipers struggled to cope with the volume of water, and I could barely see where I was going. I turned onto Lower Sunbury Road, parked outside Dad's old garage, grabbed a telescopic brolly from the door well, and sprinted over the road, fumbling with the catch. As the rain thundered on the brolly, I headed onto the footbridge, joining the north bank with Sunbury Court Island, one of the few habitable islands on the Thames. I paused in the middle, leaned on the railing, and gazed at the old timber-clad family house halfway along the shoreline.

Our beautiful Italian speed boat bought at the Boat Show in London's Earl's Court, with the winnings of a 'Yankee' horse race bet Dad had placed, was still moored to the jetty. The bright red tarpaulin was now a dirty brown.

I lit a cigarette and let my mind wander back to when we lived here only two years ago. The chaos prompted by the oil crisis changed our world forever. With petrol now over 200 per cent higher, inflation rampant, and the UK reeling after three-day weeks, it was hardly surprising that the tax-grabbing Labour Government took office in the March elections.

My parents had seen this coming, sold up, and taken a massive gamble with a hare-brained scheme to buy a half-finished hostel in Nerja on the eastern Costa del Sol in Spain. For some completely unfathomable reason, my father preferred the thought of life under a brutal dictator against that of an inept bunch of socialists determined to bankrupt the country.

"At least we'll be warm when the lights go out," he said on more than one occasion to justify it to us.

My two elder sisters, Gloria and Diana, had chosen to remain in the UK with their husbands and kids, but the rest of us had elected to go to Spain. My difficult elder brother Jim wanted to stay, but he deferred to his wife Jenny and two children, Samantha and Jim Junior, who couldn't wait. It sounded like an adventure in paradise, and I was as excited as the kids. A few months later, with everything sold, we jumped into Dad's Rolls Royce and headed for the sun with great expectations.

It was a disaster.

The hostel was nowhere near finished.

The builder's excuses were generally plausible but always accompanied by another invoice for extras we had assumed were included. We soon learned our English-speaking lawyer was a complete tosspot and the meaning of mañana.

While we waited and waited for the next pathetic excuse and drain on our resources, life in our spacious, supposedly temporary apartment became strained. However, as the months ticked by, another problem raised its ugly head – money.

Lack of work permits prohibited us from working at anything other than the hostel. With no income, we quickly became strapped for cash. Dad clamped down on the usual free-flowing money supply to which we had become accustomed. We had to content ourselves with life on the beach without sunbeds and sangria, and I had to stretch out a single beer the whole night. Living in such close quarters with my brother and his family became intolerable. An invisible line was drawn between the fridge's contents to distinguish our food from theirs.

Inevitably, it brought out the worst in both of us, causing screaming arguments and the kids running off and crying to their bedroom to escape the bad-tempered atmosphere.

Our rented apartment was on the edge of town in the La Torna building located on the corner of Calle El Barrio and the early makings of Castilla Perez. There was plenty of room, but a football field wouldn't have provided enough distance between us to deter our mutual misery. Our life had always been comfortable and under control, but now I could see my parents' strain as the endless hotel extras somehow had to be paid for. I could only respect their resilience, but we could do nothing to help them. But somehow, we never reached the stage where we mentioned packing it in.

My only light relief from this domestic cauldron was the actress Yootha Joyce. She had an apartment in the same building to escape shooting episodes of the British TV Series *Man About the House*. She enjoyed a tipple or two of brandy but was always friendly and usually departed with a slurred pithy remark and half a wave.

Then Tracy arrived.

She was with her parents. I bumped into her in the lobby, and our first exchange was almost one of relief. Someone of the same generation and linguistic persuasion was nearby to relieve the monotony of constant parental supervision. I failed to notice then, but her parents must have been pleased she was off their hands. We quickly became an 'item' and spent hours walking along the beach, swimming, and the occasional pedalo ride. She tanned quickly and attracted admiring glances with her long blond hair, shapely curves, and tiny bikini. It felt good having her around, even more so when she invited me to her room one evening when her parents were out.

She was willing and enthusiastic. I was in Heaven and soon became a dab hand at negotiating the exterior balcony railings up to her room two floors above. Thankfully, after a day on the Fundador brandy, Yootha remained oblivious and snored loudly as I scrambled past her open window in my best Edmund Hillary fashion.

Life was infinitely more bearable with Tracy as a distraction from the never-ending hostel-building saga, but I could see my parents' confidence draining daily. Failure was something they had never experienced and were ill-equipped mentally to deal with, but they soldiered on. When Tracy's parents announced they were driving their American station wagon back to the UK the following week, I saw my chance at escape and asked to go with them.

My parent's attempt to dissuade me was half-hearted. I didn't mind; I was going anyway. Not just to be with Tracy but to free my parents from fraternal tension and be one less mouth to feed.

The journey back was fun but cramped. Tracey's parents were also on a budget, so we all slept together in the car by extending the rear bench seat into a makeshift bed for our overnight stops. Lying next to Tracy was, at times, embarrassing. Finally, we arrived back in the UK.

Readjusting to the cold and grey in a tiny bedsit in Staines in one of my father's rental properties was when reality hit me. After the sunshine, it was depressing.

I worked in one of Dad's old betting shops but soon had the idea for my discotheque and, within months, was making ends meet.

A particularly heavy burst of rain shook me back to reality.

This spot on the bridge used to be my therapist, a haven well away from Jim's snide remarks and insults, where I could chew over life's mysteries. It still was. The muddy water swirling downstream was calming, and when a piece of driftwood floated by, I wondered, like me, where it might end up. The treatment was working. My mind ceased its turmoil over Tracy, and clarity returned.

Ducks and swans glided regally among the reeds, the rain not bothering them at all; a water rat scuttled down the bank and disappeared into the greenery. As my short tenure on the island flashed before me – I recalled the exhilaration when returning home from boarding school. Picnics on the lawn, racing up and down the inlet in the boat, and the sadness when returning for another term in that awful place supposed to provide the best education money could buy. Some academic nerdy types thrived there, but not me; I was more the practical type. Nobody seemed surprised when I was asked to leave. I was sixteen, and an incident involving strategically placed spuds was the cause. The exhaust pipe of our Housemaster's Hillman Hunter had proved irresistible to my friend Chris and me as revenge for detentions received for minor misdemeanours. I was allowed back to take exams and scraped through a few measly 'O-Level GCE' passes. Life would have to be my university.

Thoughts came to mind about Alison, my first girlfriend. I could see her pretty face hovering over the river. She seemed so realistic that I almost sensed her soft blond hair and inexperienced, tender lips on mine. During my early teens, we'd met on successive annual family cruises and exchanged letters for several years, but regretfully, we had lost touch. Her memory stirred something within me, a thirst for family and warmer climes.

A sudden gust almost blew me over, exposing me to the storm. I was soaked to the skin within seconds but was more concerned about my tan-brown leather jacket. In the blink of an eye, it had transformed from a stylish fashion statement into a soggy rag.

"Enough," I shouted to nobody but the inclemency. "Spain, here I come."

I shook my head to clear the raindrops streaming down my face, flicked the damp cigarette butt into the water, watched it float away, and headed for my bedsit.

I reasoned it best to inquire if the hostel was ready and if I'd be welcome. Back home, I emptied my piggy bank, inserted most of its contents in the payphone Dad so generously installed in the hall, and dialled the number Mum had sent in their last letter. There was some noise on the line as the phone connected, and then, after what seemed an eternity, the ringing tone.

"The Fontainebleau," said a distant crackling voice.

"Mum?" I said after pressing button A and listening to a fortune in coins disappear forever. I pictured her standing in the hostel lobby, the phone jammed against her ear.

"Robert, how lovely to hear your voice. Where are you?"

"At home in Staines grappling with ten pence coins, I'll keep it brief. Have you opened yet?"

"Our first busload of package holidaymakers from Wings Tours arrived yesterday."

"How is it going?" I asked.

"Hectic, we completely underestimated how many staff we needed. Why? Are you offering to help?"

"It's why I'm phoning. I've had enough here. How about me coming down like now?"

"That would be something. Is there anything wrong?"

"No, but I'll explain when I see you. I'll be there in a couple of days, ok?"

As the beeps announced more coins were required, we said our goodbyes.

FAREWELL BLIGHTY

My father's property was off Staines High Street. Originally a four-bedroom Victorian house that had belonged to my grandmother, it had been converted into various self-contained apartments. Tom, the builder and friend of Dad, had skimped on the sound insulation between rooms. On completion of the work, Tom proudly announced how well-insulated the walls were. Dad challenged him to prove it, so Tom shouted quietly in the next room. Dad fell for it. This proved embarrassing when Tracy stayed.

Sadly, I was accustomed to the consequences of my father's do-it-on-the-cheap mentality. He might drive a Rolls Royce, but when it came to choosing good builders, it was out of his scope.

I stripped the sheets and tidied up the tiny room. There wasn't much, so it didn't take long. I walked into Staines town centre, dropped the bedding and dirty clothes into the laundry, and went to Curry's to purchase a high-tech present for my parents. Everyone was raving about them on TV, and it would be a helpful gadget at the hostel. I carried the sizeable, weighty package home and found a place for it in the Jag on the front passenger seat before adjourning to The Bells on Church Street. It wasn't my local pub, but the betting shop owner, where I worked most mornings, propped up the bar on his way home and, out of respect, I felt I owed him an explanation for my sudden departure. He was a dapper, short, balding, rotund fellow with a bushy moustache and the name of Reg. By the expression on his face, he was pleased to see me.

"Not your usual establishment," said Reg. "What can I get you?"

"Thanks, a quick pint of Guinness; I must collect my laundry before it closes."

"Going somewhere?" said Reg.

"I'm done here," I said. "I'm off to join my parents."

"I wondered how long it would take," said Reg. "Unlike your father and grandfather, you were never cut out for the Bookie Trade. Your Grandfather started taking bets at Kempton Park racecourse. He and your Dad were pioneers."

"I remember Grandfather was a Tic Tac man and wore white gloves. He stood by his blackboard near the ring where stable hands led around the horses so punters could gauge their fitness. Secret codes representing the odds were gestured by hand between officials and other bookies. Evens was also referred to as straight up. A Pony was a 25/1 shot, and A Century was a 100/1. When I was younger, I thought Dad ran a toy shop."

"That was just a cover. The real business was done upstairs. Before off-track betting was legalised in 1960, bookies disguised their illegal bet-taking behind a kosher activity. From his toyshop, your Dad had runners covering every pub, office, and factory in the area, including film stars from nearby Shepperton Studios. As soon as the law was changed, he was among the first to obtain a license. The toys went out the window; he stuck up a new sign and moved downstairs."

"Much to the dismay of model train lovers," I said, finishing my beer.

"I don't think he worried about them. As you know, the business thrived and expanded to the four shops I bought from him two years ago."

"Anyway, thanks for putting up with me."

"My pleasure, but you're right; it's time for you to move on. I only employed you out of respect for your father. I would have preferred someone dedicated to the long term, but let's shake on it, and I wish you luck."

"Thanks, Reg," I said, grasping his hand. "I only came to you because Dad suggested it. He wanted me to make sure you continued his legacy."

"Ha, he fooled us both. He always was a devious one."

"So, I'm learning."

"What will you do in the hostel? I mean, you can't have had much experience."

"Coincidently, I was a commie-waiter at the Connaught Hotel in Mayfair for a year when I was sixteen. I worked the breakfast and luncheon shifts, and it was a real eye-opener. One morning, Rex Harrison, the actor, came into the restaurant. I was serving him coffee from an antique silver pot when the lid popped, spilling hot coffee into his lap. He was surprisingly understanding, saying they needed to upgrade their silverware. I thought I'd be shown the door but managed to survive. Then, at seventeen, I ran the restaurant at the Magpie Hotel in Sunbury-on-Thames, which belonged to our next-door neighbour. We had a Turkish chef whose most popular starter was *gambas al pil-pil*. I might not be the Galloping Gourmet, but I learned a few things."

"Just as well. You'll need to sell bucketloads of gin and tonics to make any real money, and while I hope the hostel goes well, it won't be easy under a fascist regime."

"And Dad said it would be a snip after being a bookie. Cheers Reg."

"Bye, Robert. And Robert?"

"Yes, Reg."

"At least the weather is nice in Spain. Say hi to your Dad and tell him no. When the hostel fails, I won't be interested in selling him back the business."

It started raining again as I sprinted into the launderette, pondering Reg's parting words. Was the hostel doomed before it even began? Surely not. A fortnight in Spain with guaranteed sunshine was cheaper than two weeks at Butlins. Every other TV advert was for a package holiday abroad, and English resorts bitterly complained about the loss of tourists. Now we were open; it just had to work. Anyway, we had no choice; we burned our boats.

I brushed the negative thoughts aside. We, Edwards, never failed.

"I've even ironed your smalls," said the kindly lady behind the counter as she handed over practically every item of clothing I possessed, neatly folded into two plastic bags.

"You needn't have," I said.

"My pleasure, darlin'," she said. "Your girlfriend, or whoever washes them next, will be impressed."

"No girlfriend now. It will be my Mum."

"Never mind, dearie, a pretty boy like you, there'll soon be another one."

"Not where I'm going."

"Where's that?"

"Spain."

"Oh, you lucky bugger. Here it's pissing' down as usual. But surely those Spanish girls are gorgeous? All steamy and passionate. Know what I mean?"

"I agree, especially in those tight, curvy dresses, but when you can't speak a word of the lingo, you don't stand a chance of seeing what's underneath."

I left her cackling, ran back to the car, and squeezed the dripping bags onto the floor in front of the passenger seat. I took one final check of the flat, picked up the rest of my stuff, jammed it any free space I could see and was off.

I prodded an Otis Reading tape into the player and headed for Portsmouth as the opening refrains of *Dock of the Bay* echoed around the overloaded interior.

I had yet to learn how much petrol costs in France. Knowing my luck, it was cheaper, but I stopped just before the harbour and filled up the Jag. Ouch, I thought, handing over my newly acquired Access Credit Card to the pump attendant.

I drove up the ramp onto the ferry, parked where instructed, and entered the lounge. I stood at the window as the ship pulled out of port. As Portsmouth disappeared into the mist, I wasn't sad to leave my homeland—not one bit.

HOLA ESPAÑA

After eight hours of choppy seas, the Portsmouth ferry arrived at Le Havre in Northern France. My concerns about sound equipment and officious French customs officers proved unfounded as they waved me through with a disinterested frown. I headed south along Routes National, aiming for Paris, Lyon, and Montpelier. At the Spanish border south of Perpignan, there was a massive queue. Several hours later, I apprehensively handed over my documents to an alert official who prowled around the Jag as if he were about to pounce. "Que es?" he said.

"Jaguar," I said.

He nodded approvingly, returned to his booth, stamped my passport with a temporary visa, and I was through.

Winding my way down the coastal road toward Barcelona, I couldn't fail to observe the ever-increasing numbers of builders' cranes and hotels under construction. It was nonstop from San Feliu, through our old favourite Tossa del Mar, Calella de la Costa, and on to Arenys de Mar, forming the early makings of the Costa Brava.

The holiday brochures for our hotel in Tossa never ceased to amuse me. The front cover had been taken from the beach, with clean golden sand in the foreground and a sparkling white building nestling against a clear blue sky. However, they cleverly omitted revealing or mentioning the busy main road and railway line between the beach and the building.

It was noisy, dusty, and hectic. Even during this early season, bikini-clad blonde girls were sunbathing and playing volleyball as crowds of Spanish boys ogled their every move. I presumed they must be German or Scandinavian here for the Easter break.

The building work petered out the further south I drove and disappeared entirely after I turned inland at Alicante toward Granada.

All those hotel builders can't be wrong, I thought as Barry White's deep bass tones thumped around the car. Surely, we must be doing the right thing. The climate in Nerja is even better than the East Coast, with balmy winters, and our beaches are far more intimate and beautiful than these long, boring stretches of sand.

I've been visiting Spain since I was a young boy. Sometimes, we flew, but we mostly drove down in Dad's Rolls-Royce. The journey was an adventure, and the vehicle attracted many admiring looks as we went through populated areas. However, with many socialists and communists among Spanish people, some remarks weren't particularly flattering. Thankfully, we failed to understand most, but fist waving was not a rare occurrence. Perhaps they assumed we were hated landowners or friends of

Franco.

We had discovered Nerja quite by accident.

My parents had friends in Gibraltar, and before Franco closed the border in 1969, we visited them and took a day trip to the small town of Marbella. There wasn't much to see except construction along the beach. Those were the glorious days of Principe Alfonso Hohenlohe. A German Mexican aristocrat touring the Mediterranean coast not long after the Second World War, seeking opportunities to replenish the dwindling family coffers. The cigar lighter in his Rolls Royce was on the blink, and he stopped at the only garage to see if it could be repaired. It took longer than anticipated, but it gave him time to meet local dignitaries and discuss the possibility of tourist development.

The Golden Mile and Marbella Club were his first investments. Through his star-studded contacts, he attracted celebrities such as Stuart Grainger, Deborah Kerr and eventually Sean Connery, and somewhere wallowing at the bottom of the pecking order, Dad.

When I was thirteen, we chased hotels down the coast in the Rolls, racing against a hoard of Seat 600s with roof racks loaded to the hilt. Every accommodation we tried, from Torremolinos to Fuengirola, was fully occupied, but Marbella Club could accommodate us. There was a disco every evening, and while my parents imbibed at the bar, I wandered off to listen to the DJ in the ballroom. He was a young English guy imported for the summer season with long hair, high heels, and a shiny silver jacket. I stood close to his equipment, fascinated by how it worked, and asked him questions while the music played.

"Why two turntables?" I said.

"To start the next disc playing as the previous one fades. Nothing kills a dance floor quicker than a pause to change the music. Let me show you."

He placed the disc onto the turntable and cued it, ready for the next song. As the current one finished, he would lower the arm onto the waiting disc, fading the volume levels between the two.

"Listen, I need to go to the men's room. Would you like to have a go?"

"Wow, yes."

"These are the discs to play," he said, pointing at a pile of singles beside the deck. Just keep changing them until I return?"

There was no sign of him for twenty minutes, and I was worried the pile was nearing the end, but he reappeared just in time.

"Well done," he said. I felt chuffed with myself, eager to try again. "Come back tomorrow. You can give me a break and a chance to chat up some girls."

So, I did, and thus, the seeds were sown for my love of music and, later, a disco.

During this stay, Dad purchased a plot of land on the fringes of Marbella, intending to build a retirement villa. The price was incredibly low when compared with our house by the Thames. Several years later, when he was ready to go ahead, the Puerto Banus marina project was in full cry, so finding a construction company interested in giving us an estimate proved impossible. He approached the developers who sold him the land for help, but their only solution was to offer an exchange for a penthouse in Nerja, where they had recently completed the Parador Hotel.

We had never heard of 'Nerger', as we initially

pronounced the town. After a six-hour drive along a narrow and curvy coastal road, it was immediately apparent that Nerja was precisely what we had dreamed of. It was our ideal Spanish retreat: quiet, quaint, quirky, and much cheaper than Marbella. They bought the apartment even though construction had barely commenced. It was the beginning of our family love affair with one of Spain's most beautiful places.

Not much had visibly changed in the interior landscape of Spain since our first visit. The views to the left and right of the road while driving through France had been noticeably different. Lush green fields growing everything from grapes to garlic covered the terrain as far as the horizon. In Spain, there was nothing, just dry scrub, a few random olive trees, and scattered allotments on the fringes of each town and village.

Other than fuel and potty stops, I hadn't had a rest since hitting French territory. I was exhausted but stubbornly soldiered on wanting to reach Nerja in record time. Just outside Granada, I fell asleep at the wheel but woke in time to swerve back onto my side of the road. Thankfully, nothing was coming, but I pulled in and slept for a few hours at the next layby.

Some thirty hours after leaving Staines, I turned another sharp bend on the narrow coastal road near Rio de la Miel, and Nerja was in front of me. I pulled over onto a patch of rough ground and climbed out, my voice husky from hours of singing along to mainly Motown hits. While I puffed away at my umpteenth cigarette of the journey, I drank in the vision of my new abode.

The Nerja coastline differed from almost everywhere on the Costa del Sol. Stark limestone cliffs formed a backdrop to small, intimate coves where the blue Mediterranean kissed the sandy shore. It was an active fishing region, and at night, lines of boats bobbed up and down in a long line parallel with the coast, their bright lights often being confused with low-lying stars.

Nerja caves were rediscovered in 1959 by five boys who were out bat hunting. They fell down a hole, landing on a Neanderthal skeleton and 45,000-year-old ceramics. The caves rapidly became one of Spain's most popular attractions.

What appealed to me more than anything was the surrounding landscape. Only several kilometres inland, the Sierras Tejeda and Almijara mountains, over two thousand meters above sea level, defined a sense of horizon protecting the town against imaginary invading hordes from the north. Somehow, I felt safer here than ever in the densely populated city of my birth, where the most prominent landmarks were church steeples and stinking gasworks.

During the nineteenth century, a thriving sugar industry existed in Nerja. The ruins of several mills with tall chimneys to process the cane were dotted around the fringes of the town. Most of the plantations had disappeared, but remnants existed. One was growing right up to the edge of Playa Burriana, where Ayo, a flamboyant local character, had recently opened the first merendero - beach restaurant. Some of the earlier English residents, Ken Taylor and his son Chris, ran a water-skiing school in the warmer months.

The centre of Nerja was dominated by a promontory, The Balcón, as the locals had christened it. It earned its name thanks to a visit by King Alfonso XII. In 1884, after a massive earthquake, he'd stood among the ruins and issued a decree that this central area of the town was to be rebuilt and referred to as El Balcón de Europa. The broad promenade is lined with palm trees and projects over the Mediterranean, providing stunning vistas of the Sierras and the blue Mediterranean. On a clear day, the Rif mountains in Morocco were visible.

Most evenings, families strolled back and forth arm in arm, nodding and smiling politely at each other and often stopping for a chat. This centuries-old tradition was how boys and girls met each other under the watchful eye of their loved ones. This courting system was completely different from what I was accustomed to, as I would eventually experience it for myself.

Next to the Balcón stood El Salvador, the imposing Seventeenth Century Baroque-Mudejar church and bell tower. Some fifteen meters in front of the massive timber doors was the courthouse dwarfed by a giant Norfolk Pine tree roughly half the steeple's height. It provided shade to churchgoers. Opposite the courthouse stood the town cinema with cars parked in front. At the far end, opposite the church doors where the town hall used to be back in the fifties, was a picturesque open-sided building decorated with geranium pots. Arches on three sides provided spectacular views over Playa Calahonda, one of Spain's prettiest beaches, where the fishing boats parked up on the sand during the day—various buildings housed fishing nets, fuel, and spare parts for boat engines.

The beautiful actress Raquel Welch starred in *Fathom*, a spy film made in Nerja during the mid-sixties, with Anthony Franciosa and Richard Briers. There's a seductive scene of her slinking down the steps to Calahonda in the briefest of bikinis, surrounded by hunky, half-naked men. Juan Manuel Fangio, the Argentinean Formula One driver, also frequented Nerja. He was a good friend of the owner of the Balcon de Europa Hotel, which opened in 1963.

I stubbed out the cigarette and resumed the final few kilometres of my long journey. I wound slowly through the tiny hamlet of Maro and approached the outskirts of what was to be my new home.

A few signs of expansion were visible on the eastern edge of town: a new school and a development known as Pueblo Andaluz were underway. The Parador was visible from the main road, and a few large villas lined Calle Rodriguez Acosta, the road leading down to it. One of Franco's ministers was reputed to own one of the villas. The Guardia Civil's presence was more evident whenever he was down from Madrid.

The west side of town ended at Calle Castilla Perez, the north at Calle San Miguel and Plaza Ermita, where a few residential properties surrounded the municipal market and Ermita de Nuestra Señora de las Angustias. The population stood at around ten thousand, with about a hundred foreigners.

At Plaza Cantarero, I headed down Avenida Generalissimo Franco, which everyone still referred to by its original name, Calle Pintada, and turned left into Calle Alejandro Bueno. I parked up behind Dad's Rolls Royce in the cul-de-sac to the side of the hostel.

Finally, I thought, standing in the middle of the street and appraising the Fontainebleau façade. The finished product was far better than I expected. Three floors rendered with white pebble dashing, surrounding an open patio with twenty-eight bedrooms and en suite bathrooms accessed by galleried landings. Each window was secured with ornate black wrought iron bars and garlanded with colourful window boxes. The solid timber front door had a glazing panel to the side. A long vertical sign was mounted from the top floor to just above the main entrance. Hostal FONTAINEBLEAU in black text was on a yellow background, which certainly caught my eye. A separate sign for BAR was above the front window.

Despite my exhaustion, my heart soared.

Coming here had been the right decision. We just had to make it work.

WELCOME TO THE FONTAINEBLEAU

I peered into the small lobby through the glazing panel. What a difference from the builder's mess when I was last here. Opposite the main entrance, double doors provided access to the patio dotted with ferns in giant terracotta pots where the infamous blue fountain trickled gently. Another door to the left led into the bar. Picturesque floral-patterned tiles lined the floor, and the pebble-dashed walls were sparkling white. I spotted my mother, as elegant as ever, sitting behind the desk, tapping on a calculator. She didn't seem her usual jolly self, which concerned me. My grandfather's picture hung on the wall behind her. It was askew, a classic sign Dad had mounted it.

I pushed the door open and entered. She looked up.
Her loving smile lit up my world.
Dorn Edwards was an attractive, deeply tanned woman in her late fifties. She wore massive sunglasses and was dressed exquisitely in a sleeveless black dress. Her perfectly lacquered dark hair was cut to curl under

her chin.

Tracy was instantly forgotten.

I was home.

Dorn burst into tears.

I rushed around the desk and hugged her. She shuddered and regained control.

"Pleased to see me?" I said, concerned I might be the cause of the problem.

"Oh, Robert, thank God you're here," whispered Dorn into my ear as a man came in from the patio and stood before the desk glaring at her. "I desperately need your help with this pest."

Dorn smoothed the front of her dress, took a deep breath, and smiled before speaking in her best BBC newsreader voice. "Mr. Hancock, how may I help you?"

Amazed by her rapid transition, I moved alongside her and smiled at the diminutive, skinny man in his early fifties frowning at Mother through squinty grey eyes. He wore a white short-sleeved shirt with a row of cheap biros clipped neatly in his breast pocket. Khaki shorts covered his knees while long white socks disappeared up under the shorts. Plastic sandals and a white floppy hat completed the quintessential outfit of a particular breed of English gentlemen on holiday in warm places.

"Any news?" he said in a squeaky-clipped voice with a broad Essex accent.

"None, I'm afraid," said Dorn.

"What sort of hostel is this?" said Hancock. "I've never been so mistreated in my life. Now, when am I going to get my suitcase?"

"What's the problem?" I asked.

"Who is this?" said Hancock.

"My son," said Dorn. "Robert, this is Mr. Sydney Hancock, an honoured guest staying for two weeks with his wife, Gladys."

"Perhaps he could help discover where my luggage is. Nobody else has, only I'm running out of clothes."

"First trip abroad, is it?" I asked.

"Yes, but what has that to do with my suitcase? When we go to Southend, British Rail never loses a thing."

"Can't beat the Brits, eh? Do you have travel insurance?"

"I do, but I fail to see how insurance will help locate my suitcase, young man."

"Maybe not, but at least you could buy whatever you needed and claim it back."

"I want my specific case. It belonged to my grandfather, and the clothes to my father. We're talking irreplaceable family heirlooms here."

"The Wings representative is doing her best, Mr. Hancock," said Dorn, biting her lip. "They promised to ring me as soon as they've found it but rely on information provided by the airport and airline. It's in their hands, I'm afraid, and there is absolutely nothing I can do about it except wait for a call. Please try and relax and enjoy yourself. You are on holiday, after all."

"But I can't wear these again. They stink?"

"Have you anything you can wear?" I ask.

"The suit I travelled in."

"May I suggest you wear it this evening, and we'll run your er… beach outfits through our laundry."

"Good idea, son," said my father, squeezing into the lobby next to me and punching me lightly on the arm with one hand while holding the other close to his chest, covered by a large bandage. Jimmy Edwards was a tall, elegantly dressed man in his late fifties with greying dark hair and black-framed glasses. Yet this innocuous appearance belied a rugged interior. He had diplomatically handled all sorts while running his betting empire. The bullying tactics of arrogant lords, demanding actors, popstars with more money than sense and hardened villains washing their ill-gotten gains through his shops had failed to penetrate his thick skin. His hotel experience and language skills may have been inadequate but he more than compensated with people awareness. He ignored Hancock completely.

"Glad you're here. Every room is full, and as you can see, I'm hors de combat. We could do with the extra hands."

"What happened?" I asked.

"Spot of picture hanging," said Dad, glancing at his father.

"I accept there isn't much you can do," said Mr Hancock, irritated by the lack of attention. We will take you up on your laundry offer. My wife will deliver it later, but don't stop calling Wings. I want my suitcase, and I insist we keep the pressure on them. Otherwise, I'll be suing everyone, including this hostel."

We waited until Hancock was out of earshot before having a three-way hug.

"Are they all like him?" I asked.

"Thankfully not," said Jimmy. "Most are middle-class white couples mainly from East London because that is where Wings are marketing our business. They are pleasant, but some of their stupid questions stretch my patience beyond belief. I'll scream if asked again for directions to the Balcón de Europa. Are you here to stay, son, or passing through? Did you bring gold-digger or…?"

"Yes, I'm here to stay," I said. "No, Tracy is no longer on the scene, and I've brought all my DJ gear, the latest discs, and bubble lamps. I thought installing them in the bar should attract the locals to keep us busy in low season."

"Great idea," said Dorn. "It's a bit flat on atmosphere because Dad and Jim aren't exactly Mister Sparkling Barman of the Year, plus their Sangria tastes like old socks."

"Talking about me again," said Jim, standing at the bar door. He was a slender man of twenty-six with longish dark hair and the Edwards brown eyes.

"Oh," he added as we three separated, revealing me. "Check what the cat dragged in."

"Nice to see you, bro," I said with as little enthusiasm as I could muster.

"To see you, nice," Dorn and Jimmy laughed.

"Mum, Dad, please; no more Bruce Forsyth," said Jim, scowling. "The one thing I do like about living in Spain is the absence of *give us a twirl* on Saturday evenings. Anyway, where's it going to sleep? We don't have any spare rooms."

"We do," said Dorn. "Room three is being used as a storeroom for the drinks."

"Do me jush fine," I said, mock swaying.

"All you are good for," said Jim. "Women and booze."

"You're a married man and father now," I said. "You need to forget about the freedom us bachelors enjoy and get on with your paternal responsibilities with at least some pretext of enjoying it."

"As usual, no respect for your elders," said Jim.

"Three seconds, and they're at it again," said Dorn,

laughing. "Robert, you'll have to make room in the kitchen storeroom and move the drinks in there, but it can wait until tomorrow. Jim, fetch Jenny and the kids and let's have a quick glass of champagne to celebrate Robert's arrival before the punters return from the beach. Where did you park your car?"

"I didn't want to leave it too far from the hostel, so I squeezed in behind the Rolls. It's jammed full of my gear and a rather special surprise."

"Something along the jewellery line?" said Dorn. "Or even better, decent tea bags?"

"Or Marmite?" yelled the kids as they rushed in and jumped into my arms. Samantha was five years old with shoulder-length dark hair, twinkling brown eyes, and a smile to melt most hearts. Jim Junior was six, slightly taller than his sister, but with similar hair and eyes. His two front teeth were missing, and he spoke with a lisp. I hugged and kissed them both. They smelled of coconut sun lotion.

"You pour the drinks, Jim," I said, lowering the kids. "I'll go fetch."

Jim stomped off to open the champagne. Two minutes later, I returned carrying the large, heavy box from the front seat. I plopped it on the bar, ripped off the sealing tape, and heaved out a white machine with a window in the front door. Everyone gathered around, straining to see what it was.

"Duh, English TV doesn't work here," said Jim, popping the cork and spilling half the champagne over the bar.

"It's a microwave oven," I said.

"We have an oven," said Jim.

"It's the latest technology," I said. "It can defrost frozen food in three minutes."

"Ooh, it will be handy for our cottage pies," said Dorn.

"Amazing," said Jenny, Jim's wife, joining us. Thankfully, Jim had married a lovely lady in her mid-twenties with long blond hair and hazel eyes. She tolerated my brother's mood swings and was organised and practical. "Now the chef can batch-make everything in advance and pull out a frozen one when needed. It's a game-changer and the first I've seen in Nerja."

"Was it expensive?" asked Jimmy.

"Don't worry, Dad," I said. "My treat."

"Must be money in this DJ lark," said Jim.

"Can't complain," I said.

"Then why give it up?" said Jim. "Don't expect to make much money here."

"Now, Jim," said Jimmy. "That's not the way to think. We are investing time and money into building our business, which should yield a substantial capital gain when we sell it."

"I doubt much will come our way," said Jim. "Meanwhile, we are just cheap workers."

"Nonsense," said Jimmy. "Of course, you will share the profits. And don't forget you have a wonderful life here, a free roof over your head, a full stomach, and no commuting or stress. Your kids and wife love it to bits."

"Harumph," said Jim, scowling. "He's just another mouth to feed."

"On the contrary, my sound system will attract customers," I said. "Rather than go elsewhere, they will stay in the hostel bar and spend their holiday money with us."

"And most of them will stay up drinking all night,"

said Jimmy, rubbing his fingers.

"You catch on quick, Dad," I said.

"What's the secret to this DJ lark?" said Dorn.

"Lots of banter and powerful speakers," I said.

"Not too loud," said Dorn. "Otherwise, Mr Hancock will be complaining."

"Bloody cavalry arrives in the nick of time," mumbled Jim.

"What, Jim?" said Dorn.

"Champagne is ready," said Jim, passing the overfilled flutes around and slopping the excess onto the floor.

"Then welcome home, son," said Jimmy, raising his glass. "And thanks for the microwave."

We chinked and sipped.

"I don't want to leave my gear in the car overnight," I said, savouring the Spanish Champagne's crispy tang.

"Better safe than sorry," said Dorn. "If you rearrange the drinks cases, there's enough space in your room for tonight. Jim will help you bring it in."

"Jim will not," said Jim. "I have enough to do behind the bar and serving dinner. I can't do both."

"We can't tolerate such attitudes," said Jimmy. "We all pull together here. Robert has worked in two hotels and is far more personal with the customers than you or I will ever be, so he can take over the bar. You concentrate on porter duties, taking food orders, and waiting tables. We will help Robert unpack his gear when we've finished these drinks. He can set it up tomorrow and work on an entertainment program."

"Is Mick Jingles here?" I ask.

"He went back to England yesterday," said Jimmy. "But will be back next week. Did you think he could play guitar?"

"He's certainly improving, said Jim. "He's been practising for days, strumming the same notes repeatedly. He was driving us mad, so we put him in a room far from the bar."

"Shame, we could have had a Flamenco evening," I said.

"Discuss it with the chef," said Dorn. "He's bound to know someone."

"The chef?" I said.

"La Rubia," said Dorn. "He is er..."

"Like you boarding-school boys," said Jim, glaring at me. "You know, queer. A poof. Bent as a nine-bob note."

"Stop your bigoted crap, Jim," said Jenny. "The word is gay. La Rubia has more charm in his little finger than you will ever have, and his cottage pie is amazing."

"After three days of practice, I should hope so," said Jimmy. "Had to throw the first four batches out. While you're with him, install the microwave and teach him how it works."

"I'll watch, too," said Jenny. "Then I can speed up the kids' meals and keep me out from under his feet. He's a bit temperamental when I invade his territory. Who knows, such hi-technology might improve my culinary delights."

"Miracles can happen," said Jim, laughing.

Jenny scowled.

"Where is er, La Rubia?" I asked.

"He starts at seven, preparing breakfast and lunch. After a break, he returns at six for the evening meals," said Jimmy. "He is also an adept handyman, and with this building, we can't function without him. The electrics are capricious, the plumbing erratic, and cracks appear at will. Without him, the repair bills would be punitive."

"I see there's a dartboard," I said. "Have you thought of arranging a match with a local bar?"

"Great idea, son," said Jimmy. "As entertainment is your thing, arrange it when you want, but don't clash with the street market on Tuesdays or changeovers on Fridays."

"Next week is Easter," said Dorn. "We shouldn't have any raucous evenings while the processions are on."

"And Robert, you should be warned," said Jim with a snide grin. "A Spanish bar opposite called Bar Bilbainos opened three weeks ago. When they close, some of their drunks' stagger in here and cause havoc, pestering the young foreign girls. Thankfully, they are not aggressive, but if your music encourages guests to stay late, they won't resist the temptation. You'll need to learn to eject them as diplomatically as possible; otherwise, they'll end up dancing Flamenco on the tables."

"One more thing," said Dorn. "We had no idea how many English-speaking residents were in Nerja and the surrounding area. They seem to be adopting us as their place of solace."

"Which means?" I ask.

"The bar is full at midday and every evening from about seven," said Jim, smirking.

"Then we should finish these and unload Robert's car," said Jimmy, draining his glass and putting it in the sink. "There's work to be done."

With the sound gear stacked in my bedroom, I went behind the bar to familiarise myself with my new workplace. I hadn't realised the room was so small. It appeared much larger on the plans but was about sixty square meters. I immediately identified my mother's interior design touches. I approved of the plain brown sofas and glass-topped wooden coffee tables by the window at the front of the building. They complemented the floor tiles. The most obvious problem was the seven dining tables of four around the edge of the bar. If the hostel was packed and everyone came to breakfast simultaneously, there wasn't enough space to seat them all. We'd have to add more tables to the patio, but what do we do when it rains? Thankfully, that rarely happened in summer, and we would probably be quiet in winter.

The freshly varnished bar counter sat atop a brick and ceramic tiled support. Shelves full of spirits lined the wall behind; glasses hung from racks above. The San Miguel beer taps were in place and connected to kegs underneath. However, the taps took up more room than planned, and the small domestic filter coffee machine had a capacity of eight cups. "Totally out of touch with the needs of forty thirsty clients," I tutted. "Let's hope they all drink tea; at least we have enough pots."

To the right of the bar was an open passageway leading to the kitchen, toilets, and storeroom. A door in the cul-de-sac to the side of the building provided additional access. The dartboard with blackboard side panels was mounted on the outer toilet wall, but where would players stand to throw?

Through the double doors leading to the open-topped patio, comfy chairs were interspersed between bushy ferns. Several patrons were relaxing and enjoying the ubiquitous sunshine and the hostel's main feature, a large blue ceramic fountain. The water gurgled gently.

"Robert?" said a soft male voice.

I looked up from trying to work out the mechanics of the beer chiller to see a short, slender man in his mid-twenties with swept-back fair hair and blue eyes wearing chef's clothing, appraising me a tad too closely.

I nodded.

"Hola, hi am La Rubia, cocinero. Nice to meet you," he said in extremely camp, broken English, holding out his hand delicately. I was in two minds to shake or kiss it.

"Unusual name," I said.

"La Rubia is namenick for persons with fair hair. My real name is Dario, but nobody call me that. You is serious. What think you?"

"We haven't thought this through," I said, indicating the bar. "It isn't big enough to lay out the breakfast buffet. The coffee machine is pathetic, and there aren't enough tables if all the guests come down for breakfast simultaneously."

"I say same ting your father," said La Rubia. "But he tells me to make do with what we have."

"That's what he usually says when more money is required. What is on the menu?"

"Breakfast continental, peoples help themselves to bread, jam, ham, cheese and pastries, we heat croissants and top up coffee," said La Rubia. "Lunch and dinner menu is all English stuff. The beef stew excellent but hi not know how peoples eat cottage pie or fish and chips. Why they no want paella?"

"Plenty of Spanish food in the bars and on the beach," I said. "I can only assume my parents wanted to provide something familiar in the hotel to make the guests feel at home."

"Then why they come Spain?"

"You ever been to England?"

"Si," said La Rubia.

"You like rain?"

"Crikey, no and it ice-cold."

"That's why the English come here for a holiday, not for the food. Where were you?"

"Hi were in London working in Spanish restaurant. It where hi learn English."

"You went to classes?"

"No, hi 'ave English friend. 'e taught me pillow talk. Perhaps you also teach me?" said La Rubia gazing at me.

"We can learn while we work together," I said. "Maybe a Spanish girl could help with my vocabulary."

"Not so easy," said La Rubia. "Spanish girls difficult."

"Why?"

"They need chaperones, us boys not."

"Chaperones?"

"Si. You not allowed to take out girls on own, always someone like parent or friends to follow you about."

"Really? But this is 1974; surely those days are long gone."

"Crikey, not in Spain," La Rubia moved close to me, put his hand on my shoulder, and whispered into my ear. "Persons try break our traditional code of conduct disappear. I could be taken concentration camp just for saying you."

"You serious or just scaremongering to get in my pants?"

"Crikey Robert," said La Rubia, deeply offended. "I warn you this as friend. If you want Spanish girls, you must be carefuls. They not easy like English and obey parents all time. What bad for you is they keep knickers locked firmly for honour of family."

"It can't be as bad as all that."

"You will see," said La Rubia.

"Thanks for the warning. Now come into the kitchen, I need to show you a new machine I brought from England."

"Hi like machines," said La Rubia as we entered.

"Dad said you were a good handyman," I said as I tried to plug in the microwave and hunted around for an adaptor.

"You Edwards all same, you not think about plug when you buy this?"

"I didn't realise they would be different."

"I have adaptor here," said La Rubia extracting one from a drawer.

"Most practical."

"Hi learn from my father. We live in old house. Always something breaking. We 'ave no money so I fix."

"This is a microwave oven," I said, plugging it in and switching it on. "It cooks incredibly fast. You can heat a cottage pie in around three minutes."

"Crikey is quick. It means I don't have to guess how many we sell each day. Just take out from freezer when need."

"Exactly."

"Crikey."

CHAPTER 5

THE ENGLISH REVOLUTION

"Has Dad approved of your decoration project?" I asked, entering the hostel bar from the patio after my siesta. Jim stood on top of a rickety wooden ladder in the centre of the tiled floor between the dining tables. He held a grey plastic bucket in one hand, and a paintbrush in the other. He stretched to his full height to reach the ceiling, which he splattered with what appeared to be thin globules of wallpaper paste. It went everywhere. His aggressive arm movements caused the ladder to lurch from side to side, yet he seemed oblivious to the danger.

"I'm bored to tears with bare white walls and ceilings everywhere, so I'm jazzing the bar up a bit. Dad said it was fine to stick my favourite racing car posters on the ceiling and mount some pictures on the wall. Can you give me a hand?"

"Only if you help me install the sound equipment after."

"Fair enough, pass me, Brands Hatch?"

I gave him the picture of Brazilian Formula One driver Emerson Fittipaldi screeching around Druids Bend in a Lotus.

"Don't take this wrong," I said. But if we want to impress our guests, surely the theme should be flamenco artists, bullfighting posters, or Spanish cityscapes, not something they can see any day back home."

"I don't care what our guests make of them. These are for my enjoyment to help me cope with working in this place. I thought you liked Formula One?"

"I love it," I said, choking back a giggle as the Brands Hatch poster peeled ever so slowly off the ceiling and wrapped itself around Jim's head. "And I have no objections to your posters, but may I respectfully suggest they adhere more effectively if the paste is thicker."

"It's fine," Jim snapped, untangling the poster and reapplying it to the ceiling. He held the paper until it stuck, then brushed out a few air bubbles. "Next."

Eventually, the ceiling was half-covered with an overlapping collage of Silverstone, Thruxton, Cadwell Park, Mallory Park, Snetterton, and others. The floor, tables and bar stools were covered with wallpaper paste. Happily, the poster arrangement met with Jim's approval. He returned the ladder to the storeroom and staggered back with an electric drill and several framed photos, mainly of him racing Mini Cooper S cars around Silverstone, which he'd started when he was seventeen. He'd shown some talent.

The walls were rock hard and challenged Jim's hole-boring dexterity. Four drill bits broke, and the electric motor smelled burned out by the time he'd finished. The pictures were crooked.

"I see you've inherited Dad's skills around the house," I said, mopping paste off the floor and furniture while Jim stood in the middle of the bar and admired his handiwork.

"They are up, aren't they?" said Jim.

"Almost," I said. "Except for those peeling away at the corners."

Jim peered up and saw nothing of the sort.

"Damn."

"Didn't he do well?" I said, laughing. "Now, where can we mount the speakers and park the deck?"

Surprisingly, we laughed while transporting the gear from my room and discussing where everything should go. Within half an hour, the *Yellow Brick Road* album by Elton John was playing.

My Mum stuck her head through the lobby door and joined us, dancing for a minute or two. We took turns to twirl her around. Dad joined us, just like in old times back in our riverside home.

Dad checked his watch, turned down the music, and said, "It's time to open for the evening."

The mood swung to tense as my parents exchanged worried glances.

Jim stomped off to shower.

I mopped up more paste. Jim returned in black trousers and hotel polo shirt just in time to make the final tweaks to the tables for the evening session. The chef had prepped the food, and I had filled the ice buckets. At precisely seven p.m., the first guests of the evening came through the bar door rubbing their hands, eager for their first drink. They were a well-dressed couple, he, tall in his forties in a dark blue serge blazer and beige slacks, she a little shorter, slightly younger, in a loose blouse and skirt.

"A new face," he said in a well-spoken voice, holding out his hand and gripping mine firmly. "Charles Bishton, my wife Jean. Let me guess; you must be Robert, right?"

"Are you hotel guests?" I asked.

"Good lord, no," said Jean. "We're your first regular locals. We run an estate agency called INFO on Calle Granada. We pop in every evening on our way home and often at lunchtime, so you'll see a fair bit of us."

"Can you mix cocktails?" said Charles as they slid onto bar stools.

"Of course," I said. "I worked in London's Connaught Hotel. What would you care for?"

"Two dirty Martinis, please," said Jean. "It's been a heavy day."

It took a while to track down a cocktail shaker and olives, but eventually, I found them. I then made a complete fool of myself with a pathetic attempt to add drama to the occasion. I threw the gin bottle into the air, the idea being to catch it and then dispense a measure of spirit into the shaker with flair and style. I dropped the bottle. But kicked it back up before it smashed to pieces on the tiles, caught it, and poured as originally intended. Jim watched my every move, and I could sense his glee as the bottle hurtled to the floor. When my lucky footwork rescued the situation, he scowled, stomped off into the kitchen, and yelled at the chef. I continued mixing the cocktail, poured the drinks, added an olive on a stick to each, and passed them over.

The Bishtons took a sip and nodded their appreciation. They chatted briefly about the real estate business in Nerja before Jean excused herself. She attempted to climb off the stool, but it was firmly stuck to her skirt.

"Is this your new strategy to keep clients drinking?" said Charles.

"I am so sorry," I said, stifling a laugh. "We were decorating the ceiling earlier. Regretfully, my brother was a tad over-generous with the wallpaper paste. I thought I'd cleaned it all but must have missed her stool."

"Pass me a cloth and some hot water," said Charles. He dabbed his wife's backside with the damp cloth and gently peeled off the material from the stool inch by inch.

"Charles, darling," said Jean after several minutes squirming with discomfort. "Could you speed it up? Only I need to…"

"Hold on, dear. Nearly there," said Charles. However, the skirt refused to be separated from the stool as Jean wriggled furiously.

"Wait," shouted Jean. She turned back, grabbed the material, and yanked it hard.

The bottom half of the skirt remained glued to the stool, but such was her desperation; it ripped below her petite derriere, and she was able to grab her bag and sprint to the ladies, her damp pink underwear exposed. When she'd disappeared, we howled with laughter. She returned, suitably relieved, and bashfully twirled to reveal a safety pin had provided an acceptable level of decorum.

Charles, meanwhile, had separated the rest of her skirt from the stool and presented it to her with much aplomb.

She gracefully accepted and stuffed it in her handbag after a curtsey.

"How gracious," said another new voice as a man

of medium build and height joined them. He was in his fifties and spoke with a northern English accent. "I have no objections to unusual fashion statements, but may I inquire why half your skirt is missing?"

I stood waiting, eyebrows raised.

"Robert, this is David Rowcroft," said Charles.

We shook hands, and I put on another album—the Carpenters singles.

"Along with astute fashion awareness, David is also known as Mr Ten Percent," said Jean, pausing to hum. *It's Only Just Begun.*

"He is an accomplished Spanish speaker," said Charles. "Keen to introduce English-speaking newcomers needing help to his pool of friendly and capable Spaniards. Surprisingly, they are efficient and reasonably priced, so we use them regularly. His wife, Kay, teaches English to young Spanish children."

"She'll be along shortly," said David.

"Don't let the grey complexion, extended belly, and mild perspiration concern you," said Charles. "Like us, he likes his alcohol and, until around the fifth drink, continues to spout more or less intelligible sense."

"Now you've mentioned the elephant in the room," said David, chuckling, "I'm not here to discuss my shortcomings, admire the grotty new Formula One ceiling paper, or astound you with my repertoire of terrible jokes. As Charles so eloquently put it, I like my drink. Vodka and Orange is my poison. This is the only time I'll mention it. In the future, Robert, pour whenever you see me, but keep the ice to a minimum. It plays hell with my liver. Ah, there you are, darling. Robert, this is my wife, Kay. Robert is fresh off the boat and the latest member of the esteemed Edwards family to join us in our little patch of paradise. He's brought a stash of music, which I hope will brighten our otherwise tedious life in the sun."

I shook hands with the slender, well-spoken lady with an elfin face. She was smartly dressed in an elegant royal blue sleeveless dress, short blond hair, and sunglasses.

"We are easy clients," said David. "We both drink the same, except Kay prefers lots of ice. Her liver is more robust than mine."

"I look forward to chatting later," I said as the next customer pressed me for service.

The bar filled. Jim circulated menus and took food orders. I served three customers at once with pints of San Miguel when Mr. Hancock, dressed in a grey suit, barged his way to the front of the crowd. "I still don't have my case. Do you have any news?"

"As you can see, Mr Hancock," I shouted as beer froth spilt over the rim of a glass into the drip tray. "We're a tad busy. Anyway, the offices at the airport are closed so we won't be able to call them until the morning. Did you give your laundry to my mother?"

"Yes, but I still don't have my suitcase. This is most unsatisfactory," continued Hancock at full volume.

He kept blathering on and on about his luggage at full volume, completely unaware that the music had finished and the whole bar had fallen silent.

Deadly silent.

I served pints to another guest, noted his room number, and turned back to a snorting Hancock.

To my horror, two tall, burly, uniformed officers from the Guardia Civil were standing directly behind Hancock, towering over him and glaring at me. Their ungainly tricorn hats, tilted slightly forward, cast a sinister shadow over the top half of their faces. To their left was a mean-faced man in his late fifties with a scarred lip. A faded brown leather patch covered his left eye. He wore blue jeans and a black leather jacket with a prominent bulge under his left arm. All three were intimidating, exactly as Franco intended. Every customer watched them warily; you could hear a pin drop.

"As I was saying, I don't have my suitcase," shouted Hancock, failing to notice I had turned white and was looking over his shoulder. "Mr. Edwards, I'm not accustomed to being ignored."

I stared at Hancock and indicated with head and eye movements that he should turn around. "Is there something wrong with your eyes?" said Hancock. I repeated my eye movements, more exaggerated this time. Finally, something twigged. Hancock shook his head, turned, and glared at the officers. "At last," he said without batting an eyelid. "Someone in authority. Have you brought my suitcase?"

The officers were astonished.

The man with the eyepatch shoved his colleagues aside and stood glowering at Hancock as if he was a piece of something he had trodden in. Spittle dripped down his chin. He lowered his forehead until it was almost touching Hancock's. Hancock appeared unfazed by the invasion of his personal space or the man's foul breath and flying saliva.

Jim bulldozed his way through the crowd and stood by the officers. "C... c... can I help you?" he said in English. He appeared terrified.

An exchange of rapid Spanish ensued between the officers. Eyepatch handed over a piece of paper to me. I glanced at it and couldn't understand a word.

Wondering why nobody had collected the plated

meals for service, La Rubia joined us, grabbed the paper from me, and scanned it.

"What do they want?" I asked.

"The hotel, she must close immediately," said La Rubia. "You 'ave no hopening license. All guests pack cases; leave now."

"Is this a joke?" I asked. "And what's an opening license?"

La Rubia consulted with the officers. With each second, he grew more nervous.

The elder of the two officers talked to the man with the eye patch, who nodded and said nothing. He removed a notebook from his jacket and opened it while glaring at me. "*Nombre*, name?" he said, pulling a pencil from behind his ear and licking the point.

"*Por que*, why?" I said, digging deep into the shallows of my vocabulary.

The man with the eyepatch glared at me with pure contempt and opened his jacket to reveal a pistol in a holster under his arm.

"Robert Edwards," I blurted out.

"Que?" said the man.

"Robert," I paused, waiting for the man to write it down, but he did nothing but stand and stare at me, pencil poised.

"Edwards," I said. "Rob…ert, Ed…wards."

Eyepatch made to write it down but seemed to have no idea how to spell the foreign name. He scribbled something, turned back to the older officer, and nodded. The officer faced me and barked out his instructions.

"What do they want me to do?" I said.

"You m… m… make announcement," said La Rubia his knees shaking. "P… p… people must go now. If not, they go prison, you too."

I looked pleadingly at my elder brother.

Jim shrugged and turned away.

"Ladies and Gentlemen," I said. "These officers have ordered us to close the premises immediately. Hotel guests should pack their cases and leave; bar customers should depart now. Sorry, but I have no idea why this has happened or how to prevent this."

"But I do," said Hancock, hopping on tiptoe and shouting at his countrymen through the gap between the officers' shoulders. "Ladies and Gentlemen, my suitcase has still not arrived. It is an extremely precious possession, and I refuse to go anywhere until the Spanish authorities responsible for its loss deliver it here. There is no way a tiny town like Nerger has enough cells to accommodate all of us, so I suggest we sit down and don't budge until these gentlemen rescind their orders."

There was a general murmuring.

Hancock sat down right in front of eyepatch and glared at him.

"We're with Hancock," said a gruff, well-spoken Londoner, who, along with his family, joined Hancock on the floor and folded their arms.

One by one, every person except the staff followed suit, sitting with folded arms and glaring relentlessly at the officers standing in their midst.

The furious younger officer drew his pistol and slowly and deliberately pointed it at Hancock's head and cocked the trigger.

I assumed I was about to witness my first death, yet Hancock remained unfazed by the possibility of instant departure and continued glaring despite the barrel touching his forehead. He was British and, therefore, superior. The idea of a foreign police officer shooting him was preposterous.

For several minutes, nobody moved.

The Brits continued to glare at the officers.

All three aimed their weapons at the seated assembly.

A classic stand-off.

The police seemed perplexed when nobody dropped their gaze. Under such intense scrutiny from such an obdurate crowd, they shuffled their feet and, for the first time, began to appear unsure of themselves.

Hancock scrambled to his feet and slowly but confidently approached the younger officer. When near enough, he lifted his hand and, with a pointed index finger, pushed the gun barrel aside, staring directly into the officer's face.

I was terrified, aware of their formidable reputation, but as I peered around surreptitiously, my fellow citizens continued their protest confidently.

Ignorance must be bliss, I thought.

"Can someone point out as delicately as possible to our dear friends," said Hancock, now peering up the nose of the younger officer. He spoke loudly and clearly as if he was addressing a council meeting. "There are over four hundred thousand British tourists in Spain, with a further three million to follow throughout the summer. If you insist on us leaving now, this story will be published in every newspaper worldwide and broadcast on every TV station. It will cause an international incident. Nobody will visit Spain for decades, and the income of every hotel and tax revenue will plummet. How do they think Generalissimo Franco will react? Do they think he will sit by and ignore your shortsightedness? No, he is desperate for the foreign currency. I think it is more than likely that you will lose your jobs and pensions and may even face imprisonment. Do you want to be held personally responsible for this, or would you kindly reconsider your orders and let the lawyers sort the paperwork out in the morning?"

"Did you understand, La Rubia?" I asked. La Rubia nodded. "Translate every word, and don't hold back."

La Rubia stepped nervously toward the officers and blurted out the translation. For a moment, there was no reaction.

The one with the eyepatch exploded in a rage and waved his pistol erratically at the seated assembly. "How dare they speak to us like this?" he shouted, spittle flying everywhere.

The older officer calmly placed his hand over the pistol. "There might be a mistake here," he said. "I suggest we allow our superiors to sort this out tomorrow."

The older officer and eyepatch had a heated but whispered discussion. Franco's name was often mentioned. Gradually, the man with the eyepatch calmed down and nodded in reluctant agreement.

"*Mañana*," said Eyepatch.

"*Mañana*?" said The Younger, holstering his weapon.

"*Mañana*," said The Elder and led the way out.

Eyepatch put away his pistol, followed them, paused at the exit, and glared at everyone.

His exaggerated sneer of contempt at the seated assembly left everyone in no doubt that this was not over.

"*Bastardos Ingleses*," he shouted and tried to spit on

the floor, but due to his constant dribble, he lacked enough spit to form enough ammunition. What little he did manage to collect dribbled down his jacket onto his blue jeans. "Harrumph," he grunted, wiped his mouth on his sleeve, and headed out. I watched him as he entered the lobby. He stumbled against the wall and out into the street.

Glances of relief were exchanged among the seated gathering. They waited until Eyepatch had disappeared and scrambled to their feet.

"Three cheers for Hancock," said someone.

After the applause faded, I turned to La Rubia. "What happens now?"

"This nightmare. You disobey biggest shits in Franco regime. When people disappear, them three involved."

"Who are they?" I asked.

"Elder, Guardia Filipe Álvarez, other, younger brother, Javier. Everyone call him 'El Cuchillo.' knife. He scalp victims before burying alive. Man with eyepatch is Diego Cienfuegos, jefe secret police. A dangerous hombre. Notebook full of names of people he no like. When they disposed, he cross them out."

"What's with the eyepatch?" I said.

"He injured during civil war," said La Rubia. "He lost eye, took shrapnel in mouth and has balance problem but he still mean as shit."

"And now my name is in his book," I said, pouring a large Cuba Libre and gulping it down.

"Yes," said La Rubia. "You need watch out."

CHAPTER 6

A QUESTION OF LEGALITY

The Hancocks were the first to appear for breakfast at nine o'clock when the doors opened. They approached as I restocked the fridges.

"Laundry, okay?" I asked, seeing him wearing the same fashionable 1920s outfit as yesterday but beautifully ironed. The pens in the breast pocket were, as usual, perfectly aligned. Mrs Hancock wore an almost see-through wrap over her tiny red bikini. Her skinny legs and arms were bright pink.

"Fine, thanks," said Mrs. Hancock. "We're going to wander the market today and maybe buy a few clothing items for my husband. What kind of stalls do they have?"

"The market covers four of the surrounding streets," I said. "Last time I went, about half sold fruits, vegetables. The others provide everything you need and are amazingly cheap."

"I don't want Chinese rubbish," said Mr. Hancock. "Where is it all made?"

"Imported goods are forbidden," I said. "Everything is made in Spain. Even the typical tourist trinkets, such as giant donkeys, sombreros, or intricate metalwork from Toledo, including the enormous swords. But beware: you may have a problem taking one on the plane going home. They also have the finest leather goods in Europe. I bought a beautiful leather jacket for a fraction of what I paid on Carnaby Street."

"Forget the swords," said Mr. Hancock. "And the trinkets. Will the stallholders give us receipts?"

"Probably not," I said. "They don't have tills. Best to buy a receipt book from the stationers around the corner and have them fill it out for you."

"Oh," said Mrs. Hancock, crestfallen. "We don't speak enough Spanish."

"Say *Recibo por favor*, then give them the paper and pen."

"We'll give it a try," she said.

"If they won't, bring the receipt book here, and I'll write out whatever you need."

"Fraud," said Mr. Hancock. "We couldn't possibly…"

"When will you learn to shut up?" said Mrs. Hancock, elbowing him in the ribs. "Now pour us two coffees; we'll sit by the window."

"Harrumph," said Hancock, shuffling off toward the coffee machine at the end of the bar, where I heard him mumbling. "Everyone seems to break the law with impunity in this damn country. Plus, you can't get a decent cup of tea. Ugh."

The remaining guests drifted in during the next couple of hours, initially tired from the previous night's post-revolutionary celebrations but soon perked up after coffee and the prospect of a street market outside the hotel. Nobody mentioned the previous evening's run-in with the law, but it wasn't long before English humour prevailed.

"I'll tell you what's good for bartering behind bars," said one man regarding me. "Take plenty of cigarettes."

"And don't bend over in the showers," said another.

I grimaced but was far more worried about what El Cuchillo might do to me, remembering the gory scalping in Soldier Blue, the epic 1970 film. It was inspired by The Sand Creek Massacre of 1864 in the Colorado Territory. Buffet Saint Marie's soundtrack was haunting.

I closed the bar doors after the last guest had departed and began to clear away the breakfast buffet while Jim prepared the tables for lunch. We used wicker baskets for baked goods and fruit, which we kept handy on a shelf inside the kitchen door. Sliced meats and cheeses, boiled eggs, butter, and jams were stored in a kitchen fridge. When everything had been tidied into its rightful place, I joined La Rubia in the storeroom, where we spent the rest of the morning mounting shelves onto walls and assembling rows of free-standing grey metal ceiling-high racks.

It was like playing with real Meccano. After a few hours, we proudly surveyed our completed efforts and transferred drinks from my room to the store. At last, I could unpack my suitcase and take a shower. Dressed in a hotel polo shirt and black trousers, I joined Jim and my parents in the lobby. They stopped talking as I entered, but I was so distracted by the events of the previous evening that I failed to notice their tension.

"Ah, Robert," said Jimmy. "Jim has been telling us about the worrying events with the police."

"Have you spoken with the lawyer about my work permit and the opening license?" I asked. "Only my name is in the scary secret policeman's dreaded book, and I don't want to be arrested for failing to comply with their order."

"He wasn't in when I called," said Jimmy. "I've left an urgent message with his secretary."

"Fine, but do we have an opening license?"

"We must have," said Jimmy. "The lawyer promised to take care of the paperwork, and I signed many documents at the notary last week."

"More worrying," said Dorn. "One of the guests called Wings to complain we are operating illegally. They are sending their area manager tonight, at eight, to discuss the complaint. If we can't show him an opening licence, he will demand that we relocate guests to a legal hotel at our expense. Then they will strike us out of their catalogue and seek compensation for cancelled reservations and damaging their reputation."

"We'll be ruined," said Jimmy.

"And probably deported," said Jim, disguising a smirk.

"I don't know who complained," I said. "They seemed happy last night."

"Then why are the bar takings so poor?" said Jimmy.

"I gave them drinks on the house to thank them for their support, without which I would now be locked up, and this hotel no longer exists."

"Why did you give away so much of our hard-earned cash, son? We're a business, not a charity."

"Then why did you commence trading without an opening license?" I asked.

"What's done is done," said Dorn. "What's

important is to find out where the license is so we can show it to the Guardia, Wings, and the disgruntled guest."

"Don't tell me," I said. "Hancock?"

Dorn nodded.

The phone rang. Dorn picked it up. "The Fontainebleau," she said into the mouthpiece. She listened for a second, grimaced, and passed the phone to Jimmy. "It's tosspot."

Jimmy took the phone.

"You promised to take care of the paperwork," he yelled, then listened to the reply.

"What's missing, you ask," said Jimmy, calming down. "You're the lawyer; you should know what's missing. All I can tell you is that the police tried to close my hotel last night because we don't have an opening license. Furthermore, our guests deliberately disobeyed an order from the Guardia Civil and could all be arrested. Thanks to your incompetence, we are likely to be bankrupt, out of business, and, what's worse, my son could be sent to jail."

He held the phone away from his ear as the lawyer shouted back.

"Wait," said Jimmy. "You say we have a license, then where the feck is it?" Jimmy listened before responding. "We need it by this evening. The area manager for the tour operator is due here at eight p.m. If we cannot prove our legality to him, we will be struck off their list of hotels and forced to repay them and our guests. If, as you say, the mayor signed the license last week, it should be a simple enough task for you to get in your car, pick it up, and deliver it here by eight. Then, go to the Guardia and explain why we didn't have a copy. If all works, we may survive, and your account may be settled. If not, the police will be after you for failing to fulfil your duties as our legal representative."

Jimmy listened, his fingers drumming on the desk.

"No," said Jimmy after a few minutes. "It cannot wait until tomorrow. I don't care who you have an appointment with; this is resolved today, or we will see what the English media have to say about you and the risks of British tourists being thrown out of Spanish hotels because of a piece of bloody paper. Do you understand?"

Jimmy listened. "Do it," he screamed, slammed the phone down, glared at everyone, and smiled.

"Has he agreed?" I asked.

"He assures me there is no problem with the license," said Jimmy. "It was signed by the mayor last week, but our dear, wonderful, efficient lawyer was too busy to collect it or inform the Guardia. The license is with the mayor's secretary, and the lawyer will pick it up in about two hours, take it to the Guardia, and then bring it here before the Wings guy arrives. We should be ok."

"Assuming you can trust tosspot," said Dorn.

"What else do you suggest?" said Jimmy.

"Why don't I pick it up from the mayor?" I asked.

"If the lawyer hasn't arrived by lunchtime, Jim can go," said Jimmy.

"Why is it always me," said Jim.

"As yet, Robert isn't an official employee of the hotel company," said Jimmy. "It has to be you."

Jim seemed as if he was about to explode, barged past me, and stormed out of the hotel.

"Why is he so angry about collecting a piece of paper?" I asked.

Jimmy appeared embarrassed.

"It's not only the license," said Dorn. "While your unannounced arrival is a blessing and solves our lack of resources, we have three rooms full of family instead of paying guests. We've told Jim they have to move into an apartment. He thought it unfair they had to move, not you."

"Good idea and probably the right thing," I said.

"Why?" said Dorn.

"Some of the excessive bar bill last night was down to Jim. From his constant snide comments, he resented my arrival and drowned his sorrows in vodka and tonic. Living offsite will keep him away from the bottle and me. It should help us all."

Jimmy and Dorn exchanged glances. Jimmy checked his watch.

"Eleven a.m.," he said. "Time for the bar to open."

"Yes, Dad," I said.

I opened the door from the lobby, adjusted the wonky dartboard, and stood behind the bar. I hadn't even wiped a drip tray before the first customer said in a broad Scottish accent. "I'll have a pint and a wee chaser."

"Certainly, sir," I said, pouring the beer and handing it over to the ginger-haired, overweight, short man with a full beard who was sweating profusely. I was surprised to see he was wearing a kilt, sporran, long thick socks, brown brogues, and a lace-fronted white shirt.

"I'm Robert. What brings you here?" I said.

"I'm Ken. I've lived here for a few months and like walking around the market. I heard about you from Charles and Jean. I bought my apartment through them and thought I'd give you a try. Is the renowned Cottage Pie available this early?"

"Cottage Pie, Ken is available 24/7. Shall I order you one?"

"I'm dieting, so make it two, with a large bowl of chips and a gallon of ketchup."

"Certainly," I said, filling out a food order slip, taking it to the kitchen hatch, ringing the bell, and leaving it on the shelf for La Rubia to process before returning behind the bar.

"Aren't you a tad warm in your national costume?" I asked.

"After decades of freezing ma nuts off in Perth, being warm is the main reason I'm here," said Ken. He tossed back the whiskey shot in one gulp. "A spot of sweat builds a wee thirst, and I enjoy a good drink."

"Do you wear it all the time?"

"In bed, nay."

"You know what I mean."

"Market days and fiestas. It adds a spot of colour and is usually a conversation starter."

"I can imagine. You're not married then?"

"I was but she didna want to come oot here. 'Too hot,' she said."

"Here are your pies," I said as La Rubia brought the plate over and placed it on the bar.

"Wow," said Ken. "Super speedy."

"We 'ave microwave," said La Rubia. "It fantastico. Hi like your skirt. Pretty design."

"This," said Ken, hoisting up his kilt to reveal a fat, hairy thigh. "Is nay a skirt, and the pattern is a Drummond tartan. Have you never seen a Scottish kilt before?"

"Scottish no, but señoras wear them in Galicia, and play *gaitas*."

"*Gaitas?*" said Ken.

"I tink you say *Bolsapipas*," said La Rubia playing an air bag pipe.

"Bagpipes," said Ken, moving to a table and tucking his kilt underneath his backside in a well-practised movement as he sat down. "I'd assumed they were an exclusively Gallic instrument."

"Where you tink origin of Gallic?" said La Rubia.

"What?" said Ken.

"Galicia, Gallic," said La Rubia.

"I swore it evolved from France, but perhaps it was from Galicia. You could have something there," said Ken, sitting at a table—his expression dismissing La Rubia's historical snippet as nonsense. I'll eat here, and bring me another chaser.

By the time Jim had transferred Ken's lunch and drinks to his table, the bar was more than half full. Jim rushed around taking orders, I was hectic pouring drinks, and La Rubia was at full tilt. The microwave bell pinged every few minutes as more cottage pies were ready for delivery. I chuckled at La Rubia when he placed another pie on the shelf for Jim to serve. His expression conveyed disgust at such awful British stodge.

Just as well, he didn't attend my boarding school, I thought. The mushy spotted dick covered by lumpy custard would have him heaving into the trash.

A couple in their mid-thirties had pink faces and legs. They seemed uncomfortable, unhappy and wanted to talk.

"Can I help?" I said, pouring more pints, wondering if every market day would be so hectic.

"I do hope so. Er… we're in Room 206," said the man, scratching his peeling forearm. "The Baileys from Ilford, Essex. We'd like a Babycham, a pint of lager, and a spot of lunch. And, I wondered if you could help us, please?"

"Here's the menu," I said, passing one over. "What's the problem?"

"Stop scratching, Cecil," said the wife, tugging her short sleeves further down her pink arm. "We decided to give the beach a rest today, so we wandered around the market. I bought some sandals and a…"

"Tell him, dear."

"We were stuck in a crowd of people. They were gathered around a bar stool watching a man with three cups," said the wife. "You had to guess which one the ball was under."

"It seemed so easy," said Cecil. "One man was right every time and won a thousand pesetas. So, I had a go."

"It was a hundred pesetas a guess," said Mrs. "You had to pay in advance."

"I had twenty goes and didn't win a sausage," said Cecil.

"I told him enough," said Mrs.

"So, I stopped and bugger me."

"Language, Cecil."

"The next bloke won first go," said Cecil.

"So, what's your problem?" I said, serving beers to the next customers.

"Did we lose because we're foreigners, or were we unlucky?"

I found it challenging to keep a straight face, and explained. "The only winners are the stooges in the crowd. It's one of the oldest scams around the Mediterranean, especially in the markets. Sorry, sir, but it has nothing to do with you being foreign; you are just uninformed."

"Oh," said Mrs.

"Bugger me," said Cecil. His wife stared at him. He buried himself in the menu. "Fish and chips for me, please," he said.

"Make it two," said Mrs.

"Take a seat, and my brother will bring it over," I said, noting everything on their tab.

The lunchtime trade remained hectic, with full tables until the market closed at two. The kids and Jenny returned from school as the last client finished his umpteenth chaser. It was Ken. For the amount of alcohol he consumed, ordinary folks would have been crawling out on their hands and knees, but somehow, Ken stood with dignity and headed for the bar more or less in a straight line.

"I'll take ma bill just now," said Ken.

His rather loud Scottish accent attracted the children's attention. They turned and inspected him with fascinated faces. They approached Ken, who peered at them, struggling to focus.

"Why are you wearing a thkirt?" said Jim Junior.

"It's nay a skirt, laddie," said Ken, smiling. "It's a kilt, we wear them in Scotland."

"But we're in Spain," said Samantha.

"Indeed, we are," said Ken. "But it doesna mean I stop being Scottish."

"What's that?" said Samantha, pointing at Ken's crotch.

Ken looked down with a puzzled expression. "Och," he said, somewhat relieved. "It's a sporran."

"Ith all furry," said Jim Junior.

"Aye, it's rabbit fur."

"What's it for?" said Samantha.

"The kilt does nae have pockets," said Ken, opening the sporran and taking out his wallet. "I keep ma money and keys in it."

The kids watched, fascinated, as Ken settled his bill and tried several times to reload the wallet back into his sporran. He departed slowly and almost steadily. His absence left the bar unusually silent. I put on the latest album by Simon and Garfunkel and was humming along to *Sound of Silence* when Jenny came out of the kitchen and announced.

"Lunch is served, everyone."

Jim pulled a few tables together. The family and La Rubia gathered around, and we tucked into a cold chicken salad.

"Has the opening licence arrived yet?" I asked. "Only, it's nearly two thirty."

"No," said Jimmy. "I called the lawyer. Nobody replied."

"Tosspot," spat Dorn. "Completely useless."

"Shouldn't we press the button on plan B?" I asked.

Jimmy chewed on his salad and nodded. After he'd swallowed his mouthful, he said. "Ok, Jim, as soon as you've finished your lunch, head down to the mayor's office."

"They close at three," said Dorn.

Jim scowled but nodded.

CHAPTER 7

LICENCE PROBLEMS

Calle Alejandro Bueno is an unassuming street about ninety meters long, linking Calle Cristo to Plaza Cantarero—a delightful orange tree-lined square with a fountain and pergola covered by dense bougainvillaea. It was a tranquil place to sit for a coffee and enjoy views of the spectacular mountains. The nearest peak, Pico del Cielo, at 1508 meters above sea level, looms over the town some six kilometres from the coast.

Like most of central Nerja, Calle Alejandro Bueno was transitioning from single-floor buildings to apartment blocks, townhouses, and retail premises. The few remaining single-floor buildings had been built during the nineteenth century. Most of these had white-painted facades, a timber door in the centre, and a wrought iron-barred window on each side. The windows were shaded with faded green roller blinds and garlanded by colourful pots of geraniums jammed between the bars and blind. There was no guttering, but waterspouts varying from half-broken plastic tubes to ornate ceramic gargoyles projected over the street to drain rainwater off the flat roofs, often showering unsuspecting passers-by. Despite the fantastic vistas, most terraces were used to dry laundry, store collections of human jetsam and the requisite TV antenna.

Although new, the apartment blocks followed a similar architectural formula. This was the only construction style builders were familiar with, mainly because it was the cheapest and used materials available locally.

The recently opened Bar Bilbainos, a typical Spanish bar opposite the hotel with wine-red doors, was busy from morning until night. On the corner of Pintada was another hostel.

As I stood outside our hostel entrance smoking and appreciating the beauty of our neighbourhood, La Rubia joined me. I offered him a Marlboro.

"Prefer Ducados," he said lighting up his own. "Faster to oblivion."

"Do they play darts?" I said, nodding at the bar opposite.

"I doubt," said La Rubia. "Yours first dartboard in Nerja far as I knowses."

"Do you think they might like to learn?" I said, thinking as head of entertainment.

"Crikey. No harms asking."

"Do you know them?"

"Of course, it small town, everybody knowses each bodies."

"The guy in black with beret and crutches, what's that all about?"

"He Miguel," said La Rubia. "Him sixty-two. Left

leg missing below knee from Civil War. He refuse to wear prosthesis and use crutch to remind nationalists of their war crimes. He wear old black army beret, with five-star red badge to provoke Guardia Civil. Nerja used have many men similars but most dead now. My father and him good amigos, they fight against Franco together. If you want, I can ask him about darts, but you must teach them how play first."

"Then do it, but not Tuesdays or Fridays."

"Ok, I go tonight. Tell me, Robert. I need understand. I like working with you, but why your father buy hotel? He has plenty money and fancy car, and not need do anything. Everybody think he crazy."

"Have you heard of Harold Wilson?"

"No."

"He is the current Prime Minister of Great Britain and Northern Ireland. His Labour Party has increased currency restrictions and taxes on the wealthy to nearly ninety-five per cent. We came to Spain to escape those taxes and build a new life for the whole family, with the hotel as our main source of income. However, the hotel is also a sensible long-term investment. Thanks to your beautiful climate, low-cost hotels, and flights, it is now cheaper for British people to come to Spain for their annual holiday than to stay home. Over the next ten years, the annual number of visitors from Britain will increase by millions. Eventually, the value of the hotel will increase substantially. We are among the first foreign businesspeople, but more will follow, especially after Franco dies and is hopefully replaced by someone more internationally acceptable."

"Crikey, most my family and friends no understand this. We have no idea what happen in Málaga let alone Britain. We have state TV, which controlled by Franco.

Nobody believe what they say, so we only watch football. Rest is mierda."

"Believe me, tourism is the future of Spain. It's already happening around the Costa Brava and Marbella. It's only a question of time before it spreads here, and there are more like us."

"Hopefully, they not make same mistake you. Your builder, Emilio, he so bad no Spaniard buy from him. This hotel take so long build, we thinking the Gaudi Sagrada Familia Cathedral in Barcelona be finished first."

"It's complicated, but you're right; we assumed appointing a lawyer, buying property, and setting up a business would be similar to how it was back home. Now we know better, but how could we have avoided these mistakes?"

"Talk with local people."

"We didn't know anyone we could trust, so we appointed an English-speaking lawyer to represent us."

"He from Málaga and know nothing about Nerja builders or bureaucracy. It recipe for disaster. Always use local lawyer and speak with Town Hall first, they know who good and bad and where ok to build."

"Too late now."

"Tell me, why your parents live in middle countryside? What wrong with living in hotel or in apartment nearby so easy walk work. They drivings three times a day."

"They bought an apartment in town, but the builder went bankrupt, and it's still unfinished. For their retirement, they wanted a quiet place in the countryside. When the hotel is successful, they will step back and leave the running of the business to me and Jim, then they won't have to drive so much."

"Of courses they wills. What happen when forget toilet paper or want to eat in restaurant. They have to drive."

"It's the same in England. If you want somewhere quiet you have to drive."

"I understand but is fallacy countryside quiet. With dogs, cement mixers, tractors, and mopeds, it is loud like a town."

"Cement mixers?"

"We like to build. Whole of Spain is building site. We fed up living in old stone houses full of damp, no electric, water, or plumbing. Familias buy cement mixer before washing machine. Here comes Jim; he not look happy."

"How did it go with the opening licence?" I asked.

"It didn't," said Jim. "Only our lawyer can collect it."

"Wasn't he supposed to pick it up before three?"

"He may well have done, but they wouldn't confirm if he had," said Jim. "Shit, I hate this useless country."

"Are you sure they understood your Spanish?"

"Of course they did, you cheeky bugger," said Jim. "And listen, if you carry on digging at me, one of us will have to get out of here."

"If we don't get an opening licence by eight, there won't be a here to get out of," I said. "If there were anyone to kill to ensure we get our licence, I would do it."

"Oh dear, how sad, never mind," said Jim, gloating.

"Some of us like it here. My future is shot with no hotel," I said, heading to the lobby. "I'll call Dad at the villa and let him know. He needs to locate the lawyer quickly."

"You can't," said Jim following him.

"Why not?" I said, stopping dead at the lobby door. "Why have I never seen that before?"

"Dad locks the phone when he and Mum are out to stop guests ringing home and running up our phone bill," said Jim. "We can receive calls but not make them."

"What if there is a fire?"

"The nearest fire station is thirty clicks away in Vélez-Málaga. By the time they arrive, we'd have burned down."

"Typical, so I suppose Dad expects us to extinguish it ourselves."

"Let's hope we don't have to."

"So, we'll have no license to show the Wings area manager or the Guardia," I said.

"You might end up in the clink yet," said Jim.

I glared at him hard. The phone rang. I picked it up.

"The Fontainebleau," I said.

"This is Rupert Caterham, area manager for Wings. My plane was cancelled due to a French air traffic control strike, so I won't be able to arrive until tomorrow. I'll let you know when. Have you got your license?"

"It's been signed," I said. "We'll show you when you arrive."

"Good, then everything should be in order," said Rupert. "See you tomorrow."

I replaced the handset and grinned at Jim.

"What?" said Jim, scowling.

"The Wings guy's flight was cancelled," I said. "We're reprieved for twenty-four hours."

Jim stomped into the kitchen.

CHAPTER 8

NEVER ARGUE WITH A JCB

When the early evening customers arrived at the bar, I was drying glasses and humming to *Hey Girl* from the Temptations Masterpiece album. I turned down the volume and smiled at the rough diamond standing at the bar with his pretty blond wife.

"Ted Bartlett," said the muscular, dark-haired man in his late thirties wearing white trousers and a green and white shirt. Two fingers were missing from his left hand. "This is my wife, Joyce. We want to kick off the evening with a bottle of your best champagne. Afterwards, who cares?"

They burst into infectious laughter at their joke.

Joyce was a brassy blond with a curvy figure wearing a red dress covered in gold jewellery. They were both well-tanned.

"Let me guess," I said, popping the cork. "East London."

"Correct," said Ted, winking. "But say no more. We often holiday in Nerja, and when here, we like to escape from everything. We've been coming several times a year for a while now and have been looking for an English bar with good company, fine grub, plenty of booze, and good music. If we have a good time, we'll be back. Know what I mean?

"We'll try our best. I'm Robert Edwards, and this is a family business."

"Great," said Ted. "We like family businesses. They stick together, know what I mean?"

"Do you have a property here?" I asked.

"No," said Ted. "We always stay in the same rental in Nueva Nerja. It's far enough away to be quiet but near enough to stagger home."

"Sorry, but I couldn't help but overhear," said Charles Bishton, leaning on the bar beside Ted. "Maybe you should consider buying a property; prices are low now, especially for cash buyers. When Franco dies, they're only going to go up,"

Ted turned to face this new source of information.

"Estate Agent?" he said.

"How did you guess," said Charles, extracting a card and proffering it to Ted. "Charles Bishton. My wife, Jean, will be along in a minute. We run INFO on Calle Granada. If we can help, give us a shout."

"How long have you been here, Charles?" said Ted.

"Five years this May," said Charles. "Why?"

Ted nodded. "You must have sold a fair few properties in that time?"

"Er…yes, we've had a good run, Charles said, counting on his fingers and muttering names. "Probably around thirty or so."

"Thirty," said Ted as I watched, unsure which way this was heading.

"Maybe more," said Charles.

"And at what commission?" asked Ted.

"For used properties, eight to ten per cent," said Charles, his face tightening. For new properties, we can get up to twenty."

"Twenty, wow. Then...," said Ted as Jean arrived and clasped her husband's arm.

"What?" said Charles as Ted reached for the champagne bottle sitting in its cooler on the bar. He pulled it out of the ice.

"Robert, two more glasses, please," said Ted.

Charles's face was puzzled as he watched Ted. He shrugged at his wife.

Ted poured two glasses of sparkling wine, emptying the bottle. He picked up the two fizzing flutes and placed them on the bar before the Bishton's. "Well, I think congratulations are in order," said Ted with a huge grin. "Let's drink to your success: bottoms up. Shall we leave Robert to his work and move to the sofas by the window? I want to hear about how you made it all a success."

"My pleasure," said Charles, relieved. "Come along, dear."

"Bring another bottle, please, Robert," said Ted loudly.

I delivered yet another and turned up the music. They took a sip and clinked glasses.

By the third bottle, they were in full swing. Ted and Jean started dancing.

The rest of the bar joined in.

At two a.m. in the morning, Charles staggered up to the bar.

"I'd like to pay the bill for all of ush, please," he slurred.

"Already paid by Ted," I said.

"Oh," said Charles. "How, er, how generous; I'll fetch the car and take them home."

"Er…, Charles, perhaps I should order a taxi?" I asked. "Or would you prefer I give you all a lift home?"

"No, no, I'll be jack in a biffy," said Charles, staggering back to the sofa where the others were emptying their glasses. "Wait for me in the schobby, and I'll pick you up lortly."

While Charles tottered outside, the others collected their belongings and stood giggling by the front door. Ten minutes later, Charles returned limping.

"Darling, what the matter?" asked Jean, rushing to steady him. "Where's the car?"

"Crit of a bash," he mumbled.

"Where?" said Ted, knocking on the lobby door to attract my attention.

"Jush round corner," said Charles.

"What's up," I said, bursting through the door, having heard the commotion.

"Crit of a bash," said Charles, waving his arm, indicating we should follow. Charles shoved the exit door and nearly fell into the street.

Ted watched, concerned.

"We'll skip the ride home," said Ted as he and Joyce headed toward Plaza Cantarero. "See you another time."

"Thish way," said Charles swaying back and forth.

We followed him, concerned, as he turned the corner and swayed up the street. In Calle Cristo, vehicles were parked on both sides. Some fifty meters up, Charles stopped in the middle of the road and indicated his car, a Citroen GS, parked in front of us with the engine ticking over.

"Oh my God," shrieked Jean. "How on earth?"

Charles swayed. The arm movement to maintain his balance was too much, and he fell over. Jean rushed to him, but he was fine. She heaved him up where he stood, swaying and pointing at his car. The driver's door was swinging from the bucket of a JCB. He'd seriously misjudged the gap as he drove by.

I climbed into the Citroen, returned it to where it was parked initially, and turned off the engine. Jean and I wrenched the door from the JCB and placed it alongside the gaping hole where the driver's door used to be.

"Come back to the bar," I said. "I'll order a taxi to take you home."

"Thanks, Robert," said Jean, giving me a peck on the cheek. "Come on, dear.

"Get the keys," said Charles, still staggering.

"Why the keys?" I said, shaking my head.

"Sho noone will shteal it," said Charles.

"You should be so lucky," I said.

I helped them both into the taxi and finished preparing the bar. When the breakfast items were in place, I took a final inspection, nodded with satisfaction, and went to bed, where I tossed and turned for hours.

My mind was busy exploring the possibilities of tomorrow. Would we still have a hotel, or would I be in jail?"

CHAPTER 9

HANCOCK'S HALF-HOUR

Mine was an internal room, and the only window provided views of the patio. After my morning shower, I pulled back the curtains to see the blue fountain trickling quietly in its centre. My mother loved this main feature and relished turning it on every morning and off at night. It was her baby and the inspiration behind our Spanish venture's name. I remember the discussion as if it were yesterday. We wanted a name that projected the image of a romantic holiday. Blue Fountain sounded like a motorway service station in English, and Fuente Azul in Spanish didn't tick any boxes. Then Mum remembered that when we visited Miami, the hotel we stayed in was The Fontainebleau. It rang so much better in French, so The Fontainebleau it was.

The fountain hadn't always behaved so gently.

Dear Emilio de Miguel, our builder, hadn't wired the pump correctly, so on first use, it gurgled, spat a giant jet of water two meters high, and then cut off the electricity. It was one of his many failings, but his worst was the electrical distribution board.

One wasn't powerful enough to simultaneously power the kitchen oven and air-conditioning. Under the threat of violence, Emilio had agreed to install a second circuit. Most technicians were still learning to work with higher voltages as Spain moved from the old 120 to the new 240 volts. As usual, Emilio's excuses were plausible, and the consequences were expensive, but our main complaint was that he was so slow. The second circuit was up and running only the day before we opened and continued to be the source of mysterious power outages in the middle of dinner.

Every time Dad passed the fountain, he scowled. It wasn't solely because it reminded him of the delays and extra costs he'd endured before we opened. What enraged him was what an idiot he would seem when telling his fellow bookies at their annual dinner in Mayfair.

I quickly realised that running a family hotel wasn't just about a functioning building, friendly service and clean rooms. We were only as good as well-organised logistics and reliable suppliers. Toilet rolls, for example. Although they are an inexpensive, readily available commodity, running out of stock can quickly happen with dire consequences. But there was always an alternative if we ran dry of whiskey. My mother was responsible for monitoring the stock levels of everything except the bar, which fell to me. She left her list on the lobby desk before heading home each evening, and I phoned them through to our regular suppliers the following day as soon as the phone was unlocked. Without this daily task, our hotel would quickly grind to a halt. So, there I was, as usual, sitting at the reception desk in the lobby, filling out paperwork for the orders when the phone rang.

"Fontainebleau," I said.

"Robert?" said a female voice.

"Yes."

"This is Sharon from the Wings office in Málaga airport. We have located Mr. Hancock's suitcase; it's at our office. Regrettably, because it is old, it hasn't withstood the ravages of baggage handlers. The lock broke, and everything fell out. We've packaged everything up as best we can but had a problem with a crumpled cardboard box. It was unusable, so we wrapped the contents in elastic bands and stuffed them in a shopping bag. I hope we didn't damage anything."

"Anything delicate in the crumpled box?"

"Er..., a bit embarrassing."

"Go on."

"Don't get me wrong because I'm no expert," said Sharon, trying to stifle a giggle. "But to me, they resemble sex toys."

I howled. Sharon joined me.

"Is it," said Sharon, trying to talk but forced to stop for another bout of giggling. "Is it, er… is it worth sending er... the case over to you, or shall we keep it for him to collect on his way home tomorrow?"

"Good question," I said, a plan taking shape in my mind. "Give me your number. I'll have a word with him and call you back."

Sharon dictated the number, and I scribbled it down on the notepad.

"Thanks, Sharon," I said. "Oh, one more thing, when does Rupert's plane arrive?"

"We suspect this afternoon but haven't been informed of anything definite. These strikes in France are causing havoc with our timetable."

"Really? That is good news. Thanks. Bye."

"Who was on the phone?" said Jimmy, barging in the front door with a big scowl. Dorn followed. Jimmy unlocked the phone as if he were giving away his life savings to a taxman.

"Wings," I said. "They have Chummy's suitcase. The other good news is that the area manager won't arrive until this evening. Do we have the case delivered here, or shall we leave it at the airport to be collected on his way home tomorrow?"

"Not sure," said Jimmy. "What do you think?"

"I think we have an opportunity to win back Hancock's approval," I said. "He might even withdraw his complaint."

"Go on," said Dorn.

"Why don't I offer to take them to the airport in the Rolls and then on to lunch at the historic Café Central? Rupert would have seen the opening licence by the time we are back here and hopefully approved our continuation in the Wings brochure. We can show it to Hancock and offer him a free week here at the end of the season as a gesture of goodwill. It will confirm we have no hard feelings about his complaint and are grateful for his role in keeping the police at bay?"

"Not comfortable with the free week," said Jimmy. "And for the way he keeps upsetting your mother, I'd rather string him up from the nearest lamppost. But I suppose you're right, son. Good idea. Have they gone out yet?"

"No, they've just finished breakfast."

"Then knock on their door and extend the invitation," said Jimmy, handing over the car keys. "Put a suit on so people will think you are their chauffeur."

"Ok," I said, heading off to my room. "Will you finish off the breakfasts and run the lunchtime bar? Only it's Jim and Jenny's day off."

"Fine, go," said Dorn.

I headed off but remembered the reason why Rupert was coming. I popped my head around the lobby entrance. "Do we know for sure when the opening licence will arrive?"

Dad stared at me long and hard. "The opening licence is not your problem, don't worry about it."

"Dad, it is my problem as much as yours. My future is here in Spain, and I don't intend to return to the UK. So, make sure you get the damn license in time for Rupert, ok?"

I ran upstairs and knocked on Hancock's door. Mrs Hancock opened it wearing a skimpy, unflattering bikini. She stuck out her left hip and provocatively fiddled with the bikini's side strap.

"Any news?" she said, fluttering her eyelashes.

"Er... yes," I said, squirming with embarrassment. I couldn't shake the vision of them debating furiously which toy they should try next.

"What is it?" said Mr Hancock, joining her at the door in a new pair of baggy shorts.

"W... Wings have recovered your suitcase," I stuttered.

"About time," said Mr. Hancock, shoving his wife behind him.

"They regret the lock broke, and everything fell out."

"Incompetent idiots," said Mr. Hancock, breathing deeply.

Mrs Hancock continued to flirt from behind her husband.

"However, they refolded your things tidily and have strapped it shut."

"Did they repack all our stuff?" asked Mrs. Hancock.

I looked down at the floor, praying for a *Beam me up Scottie* moment.

"Almost everything, but there was a problem with a cardboard box," I said, chewing my cheek. It broke. I'm sorry, but all your um…"

"Harrumph," said Mr. Hancock. "Are they intact?"

"The Wings staff were puzzled about the items," I said. "And hope they have done the right thing."

"What, exactly?" said Mr Hancock, on the verge of a nervous breakdown.

"They wrapped them with elastic bands and placed them into a transparent carrier bag. Unfortunately, they er… wouldn't fit in the case, you'll have to carry them as hand luggage. Alternatively, you might like to consider their offer."

"Offer?" said Mr. Hancock, having turned a deep shade of red.

"Even though they beefed up your case as best they could, they suggest it is unlikely to survive the journey back to the UK in one piece and advise you to accept their gift of a replacement. You can choose a bigger one so er… it all fits, but you can decide when you inspect the old one."

"Is there something wrong with your cheek?" said Mr. Hancock.

"A mouth ulcer," I said.

Mr. Hancock glared at me, his expression jammed with suspicion.

"The thing is," I said. "Would you care to collect the case today or wait until you depart tomorrow?"

"We'd like to collect the case today," said Mr. Hancock. "Then we can use our er clothing on the final day. Do you know how we can get to the airport and back?"

"Actually," I said. "I am happy to drive you and invite you to lunch in a historic restaurant in Málaga centre."

"About time you showed us some gratitude," he said, glancing at his wife and smiling for the second time during his visit.

She nodded.

"Fancy restaurant is it?" she said.

"No, but people dress nicely," I said.

"Then shall we say downstairs in half an hour?" said Hancock.

"The car is in the alleyway," I said. "I'll wait for you there."

Hancock nodded and closed the door.

I went to my room, changed into a grey suit with flared trousers, ran a brush over my shoes and called the daily orders through. I rang Sharon and confirmed our arrival at the Wings office before lunch.

"Good thinking, son," said Dorn as I made the call. "Fingers crossed that tosspot turns up with the licence he promised yesterday."

"Have you spoken with him?" I asked.

"Not me, but Dad rang and spoke to his secretary after your outburst. Her English isn't so good, but she said he picked up the licence and will deliver it today around lunchtime. How long will the Hancocks be?"

"Half an hour."

"*H, H, Hancock's Half Hour*," she giggled. "How fitting?"

I chuckled and headed out to the car. I was

grovelling around in the Rolls glove compartment for a map of Málaga when someone coughed and tapped me on the shoulder. I backed out of the car to find the Hancocks irritated. He was in his only suit, she in a tight red sleeveless dress and sombrero.

"You told us you'd be waiting outside with the car," said Mr. Hancock.

I took a deep breath. "The Rolls-Royce is the finest car in the world, Mr. Hancock."

"We are going in this?" said Mrs. Hancock.

"Indeed, Mrs. Hancock." "No expense spared.

"Where on earth did this come from?" asked Mrs. Hancock.

"This is my father's car," I said. "We drove it down from England. It has UK plates."

"But it's right-hand drive," said Mr. Hancock. "Is it safe to drive in Spain?"

"If we managed to get it this far without any scrapes, I said. "I expect we can safely negotiate our way to Málaga and back. Now, do you want your suitcase or not?"

"There's no need to be bolshy," said Mr. Hancock. "Gladys and I are only concerned for our wellbeing. Shall we get in the back?"

"Of course," I said, opening the door and offering my hand to Mrs. Hancock. I guided her in and left Mr. Hancock to his own devices.

He climbed in the front.

I gritted my teeth, shut the door, and started the engine. It purred as I reversed out of the cul de sac and set off.

As I drove, Mr Hancock caressed the burr walnut facia as tenderly as he would a lover's cheek.

"Always wanted to ride in one of these," he said,

admiring the leather interior. "I can see why rich people buy them now. You're higher up than other cars and can look down at the plebs as you glide along. Gladys, you alright in the back there?"

"Yes, dear. There are picnic tables and an electric screen divider I can put up should I want privacy from the commoners in the front."

"Is this a normal model?" said Mr. Hancock.

"Hardly," I said. "It's a special edition James Young Rolls-Royce Silver Cloud II, a two-tone grey model with a long wheelbase."

"Did you hear, dear?" said Mr. Hancock. "This car is like the Queen's."

"It's certainly comfy," said Mrs. Hancock. "Although it throws me about a bit when we go around corners. I hope it doesn't make me queasy."

"Need a bag?" said Mr. Hancock.

"Yes, but I'll cope if he drives slowly," said Mrs. Hancock. "I hope."

"Try and refrain from waving," said Mr. Hancock. "We don't want to mislead anyone."

Gladys giggled, put the armrest down, and settled into her corner, making mini-practice waves.

I headed along the coast road at a snail's pace, petrified that Mrs. Hancock might have difficulty holding on to her breakfast. I checked the mirror every few seconds, poised to stop if necessary. My father would be furious if she made a mess on the delicate leather.

And I'd have to mop it up.

CHAPTER 10

WHAT A GAY DAY

I returned from Málaga around five with the Hancocks and their luggage. Thankfully, the upholstery survived. After two glasses of wine with lunch, they both snored in the back for the homeward journey to Nerja. We joined my parents in the lobby. Mr Hancock was hanging on to his old, damaged suitcase as if it was his favourite teddy bear, but more surprisingly, he was nodding and smiling at everyone. Mrs Hancock showed Mum the brand-new hard-shell plastic case from Wings covered with their logo before they went up to their room.

"All good?" said Jimmy after they had gone.

"Perfect," I said. "Like kids with favourite toys."

"Finally, they can have a play," said Dorn, smirking. "What er... colour were they?"

"I didn't see anything because I had to stay in the car. When they returned, the er... accessories had been packed."

"How was lunch?"

"Not too expensive, Dad. Mr. Hancock loved the clams?"

"What a relief. Excuse me, but the bar is calling," said Jimmy, leaving us.

"With the uncertainty of when you were coming back and this wretched Wings man coming, we decided not to close for the afternoon," said Dorn, sitting behind the desk. "I'm exhausted; plus, we received complaints about the cottage pies at lunchtime. Some were cold in the middle; others, the mash too soggy."

"I'll have a word with the chef," I said as a handsome man in his early thirties with swept-back dark hair entered. He wore an expensive blue suit with flared trousers and wide lapels and had ice-blue eyes. "It's probably the microwave settings. Good afternoon. Can I help you?"

"Good afternoon, my name is Caterham," he said in a deep posh voice. "Rupert Caterham, area manager of Wings Tours. I've come to see Jimmy Edwards."

"He's serving behind the bar," I said. "I'll take you through?"

"Dad," I said, joining him behind the bar. "This is Rupert Caterham from Wings."

"Oh," said Jimmy, coming around and shaking hands. "Welcome; we weren't expecting you until later."

"Dashed frogs on strike again," said Rupert. "Anyway, I'm here now and need your opening licence."

"I'm so sorry," said Jimmy. "But it hasn't arrived yet. Our lawyer is on his way and will deliver it this evening."

"Most inconvenient," said Rupert. "On the phone, your son said it was ready."

"I had it all arranged for yesterday but put it off when we heard you weren't due until this evening. Our lawyer had another urgent appointment."

"Can't we ask your lawyer to bring it now?" said Rupert. "Only I have other appointments in Marbella."

"Regretfully, he's based in Málaga, so no, but he is due here imminently," said Jimmy.

"Why Málaga?"

"There are no English-speaking lawyers in Nerja."

"Most unlikely," said Rupert.

"Believe me, if you could find me one, I'd fire him immediately. He's not exactly reliable, to say the least."

"Hence the tardy opening licence?"

"Indeed," said Jimmy. "Listen, while we wait for the lawyer, why don't you sit, drink, and order any food you fancy on the house? Our chef, La Rubia, will take personal care of you."

"I don't have much choice," said Rupert. "But six p.m. is my absolute deadline to make my next appointment. You will lose the Wings contract if the license isn't here by then."

"I understand," said Jimmy, edging Rupert toward the window seating. "But I'm positive the lawyer will be here shortly. Please take a seat."

Rupert sat by the window and looked around with a surly expression. However, his face lit up when La Rubia handed him the menu. I exchanged glances with Dad. He grimaced.

La Rubia was blushing and seemed besotted by Rupert.

And Rupert appeared equally so.

They sat closely together while La Rubia described the Fontainebleau gastronomic delights. Rupert hung onto every word, gazing intently into his eyes. La Rubia blushed, stroked Rupert's arm, and fluttered his eyelids.

Rupert relaxed after two glasses of dry fino and a plate of La Rubia's finest microwaved beef casserole with chips on the side. He and La Rubia were deep in conversation to the exclusion of everybody else in the bar. I'd never seen La Rubia so animated. Was Rupert also gay? If so, it could solve our licensing problems.

As six o'clock approached, there was no sign of the lawyer.

I slipped out to Dorn.

"What are we going to do? Still no lawyer."

"Rupert is English," said Dorn. "He won't speak Spanish or know what an opening licence resembles. We could show him a copy of our contract with the builder. It has a notary stamp and appears official. He won't know the difference."

"Do we have it here?"

"In the filing cabinet."

"Ok, Mum, prepare it. I'll bring him out."

I rejoined Dad in the bar to outline our deception, only to discover La Rubia still deep in conversation with Rupert. The excited expressions on both their faces suggested they had found mutual interests. La Rubia glanced up and came over.

"Rupert accept invitation to me show him Nerja," he said. "I keep him distracted."

"What about the kitchen?" said Jimmy.

"Close," said La Rubia. "Keeping Rupert happy more important than profit on a few pies, and Jimmy, believes me, I makes him extremely happy."

"Really. How?"

La Rubia regarded us knowingly and smiled.

"Oh, I see," said Jimmy. "He bats with your team,

then off you go and keep him away for at least two hours; the certificate should be here by then."

"He lovely man, I might not bring him backs ever, but when I do, then we talks about increase in wages."

"Harrumph," said Jimmy, blood pressure boiling. "Just don't bring him back too early.

We resumed serving customers. When we checked again, La Rubia and Rupert had disappeared.

At seven p.m., there was no sign of the lawyer.

"No news is good news," said Dorn, coming to tell us the obvious.

"Yes, but I hate this hanging around," said Jimmy. "It's like waiting for the result of a steward's enquiry after your horse has won. Damn lawyer, why can't people do as they promised."

"Relax, Jimmy, or you'll need another indigestion tablet."

"If we don't get this licence soon, I'll need the whole bottle. Rupert and La Rubia are taking their time."

"That could work quite well," I said.

"How?" said Jimmy.

"His office may not approve of gallivanting with suppliers," I said.

"Mmm…," said Jimmy as Mr. Hancock entered the bar.

"I'm glad I've caught most of you together," said Mr. Hancock. "I just wanted to apologise for my unspeakable behaviour earlier in the week. I realise now it was no fault of yours my case went missing, but in the absence of anyone from Wings, you were the only route to finding a solution."

The bar door opened.

La Rubia and Rupert came through the front door

together, relaxed and happy.

"This is Rupert from Wings," said Dorn. "Meet Mr. Hancock."

"You're from Wings," said Hancock, turning to Rupert and advancing so close that he invaded his personal space. "The name is Hancock, and I demand to amend my complaint."

"Mr. Hancock?" said Rupert, stepping back, trying not to scowl at Hancock's garlic breath.

"Correct," said Mr. Hancock. "I confess when I lodged my complaint, I blamed the hotel for my lost luggage. Now I understand it was not their fault. It was the Wings' contracted baggage handlers. They sent it to Gibraltar by mistake. My complaint should be about your company, not this hotel. Despite my constant moaning, I congratulate the hotel staff who have been most cordial and helpful in solving your problem. Naturally, I will seek compensation for my additional purchases and laundry costs."

"Are you no longer concerned about the hotel's legality?" said Rupert.

"Yes, but Robert explained that in Spain, everything works differently from elsewhere," said Hancock. "I'm no longer worried about it, nor should you be."

"I'm not," said Rupert, turning toward Jimmy. "However, my company cannot condone illegality as it negates our insurance under the recently formed Air Travel Organizers' Licensing scheme. Regretfully, Mr. Edwards, unless you can show me your Opening Licence and the proper liability insurance, we must cancel our contract with you."

"No worry, I have it here," said Dorn, waving the builder's contract.

"*Señora*," said La Rubia, alarmed at what he saw.

"Before you present it Rupert, we needs talk?"

"What?" snapped Dorn as La Rubia whispered in her ear.

"No show paper him."

"He won't know what it is?"

"He speak a perfect Spanish, *Señora*. Pretending building contract is opening license make everything *muy malo*."

"Oh shit," said Dorn replacing the paper in the cabinet. "Er, sorry, Dario told me it was the wrong piece of paper."

"Then I must inform you," said Rupert. "Subject to confirmation in writing. You leave me no choice but to cancel our contract with the Fontainebleau."

"I should have stayed in England," said Jimmy.

"We're all doomed," I said.

"Why is everyone so glum?" said a tall, distinguished man with silver-grey hair entering the bar. He wore a blue serge blazer, beige flannels, and a Panama hat.

"I am Felipe Represa de Castro, the hotel lawyer," he said, delving into his black leather briefcase. "And this is the elusive opening license and a letter from the Guardia Civil withdrawing all charges."

Dorn slumped into the chair. My father and I hugged. Rupert and La Rubia kissed. The lawyer looked on in amazement.

"I only delivered a piece of paper," he said. "What's all the fuss?"

"Might be to you, tosspot," said Dorn. "To us, it's life or death."

"I'm pleased to say," said Rupert after reading the documents. "Everything seems satisfactory, so we can anticipate a long and profitable relationship.

Regretfully, I'll need to visit regularly to check that everything is running smoothly and that the cottage pies are up to scratch."

"Crikey," said La Rubia, blushing.

Whew, I thought. What a result. If this hadn't worked, we'd have been thrown out and our assets impounded.

And I would have to begin again.

After we closed for the night, I went for a walk, needing a breath of fresh, cool air before settling down.

The town was quiet, so I returned home and was about to unlock the front door when a dilapidated Seat Five Hundred chugged past me and stopped outside Bar Bilbainos.

The driver opened the front doors, disappeared inside and returned with a pair of timber ramps. He placed them on the step, drove the car into the bar and tidied up. He gave me a friendly wave as he closed the doors behind him.

The bar wasn't just his home but his garage.

CHAPTER 11

STOLEN STOLE

After several weeks of reorganising the bar and restaurant, breakfast finally functioned like a well-oiled machine. Instead of spreading the trays and baskets individually along the bar where the end ones were hanging over the edge, I'd made some wooden stands to double stack the baskets at a forty-five-degree angle. Thanks to the skills learned from my O-Level Maths, I analysed the beverage statistics and calculated the average percentage of coffee versus pots of tea. The British desire for their favourite cuppa overwhelmingly prevailed, leaving the filter machine to cope with the demand for coffee. I'd moved it to a new side table at the end of the bar so people could top up without hindering those queueing for the buffet. Even Jim had nodded his approval. I loved coffee but preferred the rich aromas and intense flavour of the local Santa Cristina brand made with an Italian expresso machine in a nearby café. One day, I dreamed, we would be able to afford one.

"Are you free?" said a middle-aged male guest as I passed his table.

"For you, Mr. Panter, always," I said.

"It's Painter," he said, holding up a plate with a croissant missing a bite. May I congratulate the chef on this piping hot, tasty croissant? However, it is soggy. Can you bring me a crispy one, please?"

"Straight away, Mr. Painter," I said, taking the plate and heading to the kitchen.

"How did you warm this up?" I said, showing the offending article to La Rubia.

"In micro," said La Rubia. "Why?"

"Do another one, but in the oven," I said. The micro warms croissants quickly but soft, not crispy. Can you do the same for future croissant orders?"

"Everything in micro soggy or solid ice?" said a distinctly miserable La Rubia. "It also big problem with cottage pies."

"Mum said. The machine is only a domestic model and not powerful enough for commercial use. Try giving them a minute longer on a lower power setting and then crisp them off in the normal oven."

"Crikey. You now cooks?"

"It's just a suggestion. I only want happy customers."

"Me too," said La Rubia. While we wait for croissant, I speaked with Pepe owner of Bar Bilbainos, they thinking about darts but must makes a team. How many peoples they need?"

"Three."

"Crikey, difficult but I say him," said La Rubia opening the oven door and jumping back from the heat. "Here, crispy croissant."

"You sure?"

La Rubia stuck his finger in the end and nodded.

I shrugged and took it out of the oven. The plate was too hot to hold, so I dropped it on the floor, where it smashed into pieces. La Rubia, with oven gloves in hand, looked at me as if I were a creature from outer space as I cooled my fingers under a cold tap.

"Crikey," he said and shrugged. He picked up the croissant and placed it on a freshly washed plate.

I dried my stinging hands, took the plate from him and headed to the restaurant.

"Your crispy croissant," I said, placing the new one in front of Mr. Painter.

Painter prodded it with his finger and nodded. "Perfect," he said. "Thank you. But now we have another minor issue."

"How can I help?"

"Your bread rolls are rock hard," he said, showing me a small object between his forefinger and thumb. "Regretfully, one of my wife's fillings was no competition."

"I'm so sorry," I said. "We order them fresh daily from the bakery around the corner. The Spanish prefer them crispy. Do you want me to organise a dentist?"

"To be fair, it was a very old filling," said Mrs Painter. "So, we won't make a fuss, and I'll have it fixed back home."

What appreciative guests, I thought.

I spotted my parents entering the lobby. They looked upset and beckoned me to join them.

I checked the full breakfast tables. Nobody seemed to need anything, and the coffee pot was full. I went out to the lobby, followed by Jim and Jenny.

"Hi," I said. "What's the problem?"

"We've been robbed," sniffed Dorn.

"What happened?" I said, consoling her.

"They smashed a window in the Rolls, took my cassettes, and her mink stole," said Jimmy.

"Doesn't sound too serious," said Jim.

"Cheeky bugger?" snapped Dorn. "It was a wedding present from your father. It cost a fortune."

"When did this happen?" I asked.

"During the night," said Jimmy. "They smashed the rear side window."

"Didn't you lock the garage?" said Jim.

"The up and over was closed, but we never lock anything," said Jimmy. "Even the car was open. All they had to do was try the door."

"Didn't you hear something?" said Jenny.

"How could we?" said Jimmy. "The garage is at the front, bedroom at the back. We didn't hear a thing."

"Have you informed the police?" said Jim.

"The Guardia Civil came immediately," said Jimmy.

"Most impressed," said Dorn. "However, we had to wait until a translator was available."

"The police provided a translator?" asked Jim.

"Of course not," said Jimmy. "We had to phone tosspot."

"Wait," said Jim. "He came from Málaga for a stolen stole?"

"No, son," snapped Jimmy. "It was done on the phone. They found prints and some blood on the window and suspected they knew the culprit. They're going to arrest him now."

"So, you might get your stole back, Mum?" I asked.

"Let's hope so," said Dorn, sniffing.

"Breakfasts are calling," I said, heading back into the bar, leaving Jim and Jenny to console our parents.

Two hours later, two uniformed officers of the

Guardia came into the bar. They were new faces, so I wasn't immediately concerned. Until one pointed at me. My heart raced, and my stomach churned. Here we go again. I went over and stood before them, wondering what to say.

"We understand you speak some Spanish," said the older one.

I nodded.

The younger one brought a brown paper package from behind his back and handed it over. "This is your mother's stole," he said. "And your father's cassettes. Please tell her we caught the thief who is being dealt with. He will no longer be bothering you or anybody else."

They turned and left.

I heaved a sigh of relief and unwrapped the paper. Inside were the stolen items. I took them into the lobby and said, "Mum, your stole is no longer stolen."

She heaved a sigh of relief, took it out of the package, cuddled it, and then unfolded it. She examined it closely and shrieked.

"What is it?" said Jimmy.

"There's a burn mark on it," she wailed.

Jimmy winced as he remembered one evening in London where his cigar had caught the stole as he helped Dorn out of the car. He had hoped she wouldn't notice.

"Perhaps it's moths?" said Jimmy.

"Certainly not," said Dorn, surprised at such insinuations. She prided herself on her standard of housekeeping. "I'll not wear it again."

Jimmy shrugged.

Jim smirked.

"Does this mean the Guardia have forgiven us?" I

asked.

"Maybe," said Jim. "But you're still in the secret policeman's book. Watch out when walking home alone, especially at your usual time of four in the morning."

The sense of foreboding experienced during Hancock's siege returned. I hadn't expected to feel this way in Spain. In England. I may have had the odd brush-up with police over a speeding fine, but here, they were coming thick and fast.

What next?

CHAPTER 12

WATER BOMBS

Hancock plus fellow revolutionaries had departed, and the subsequent tour group had replaced them. They were also a mixed bunch except for one middle-aged lady in room 203 travelling alone. She had a disproportionate number of annoying questions at the welcome drinks party compared to others. While most inquired about beaches and places to eat, she asked, in what seemed to me a contrived upper-class accent for someone so shabbily dressed, about where to find daily horoscopes and chocolate digestives, which, of course, had to be McVities. She reminded me of the headmaster's secretary at boarding school.

Jim and their family had moved into their apartment. After dinner, he headed home, leaving me alone to cope with the bar. This was fine because tonight was my trial music night. My sound equipment was set up permanently in the far corner of the bar to not ingress into the space needed for breakfast buffets. I'd sorted out a pile of discs earlier, which I guessed would suit the range of ages in the new group and played the top one. The Hues Corporation belted out *Rock the Boat*. Worthy of higher volume, I thought, cranking it up a bit, which spurred an instant response. One couple started dancing in the middle of the bar. The limited floor space was packed within seconds, and some dancers spilt out onto the patio. Next up was *Superstition* by Stevie Wonder.

I upped the volume yet again.

The drinks flowed.

The noise swelled.

The Fontainebleau was thumping.

The tobacco smoke wafted in the dim light as the bubble lamps created disjointed moving shadows around the bar. Finally, I thought, this was more like it. Nods of approval came my way from some of the new guests; they probably hadn't expected this on a Wings package holiday. Then, a woman screamed out of nowhere and rushed into the bar, pointing at the third floor. Her hair was drenched, and blotchy make-up ran down her face as several women surrounded her to inquire what was wrong. She was too upset to explain.

I squeezed through the remaining dancers, too wrapped in each other's arms to be bothered by this latest drama. I wondered where the water was coming from, assuming it must be another of the builder's plumbing disasters.

I looked up and… splat. A water bomb hit me on the shoulder and drenched my polo shirt. Splat, then another, and not just me. I picked up an empty plastic bag and examined it as another landed by my foot. I withdrew under the stairwell and tried to identify the source of the bombardment. It was the woman on the top floor in Room 203. She was leaning over the railing, screaming disgust at the excessive noise. Her face was screwed up with rage as she hurled more water bombs. She yelled above the music in what I can only describe as a piercing impression of a costermonger's wife, "How is a girl to get 'er booty sleep?"

Had she brought dozens of bags with her in case she needed to complain? What a contriving old cow. I retreated to the bar, where La Rubia handed me a towel. Hancock may have flown, but now we had this miserable chocolate biscuit fiend determined to spoil the fun.

Everyone crowded into the bar to escape a further drenching. Some men unbuttoned their soaking shirts to dry off. One woman's white top turned transparent. She ran upstairs blushing but returned within minutes to rejoin the dancing to a barrage of ribald remarks. I reduced the volume and shut the patio doors.

Now, there was only room for slow dancing. I changed the music to, *You Are So Beautiful* by Joe Cocker. With so many people crammed into a small space, even with the air conditioning on full, the bar temperature was stifling.

Bar sales went through the roof.

After the last client departed in the early hours, I was closing the outer doors when a couple in their mid-thirties arrived.

"Sorry," I said. "We're closed."

"We understand," said a cheeky, handsome young man, around thirty years of age. He was well-spoken with a hint of a London accent and very sure of himself. "I'm Mike, and this is my partner Eva from Sweden."

Eva was blond and ever so slightly on the plump side but attractive, friendly, bubbly, and smiling.

"We wanted a quick word," said Eva.

"We run Bar 23 on Calle Pintada," said Mike. "Charles popped in on his way home and told us about your amazing music collection."

"Come in, come in," I said. "We don't want to disturb the neighbours."

"We're in Spain, Robert," said Mike with an astounded expression. "Nobody worries about neighbours."

"The thing is," said Eva. "We run Narixa, the discotheque overlooking Playa El Salon. This Saturday is Eurovision. Spanish TV is showing it in colour, and we will have a special evening to celebrate the occasion."

"We wonder if you'd like to come and play the music for us," said Mike.

"And bring some of your records," said Eva.

"Which ones?" I said.

"We made a list," said Mike, handing it over. "Hopefully, you have most of them."

"Will you come?" said Eva.

"My pleasure," I said, scanning the list. "But it'll have to wait until I've closed the bar first."

"So will we," said Mike. "We don't start until after midnight."

"Then see you Saturday," I said, yawning before ushering them out.

At breakfast the following day, our water bomber sat alone at a table in the corner of the bar, sipping her tea, looking sad and vulnerable. I was concerned she might repeat her performance tonight because whatever her antics, everybody else in the hostel was determined to dance the night away. I pondered what I should say to her as I watched other guests on the surrounding tables. Many were in animated conversations, planning beach trips with newfound friends.

Observing relationships develop as guests progressed through their stay with us was fascinating. They arrived exhausted, escaping the stress of commuting and work, and hardly talked to each other, having become accustomed to living almost separate lives in their daily grind to survive. Many rediscovered why they fell in love in the first place and, by the time they returned home, had rejuvenated their relationships. Perhaps these romantic connotations were why many returned year after year.

Sadly, a few couldn't handle being close to each other, so they confirmed they were doomed and agreed to initiate divorce proceedings. Overall, love prevailed, so the dancing had to go on.

I approached the lady from 203 and asked, " Would you mind if I joined you for a minute?"

"Go ahead," she said without looking at me.

I sat on the chair opposite and looked at her. She couldn't return my gaze.

"I expect you want to discuss my noise abatement protest," she said, staring defensively at me.

"I'm more interested in how we can prevent a repeat performance," I said. "Look around at our other guests; they loved the music and want more. What can we do to avoid disturbing your beauty sleep?"

"I don't know, but suggestions are welcome."

"How about I buy you some earplugs?"

"I put some out to pack but left them on the bed."

"Are you going out today?"

"I thought I'd try a sunbed."

"Then, when you return, a packet will be on your

bedside table."

"Thank you, young man," she said relieved.

We didn't hear a peep from her after that, and when she departed, she hugged me and said, "Thank you."

CHAPTER 13

ROYALTY

We had a rare break between groups and decided to celebrate with a BBQ at my parent's villa. We locked the hotel around five pm, squeezed into the Rolls and drove up to La Molineta. After an overindulgent evening forcing down Dad's crucified chicken wings, we slept well but had to be up early the following day to take the kids to school. The adults felt a little worse for wear, but the kids were excited about seeing their friends and were hanging out the window waving at everyone as we passed. As we approached the school, all the parents stopped talking with each other and looked at us with questioning expressions.

"Why are those people looking at us, Grandma?" said Samantha.

"Perhaps they think we're royalty," said Dorn from the front passenger seat.

"Try not to wave?" said Jenny from the back seat.

"Don't encourage them," said Jim, sitting beside his wife. He grabbed the children's arms. "Sam, Junior, stop waving, and please close your mouths; those silly grins remind me of a horse."

"That's not a nice thing to say," said Samantha. "And you're hurting me."

"Sorry, darling," said Jim. "But this is not a toothpaste advert, and we shouldn't be waving at anybody. We are ordinary people who happen to be driving an unusual vehicle. It doesn't make us any better or different from them."

"Then why are they thtaring, Grandpa?" said Jim Junior.

"Curiosity," said Jimmy. "Perhaps they've never seen a Rolls-Royce."

"That's because we always walk to school," said Samantha. "Anyway, I want to wave to my friends. They'll be upset if I didn't."

"Never mind now, sweethearts, we've arrived," said Jimmy, pulling up outside the school gate. "Have a great day."

The kids climbed out, followed by Jenny, carrying their backpacks. As they walked toward the gate, the crowd fanned back to let them through, bowed and laughed. The kids walked through bowing, doing royal waves and giggling like crazy. They loved the attention. Jenny blushed furiously.

To me, it was a wonderful moment—finally, a sign that we were accepted. We tingled with pleasure as Dad drove us to work, where we opened up and went about our daily tasks.

While drying glasses, I studied the bar's layout to see what improvements could be made with any extension plans. What was the ideal number of heads we could cope with without increasing staff? How long should the counter be for one bartender to manage, or maybe two, when pressed to serve a more significant number of customers? How many tables and chairs are needed for diners? Where could the sound system be more logically integrated?

I spent nearly every waking moment within these four walls and needed to feel comfortable that the new layout was as efficient as possible. Then, I would be happy and content to converse with whoever needed me. The only people I ever spoke with were usually on the other side of the bar, either lecturing me with their pet rant, seeking my advice, or boring me with drunken ramblings. If I was destined to be enshrined behind this wall of bottles, glasses, and beer kegs, surely, I had the right to prepare the brief for its expansion. This was my domain and should be harmonious with how I worked.

So lost was I in my little world I failed to notice when Mum popped her head around the bar door. "Robert, we have a new guest. Could you give him a hand with his luggage?"

"Sure," I said, drying my hands. "Which room?"

"Jim and Jenny's old room," said Dorn.

I entered the lobby to find a short, skinny man in his early fifties with greasy black hair supporting himself on crutches. He wore a thick red and black plaid shirt and blue jeans.

"This is my son, Robert," said Dorn. "Robert, this is David Wilks from Canada. As of today, The Fontainebleau will be his new home. He wants to live here for the foreseeable future."

"A pleasure to meet you," I said, unsure to shake hands.

David solved his dilemma by moving both crutches into his left hand and holding out his right. We shook.

"Is this all you have?" I said, indicating the single suitcase.

"I don't need much," said David with a broad Canadian drawl. "I've been travelling the world with Bessie for nearly a year, but it's time to settle and return to work."

"Bessie?"

"Sorry, my case is Bessie, named after my well-travelled Aunt, and the typewriter inside is Marnie, a favourite secretary back home."

"You give all your stuff ladies names?"

"Sadly, it's the only way I can get closer to the fairer sex."

"I'm sure your fortunes will change in The Fontainebleau."

"You, er..., have plenty of available women?"

"All ages, shapes, and sizes, but more importantly, they are in holiday mode. After a couple of sherries, they tend to let their hair down more readily than back home."

"Then I hope the excitement won't kill me," said David.

"Nice way to go, though. Follow me, please," I said, picking up the heavy case. "What have you got in Bessie, a year's supply of Canadian Club?"

"Ha, no. Just Marnie, along with several reams of paper and spare ribbons."

"Are you a journalist?" I said as we went through to the patio.

"No, but I write."

"Wow, our first creative guest."

"I've been on a sabbatical for over a year, but now I'm suitably refreshed. My fingers are itching to stab the odd key or two. Spain is cheap enough for me to live comfortably, and your mother has agreed that the hotel will take care of my laundry and meals so I can concentrate."

"What do you write?"

"That is my first challenge. I have gathered many ideas on my travels, so I need to sort those into some package for a novel."

"How long does it take to write a book?"

"How long is a piece of string? I've mainly done screenwriting for TV until now, so this will hopefully be my first literary masterpiece."

"Please let me know if I can help."

"Eventually, I'll need a supply of A4 paper, but in the meantime, a lift onto a bar stool most evenings is fine."

"Cool. I'll introduce you to some of our regulars. Many have been here for years and have a host of tales to relate."

"I look forward to that."

"Here is your room," I said, opening the door and ushering David inside. "When you need laundry, just stuff it in the bag provided and leave it outside. If you need peace while writing, give us a shout, and I'll get La Rubia to drop in some snacks."

"Eh, thanks, Robert. Sounds perfect."

"You're welcome, David. Enjoy your stay."

CHAPTER 14

WATERLOO

Luxemburg won the Eurovision Song Contest twice in a row, in 1972 and 1973. Holding it once in their small country had been deemed too expensive, so Britain volunteered to host the second. The nineteenth contest was held at the Brighton Dome on Saturday, 6 April 1974, and was compered by Katie Boyle for her fourth and final time. Seventeen nations took part. Britain escaped the dreaded *zero point* and came fourth with Olivia Newton-John singing *Long Live Love*. Spain came ninth with *Canta y sé feliz* by Peret.

I arrived at Narixa on Saturday night after midnight, carrying a box of records, dressed in casual jeans and a shirt. Long before I turned the corner into Calle Tajillo, I heard the music thumping so loud the church seemed to vibrate in time to the music.

The Narixa building was decrepit but unheeded; I went through the open door and headed for the bar, where the dim lighting hid the damp spots and holes in the wall. The dance floor was packed with people, primarily Spanish, in flamenco dresses and other get-ups.

Eva and two other beautiful blond girls in Swedish outfits were behind the bar, rushing to keep up with the constant demand for exotic cocktails. She spotted me and indicated I should join Mike in the DJ booth. I went over, waited until the record ended, and approached.

"Guess what," said Mike as I joined him behind the deck.

"Go on," I said.

"We have a major coup here tonight," said Mike, giving me an album. "Play track three on Side A."

I removed the disc from the album sleeve, noticing the name of the group.

"Why is it a coup?" I said.

"You'll see," said Mike. "Usually, it takes six months before new records appear in the shops here in Spain, but amazingly, a Swedish friend brought down a bunch of albums he purchased in Stockholm last March. This was one of them."

The crowd was pushing closer, anticipating something special.

"Ladies and gentlemen," said Mike. "Let's warmly welcome our new DJ, who recently arrived from England to become part-owner of the Fontainebleau, Robert Edwards."

I slipped behind the twin decks, put on the headphones, and grabbed the microphone. "Damas y Caballeros," I said into the mike while loading the album onto the deck and setting the speed to 33RPM. "We have a special surprise. You all know from watching TV this evening that the winner of the Eurovision Song Contest was the Swedish group,

Abba."

I waited for the inevitable cheer. When it died, I dropped the needle precisely onto track three and set it turning. As the introduction played, I spoke over it. "At great expense, we have had their album flown over. It's just arrived at Narixa, and you are the first to hear it live in Spain. Yes, it's *Waterloo*."

There was astonishment all around. Narixa went crazy.

Great, I thought while admiring some sexy girls in Lederhosen strutting their stuff. I was in my element.

Demand was such that every half an hour, I played Waterloo.

We were still at it as the sun rose and its warm pink rays illuminated Playa El Salon.

CHAPTER 15

STRAPPED FOR CASH

"Robert," called Mum from the lobby. "Your father is back with the supplies. He's blocking the road, so can you give him a hand to unload?"

I dropped my tea towel onto the bar and rushed outside. Nobody was waiting behind the Rolls, so I relaxed and picked up a carton of Gin from the open boot.

My father heaved out some large tins of tomatoes.

"Unusual brand," I said.

"They were on special offer."

"I hope it doesn't taste bad; our gin customers are accustomed to Larios."

"Give them Larios first and this for the subsequent drinks. After one, they won't notice the difference."

"Are things that bad?" I asked as we dropped the items on the lobby desk and headed back out for the rest.

"We have to watch our costs," said Dad as we added the final cartons to the desk.

"But not at the expense of quality. Our customers aren't fools."

I looked at my mother and sensed the tension between them.

"Come, we need to clear the air on this," said my mother.

"Shouldn't I move the car first?" said Jimmy.

"We're in Spain, not Staines. Whoever needs to pass will wait happily in a civilised fashion until we're done."

My mother removed the calculator from the desk drawer, tapping in a few numbers.

The photo of my grandfather adorning the wall behind the desk was still askew. Dorn straightened it every morning, but after a delay of a few seconds, it swung back to its original position.

Jimmy perched on the desk and peered sheepishly at Mum. I'd never seen him so down. Was I about to hear a revelation?

"Look," said Dorn, holding up the calculator screen and waving it before me. "When you see the total picture, we aren't so badly off considering. We survived over a year without income and still made all the outstanding stage payments for the hotel. Our villa and half-finished penthouse are fully paid for, and we have many bookings for the summer with Wings Tours."

"I know, sweetheart, but it doesn't change our situation," said Jimmy, studying the calculator display. "Yes, we have some clients, but what about the winter when the package tours stop? We must face the reality of no bookings for at least six months, yet we still have to pay Emilio de Miguel, the builder, one more staged payment before the hotel is transferred to our name. If we don't have enough, Emilio will repossess the building, and we lose everything."

"Surely, we have sufficient money?" I said.

"Assets, son, but they are tied up in the UK for another three years. They will cost a fortune to cancel, let alone the massive dollar premium when buying foreign currency. Our only option is to generate cash with the Fontainebleau."

"We could sell the properties and move in here," said Dorn. "As you said, it would only be for three years."

"With taxes and a fire sale price, we might lose up to sixty per cent of the value and still struggle to pay. Darling, we have only one option: to make this place work. Three years of hard work and with a fair wind, we should be okay."

"Not quite how we envisaged our retirement."

"We'll still have plenty of years to enjoy the sun."

"I'm beginning to think we should have stayed at home. I might not be decrepit, but the stress is killing me."

"With Wilson in charge, the challenges in the UK of hanging on to what we have would have been equally as hard. Here, at least if this place succeeds, we can make some money and don't need much to live on."

"True, but what a come down," said Dorn. "From luxury living in our beautiful island home on the river Thames with no care in the world to this. I told you not to commit so much to investments,"

"You were right, but at twelve per cent, the interest rates were so high it made sense at the time," said Jimmy.

"What a mess," said Dorn. "At this rate, we'll be the only millionaires living in a cave."

"As I've said before, with the climate here, we'll be warm troglodytes," said Jimmy, shaking his head.

Dorn smiled at him. "I do hope you are joking. Our biggest mistake was completely underestimating how much we needed to set up this hotel."

"Nobody could have envisaged the delays," said Jimmy.

"Nor the staggering extra costs," said Dorn.

"Anyway, we are where we are," said Jimmy. "On a knife edge, and now I've tipped us over because I've had to borrow to keep us going. For the first time in decades, we are in debt with no way of paying it back."

"But not for long," said Dorn. "The hotel income forecast is promising. When Wings pay what's outstanding, we'll be in credit again."

"Only temporarily," said Jimmy. "Our room rate is 235 pesetas per night with continental breakfast, but when we sell through Wings Tours, we must discount to 165. We need to sell many room nights to raise enough to pay for everything and save up for the final payment to Emilio. Don't forget we have things to buy and staff to pay for. I'll have to borrow more for those unless I can persuade Emilio to accept part payment."

"You'll find a way, dear," said Dorn. "You generally do."

"Thank you for your faith, but I've never been up against it like this. Let's hope the German Club 18-30 also signs up. If they go ahead, the hotel should be full until October, and it needs to be because the interest on the loan is extortionate," said Jimmy, his eyes welling up. "We might even have to sell the Rolls."

"Am I hearing this right?" I said. "We've gone from millionaires to paupers in just over a year."

"I wouldn't put it quite so extreme, son," said

Jimmy. "We are asset rich but cash poor."

"Then it's pointless making suggestions to improve things," I said.

"Depends," said Jimmy. "What did you have in mind?"

"We proved entertainment is how to increase our weekly earnings last week, but the lack of space seriously hampers us. Just imagine how much we could have taken with a bigger bar?"

"I agree," said Dorn. "We made more in one night than a week's worth of full bedrooms."

"I have no argument with you," said Jimmy. "However, a bigger bar costs money we don't have."

"Then borrow more against your properties," I said.

"No," said Jimmy. "I've already overstretched my loan limit. The bank wants to see a history of positive cash flow before advancing me more, which will take time. Our biggest problem is that unless we can pack in more successful weeks before the season ends, we won't be able to repay the bank loan or make the final payment to the builder. Then we lose everything."

There was a loud noise outside, this time like a squealing pig. All three of us moved to the door and peered out.

Two ancient mopeds had stopped behind the Rolls and were sounding their pathetic klaxons.

People in the recently built four and five-floor apartment blocks opposite were lining their balconies to see what all the fuss was about. Customers spilt onto the pavement outside Bar Bilbainos and from the bar in MonteSol on the corner of Pintada. Its owner, Manolo, '*El Cateto*,' the peasant, led the crowd.

Each driver carried a huge sack of potatoes perched precariously on top of the gas tank secured between their thighs. The middle-aged farmers, wearing battered blue overalls and wide-brimmed straw hats, seemed unperturbed by the empty vehicle in front of them. Their noisy engines ticked over, billowing stinking fumes from half-rusted exhausts. They shouted between themselves, shrugged, and gestured good-naturedly while pressing their klaxons and waiting for the road to clear.

"Sorry," shouted Jimmy, waving at the moped drivers, but they were busy chatting and didn't notice. He hurried to the driver's door, climbed in, and set off. He wasn't going far, only around the block, planning to park in the cul de sac at the side of the hotel.

He needn't have hurried.

The two gentlemen on their mopeds were so engrossed in conversation that they failed to see the way ahead was free until a large truck transporting builder's rubble crept up behind them and gave them a long blast on twin air horns. They jumped like startled rabbits, patted each other on the shoulder, and set off in a cloud of fumes along the street. They hadn't gone but a few meters when one of their precariously perched sacks split open, spilling potatoes of all shapes and sizes. They bounced and rolled everywhere. The carefree laughter as onlookers dived in to save the spuds was infectious. Nearly all were rescued. A few disappeared mysteriously, but not because some had found their way into people's pockets. Nobody stole food from a neighbour in a practically crime-free Nerja, but a few of the smaller ones disappeared down a drain where a grateful rat popped his head up, thinking it must be Christmas.

For the recovered potatoes, however, there was a problem. There were no containers. The helpers surrounded the mopeds with arms full of potatoes, hunting around helplessly for someone to solve the situation. The conversation was loud, mainly covering implausible suggestions for where to put them.

Thankfully, the rubble truck driver provided an empty cement sack from his cab. The potatoes were repacked and perched on the moped petrol tank within minutes. Muchas gracias was exchanged umpteen times, and the drivers resumed their short journey to the greengrocers just around the corner on Calle Cristo.

I returned to the bar, chuckling.

But the distraction hadn't stopped me from worrying about our financial situation. I knew we were haemorrhaging cash, but I had no idea we were on the brink of disaster. How were we going to resolve this?

CHAPTER 16

BROTHERLY LOVE

With the breakfast items cleared away, Jim and I sat about as far away as possible from each other at the bar, pretending to study the dregs in our cup of coffee. He was probably dreaming of racing cars around Brands Hatch, whereas I was psyching myself up for another hard day wiping tables, drying glasses, and tolerating drunken ramblings.

"Were you aware of how bad Dad's finances are?" I asked, not as an attempt to break the usual tense silences between us, but he was the only other person with whom I could discuss such a sensitive subject.

"Yes, but I didn't take much notice," said Jim, almost relieved at having an audience interested in his opinion. "As you know, I didn't want to be here in the first place. If bankruptcy forces us to return home, I will be delighted."

There was a loud phut, and a smell of electrical burning wafted into the bar from the kitchen.

"Joder," screamed La Rubia. "Help."

Jim and I rushed into the narrow kitchen to find La Rubia frantically pushing buttons and twisting dials on the microwave situated on the marble worksurface in the far corner. Black smoke belched out from the supposedly airtight door. The smoke was wafting up and hanging below the ceiling so densely that I couldn't see the row of spotlights. It was sinking lower by the second, and the tops of the wall-mounted cabinets were disappearing fast.

I tentatively touched the microwave; it was red hot. I yanked the plug out from the socket and grabbed a tea towel hanging on the rail on the front of the oven. I wrapped it around the machine, picked it up, and hurtled toward the back door.

"Jim, fetch a blanket or something to cover it," I yelled as the tea towel burst into flames.

I dropped the oven onto the middle of the cul de sac with a sickening crunch of metal on concrete and turned back to Jim. He was standing at the door doing nothing except smirking.

"Idiot," I said, sprinting into the storeroom. I glanced around and picked up a dust sheet. I unfolded it as I ran back outside.

I threw the sheet over the oven and wrapped it tightly around. The flames went out, but smoke continued to billow out from under. I withdrew, and we stood and watched as the smoke died down. When I deemed it safe, I approached the oven, removed the sheet, and opened the door. More dirty smoke revealed a blackened open tin with burned baked beans inside.

"Who put this in the microwave," I said.

"I did," said Jim. "I fancied beans on toast for my breakfast. What of it?"

"Damned fool," I said. "You can't put metal in a

microwave. La Rubia, why didn't you stop him?"

"I was in the restroom," said La Rubia. "The timer was ticking when I returned, so I assumed someone was heating some water for a mug of tea or something."

"Perhaps we can claim it on the insurance," I said. "Jim, as you broke it, you can carry it into the storeroom and leave it there for the insurance assessor."

"Fuck, you," said Jim. "Carry it yourself. You bought the damn thing."

"And thanks to you," I said, shrugging and picking it up. We'll have to buy a new one. Dad will be delighted."

I carried it into the storeroom, heaved it onto a shelf, and heard the door close behind me. I turned. It was Jim. He was white with rage, picked up a small tin of paint, aimed at me, and threw it hard. I ducked. The tin smashed into the wall behind me and burst open. White paint splashed everywhere, including over my clothing and hair.

"What is wrong with you?" I screamed, watching Jim pick up another tin and aim.

"I've had it with you," shouted Jim. "Always thinking you know best, bossing me around, bullying my wife to cook your lunch. Life was almost bearable until you turned up; now, it's pure hell. It's best if you fuck off back to England."

"Still resenting me," I shouted. "You've been doing it ever since I was born and replaced you as the baby of the family."

"Rubbish," shouted Jim, hurling the can. It missed and smashed into the wall, splattering me and the shelves with cleaning materials. "You're a spoiled brat demanding everything your way."

The door opened, and a timid La Rubia came in as Jim picked up another paint can. He jumped on Jim's back, scratched his cheek, pulled his hair, and screamed, "Leave him alone, you big bully."

Jim made to throw the can, but La Rubia restrained him.

"What's going on?" said Dorn from the doorway.

"Jim didn't like the colour of the storeroom and decided to repaint," I said. "Sadly, his brush skills haven't improved, and as you can see, I have a new look."

La Rubia went over to Dorn and whispered into her ear. Jim stood defiant, glaring at me with his fists clenched.

"Jim," said Dorn. "You made the mess; you clean it up. Then we need to talk with your father."

"No," said Jim. "I will not clean it up. I'm done here. I'm a twenty-six-year-old married man being treated like a bloody three-year-old lackey. It's about time I made my way in the world. Me and the family are going back to England."

"I don't think Jenny..," said Dorn.

"I don't care," said Jim. "I'm off."

He stormed out, slamming the door behind him.

CHAPTER 17

GOODBYE SAMANTHA

It was challenging to have a serious family meeting without interruptions from guests with fatuous requests that most idiots could have resolved themselves. However, we urgently needed to sort out the situation with Jim before war broke out and disturbed the superficial calm we usually managed to hide behind. We adjourned to room two near the lobby. It was opposite Bar Bilbainos, whose rowdy customers should drown out our conversation.

"Jim," said Dad after moments of silence caused by everyone's reluctance to begin. None of us wanted to be here or reopen this smouldering can of worms. Thankfully, Dad commanded the respect of the room, so we listened and said nothing. "Son, irrespective of why you used our entire stock of white paint to make your point, we need to resolve what you want and what is best for the business."

"I cannot work with him," said Jim, glaring at me with intense hate. "Until he arrived, everything was fine. He must go."

"No, Jim," said Dorn. "Everything was not fine before Robert arrived at my invitation. We had underestimated the staff we needed and were working twenty hours a day, even though this was meant to be our retirement. You and your brother bury the hatchet, and we work as a team, or someone has to go."

"We can do this voluntarily," said Jimmy. "Or I will decide, bearing in mind we desperately need to reduce our costs. Robert, do you want to go back to the UK?"

"No thanks. I quit everything to come back, so I want to make a go of it. My music evenings prove I attract customers, which we can continue to build on with the residents during the difficult winter months. Jim adds nothing to the business and scowls at the customers because he is unhappy in Spain. He was like it before I returned last time and was still the same on my return. If I may, I'd like to suggest an idea for Jim and Jenny to consider."

"I'd like to suggest," mimicked Jim in a fairy-like voice.

"Be quiet, Jim," said Jenny. "Go on, Robert."

"To be fair, Jim never wanted to come here," I said. "So, whatever we do to make him happy won't work. He really should go back to England."

"But what could I do?" said Jim.

"You could get a job," said Jenny.

"As what," I said. "Second-hand car salesman in Twickenham like before with Mick Jingles? I don't think so. Times have changed since then. Car sales are on the floor. Mick has had to wind down the business and now spends most of his time here playing guitar. Furthermore, what skills could he write in his CV to attract an employer? Surly waiter, painter, poster hanger?"

Dad stifled a chuckle.

"There is something I've been thinking about?" said Jim, glaring at me with less animosity. You all know I love driving, so why not set up a removal company? Start with me and a van and grow from there, Dad. You could guarantee a loan from your rental income to buy the van. We could live rent-free in the Staines property and pay rent as income grows. I would be self-employed and in charge of my destiny."

"Are you sure, son?" said Dad, glancing tenderly at Jim.

"Yes," whispered Jim.

Jenny hugged him.

"Why didn't you say?" she said.

"Because you and the kids love it here," said Jim.

"You can come back any time you want," said Dorn, relieved a solution had been found.

"You'll have to share a room with the kids," said Jimmy.

"Nonsense," said Dorn. "You can stay in the villa."

We all heaved a sigh of relief.

We had agreed upon something together for the first time since our arrival in Nerja. With the bonus that we had substantially reduced costs.

I exchanged glances with Dad.

He nodded and tried to hide his satisfaction.

CHAPTER 18

HELLO HARRIS

After our amicable decision for Jim and his family to return to England, the day dawned for their departure. Half of me was delighted. Without my daily cause of conflict and snide remarks, I could get on with the job, but I could see my mother was hurting at the loss of her grandchildren. She knew how much they loved living in Spain.

I stood at the back of the lobby, watching while they hugged. Even Dad's eyes were watering, although not out of sadness about Jim going. He was annoyed at himself for all the disasters and the breakup of the family, something he had hoped to avoid. His drive and enthusiasm for our Spanish business had excited everyone to come and join him, me included. Now, I worried he might jack it all in.

What could I do if he did?

He spotted me watching and sidled over.

"I had a call from Club 18-30," he said. "The first of seven German groups arrive next Wednesday.

Without Jim and Jenny, we have to find a way to deal with them without employing extra staff. It will mean some changes. Meanwhile, say a fond farewell to your brother for your mother's sake."

Amazing, I thought, a dicky digestive system, family falling apart at the seams, business on the verge of bankruptcy, and still he wants more. There was no chance my father would give up, which was reassuring.

I hugged the kids. They didn't know whether to laugh or cry. They had loved their time in Nerja, were both fluent in Spanish, and had many friends. Most of all, they enjoyed the freedom of living in a safe place with few vehicles and happily walked themselves to school and back. Adjusting to the English way of life would be hard, and I suspected Nerja would always sit in a corner of their mind as they grew older.

I kissed Jenny on both cheeks, and she smiled, but I could see she was hurting.

"Come back as often as you can," I said. "It won't be the same without you, and I'll have to make my lunch."

"About time," she said.

"Take care of Jim, and good luck with the removal business."

She nodded and wiped her eyes. I turned to Jim and held out my hand. He took it, and we hugged.

"All the best," I said. "I hope there are no hard feelings

"I'm sure we'll recover over time," he said.

The profound exchange was one of our rare finer moments.

Dad stopped the Rolls in front of the hotel. We loaded their many cases into the spacious boot. Jenny and the kids scrambled into the back seat, hanging on tightly to their teddy bears. Jim and Dad hugged and then climbed into the front. Mum and I watched, a little sad, and waved as they drove off.

Seconds later, a taxi arrived; it deposited two couples and their cases at the front door.

"Must be the Harris family," said Dorn, smoothing her blouse and wiping her eyes. "Robert, this is relentless; I can't even say farewell to my family without interruption."

I knew exactly how she felt. I hugged her, and we went back inside. Dorn sat down behind the lobby desk and tried to compose herself.

"I don't wish to be insensitive," said one of the men entering the lobby, spotting my mother's distress. He was a mid-height, medium-built man in his mid-thirties with longish, mousy hair as they heaved their cases into the lobby. "Is there anything we can do to cheer you up?"

Dorn smiled and sniffed. "Sorry," she said. "My grandchildren have just left."

"Quite understandable," said the older man with a beard. "Hopefully, a few of my brother's jokes will do the trick."

"Forgive their crassness," said one of the wives—an attractive, slim, dark-haired lady in her late twenties. "We are the Harris family from London. This is my husband, John; he's a printer. I'm his wife, Sally. We've recently purchased the top floor of the Rocamar apartment block on Calle Carabeo. We hope to complete the paperwork and move in sometime this week."

"I'm his younger brother, George Harris, and this lovely lady is my wife, Cheryl; I'm a jeweller in Hatton Garden. We're just along for the ride. We also have two other brothers who will likely be bothering you. Bob is a cabbie, and the other is Dougie; he does his own thing."

"We look forward to having you with us," said Dorn. "This is my son Robert, who runs the bar and restaurant."

"Hi, Robert," said George. "You will be seeing a lot of us. We need to pick your brains. My brother will be furnishing his new penthouse. Maybe you can help?"

"I might just have somebody in mind for that," I said.

"Perfect," said George. "We can talk about it later."

"Then let's sign you in and take your passport details for the Guardia Civil Book," said Dorn. "Robert will give you a hand with your luggage."

While I humped their cases up to the top floor, I couldn't help but sense the brother's jovial character. It could be a good week.

CHAPTER 19

DON'T MENTION THE WAR

Despite having lived through the Second World War, my parents had never revealed how they survived or their opinions about Germans. I'd never met any Germans, so my perception of them was typical of our generation indoctrinated by war films and winning the 1966 World Cup at Wembley. I was, therefore, intrigued to learn what made them tick. Our first Club 18-30 German group were checking in, and from what I could see, there were more girls than boys.

My opening conversation was with a huge, muscular, blond guy who approached the bar not long after they had settled in.

"I am Hans," he said in good English but with a thick accent. "Ze girls haf sent me to ask about good Spanish bars and restaurants."

"We have a good restaurant here," I said, handing over the menu.

Hans read it. "Zis is English food. Vi want Spanish."

"Try Pepe Rico on Calle Cristo. They have a German chef, or Udo Heimer on Calle Andalucía. He is from Hamburg."

"No, vi are in Spain, vi want Spanish food not more wurst, kraut or kartoffel."

"Do you speak Spanish?"

"Of course, most of us speak a little. Vy?"

"Because the typical Spanish establishments only have menus in Spanish."

"For us, zat is no problem. Vi are here to improve our Spanish."

"Here is a map of the town. Try Rey Alfonso Restaurant. It's built into and below the Balcony of Europe overlooking the sea. We also have music and dancing here, but if you want to see real Flamenco, try Burro Blanco or El Molino."

I pointed out the locations on the map, and Hans went off happy.

He was less amicable when I was behind the bar the following day, admiring the sparkle on a highly polished wine glass.

"Breakfast vas late," he said glaring at me as if I had committed murder.

"Hopefully, it won't ruin your day," I said. "We had a problem with the hot water system. It was a choice of a hot shower or slightly delayed jam delivery."

"Vot is jam?"

"It's the sweet fruit spread for your toast."

"You mean marmalade?"

"Marmalade is made from citrus fruit. We can't import it from England, so use jam instead."

"You English are zo difficult, marmalade, jam, zay are all marmalade. Never mind, vot is ze problem with ze plumbing?"

"Our plumbing is perfect, even I understand it," I said, refilling the coffee machine with water. "However, even the BMW of hot water systems won't work without propane gas cylinders."

"You don't haff town gas?" said Hans.

"No vi do not," I said failing not to mimic the giant of a man. "We leave our empty gas cylinders on the backdoor step, signalling to the delivery man that we need more. Sometimes, he forgets, like this morning. This means we must borrow one from a neighbour or drive to the gas depot in Calle Cruz to fetch one. As the depot doesn't open until after breakfast, we had to knock on every door in the nearby streets to beg, steal, or borrow one. It's part of the joys of running a hotel in Spain. Sorry if our three-minute delay has disturbed your morning plans."

He nodded and smiled. "For me, it's no problem," said Hans. "But ze girls will be ferry angry."

"Vi, er why?" I asked.

"It is my job to put towels on ze front row sun loungers at ze beach," said Hans, shrugging. "Now the verdammt Englanders vill beat us to it."

"Makes a change," I said.

"Vot?"

"Since 1945, you win everything against us. Well, apart from the freak occasion in 1966. And this year, we didn't even qualify for the finals."

Hans returned my gaze blankly, then twigged.

"Doch ja, you mean ze world cup," said Hans, leaning forward and whispering. "My friend, let us agree. If you don't mention ze var, I won't talk about ze football. Now vot I need is a thermometer. Do you haff one?"

"Do you have a fever?"

"No, I am fine."

"Then why do you need a thermometer?"

"To measure ze sea temperature."

"Why?"

"Because below twenty-eight degrees Celsius, ze ladies vill not swim."

"Could they try dipping their toes in the surf? Then, they will know if it is too hot, too cold, or just right. Then you won't need a thermometer."

"You have no idea about German ladies," said Hans with an expression of horror. They need to know precisely how hot it is before they get off their sunbeds to swim. Toe dipping does not provide enough accurate information. Alzo, I ask again, do you have a thermometer?"

"No, just toes."

"Mein Gott, ve Germans are zo different. Our reasons for living are precision, machines, and medicine."

"It's why you make such excellent cars, whereas we English follow our creative instincts," I said. "Our reasons for living are poetry, love, romance, the arts, and not forgetting dogs in all shapes and sizes."

"Vot are you two discussing?" said a tall, slender blond German girl coming behind Hans and smiling warmly at me. I gauged she was around eighteen.

"Ah, Bettina," said Hans. "Vi is having a philosophical discussion."

"How sexy, boys not talking about football or girls' tits. Who is this?"

"Robert," said Hans. "He is English but as he owns ze hotel, vi vill be nice to him. Who knows, we may efen get breakfast on time."

"Hallo, Robert," said Bettina, reaching out her hand

and grasping mine firmly. "Nice to meets you. You ver coming out of room three earlier?"

"Hi, Bettina," I said, mesmerised by her ice-blue eyes and wondering why such a gorgeous girl was holding my hand. "Yes, it's my room."

"Achso, you sleep in hotel?" said Bettina.

"Indeed," I said.

"Ferry interesting," said Bettina, giving me a lingering gaze. "Hope to see you later." She turned and joined several other German girls heading out to the beach.

"I zink you vill be alright mit Bettina," said Hans, winking several times. "She likes ze tall dark men mit beards. Try leafing your vindow open tonight."

"I leave it open every night," I said. "We call it air conditioning."

"Ach so," said Hans as he headed out the door, muttering to himself, his expression clouded by confusion.

CHAPTER 20

A DICTIONARY IS ALWAYS USEFUL

As I crossed to my room after clearing the lunch tables, the July heat on the patio was fierce. All the guests had adjourned to the beach for cooler sea breezes, so the hotel was tranquil.

As I settled down for a siesta, I decided I liked Germans.

They were not how I had expected. At first, I found their directness unsettling, but I soon learned they just wanted accurate information, for which they were extremely grateful. Punctuality was good manners for them. Adjusting to the Spaniard's less rigid mentality was difficult. They were polite and enjoyed a drink but didn't overdo it. If subsequent groups followed suit, we should press Club 18-30 for more because they were less trouble than fellow citizens.

Since my brother had departed, my parents had become obsessed with reducing costs. I worked from dawn until well after midnight seven days a week. Mum had taken over the room cleaning. Dad flitted between the two but with his two left feet proved more trouble than help. The afternoon tranquillity was often interrupted by door slamming, vacuum cleaners, and curses as I attempted to nap. Before opening time, they joined me and La Rubia for an early supper, dripping with sweat.

I peered at them, shaking my head as we tucked into a tropical salad and jug of ice-cold lemonade.

"La Rubia," said Mum. "We need a full-time cleaner. Do you know anyone?"

Dad scowled.

"Yes, your neighbour, Irena," said La Rubia. "She live opposite apartment and clean Nueva Nerja school but only in term, and occasionally in Bar Bilbainos. She need full-time job with contract."

"Does she speak English?" said Dorn.

"Crikey, not a word," said La Rubia. "But she is woman with two teenage children. Believe mees, she know how clean."

"Could you ask her to come and see us?" said Dorn with a huge sigh of relief.

"How much does she charge?" said Dad.

"Whatever it takes," said Mum.

"The price for cleaners is thirty pesetas an hour," said La Rubia. "If you no offer, I no ask. I not want get her excited if you disappoint her with cheap offer."

"Then we'd be delighted to meet her," said Mum.

Dad scowled, but Mum had browbeaten him on this one. They left utterly exhausted just before I opened the bar for the evening session.

"We've completed our purchase," said John Harris, sticking his head in the bar door as I filled the ice bucket. "We will be down shortly to celebrate. Perhaps you can introduce us to this friend of yours?"

I nodded and waved as I put on a newly arrived Roxy Music album brought over by Mick Jingles. He was always back and forth to England. We let him stay in the hotel at a special price in return for playing guitar some evenings before he went off to perform in other bars and clubs around the town. But in exchange for the particular deal, we sometimes had to change his room at short notice. He wasn't paid much for his work and was usually short of cash. He didn't own many clothes. With only two pairs of trousers, he kept the best pair for evening performances. We had to move him once because a family had requested adjoining rooms. Mick was accustomed to this, so didn't object to my mother moving his things. One late afternoon, he returned from having been out all day, and my mother told him she had moved him to room 111, gave him the key, and up he went. A few minutes passed and Mick returned, claiming he'd lost his best trousers. He was a slender man of gypsy descent in his late twenties with a chiselled face, brown eyes, and long curly hair.

"I moved all your stuff to the new room," assured Dorn.

"Well, you forgot my best trousers," said Mick. "I left them between the mattress and bottom blanket to press them."

Thankfully, the room was empty when my mother went to recover them.

The Harris tribe certainly knew how to celebrate. When settling their enormous bar and food tab, they presented me with a list of items needed for their penthouse. It included everything you could imagine for a new apartment, including curtains and sunbeds. They wanted someone to escort them to the various shops to translate. It was perfect work for David Rowcroft, from whom I would eventually receive a percentage.

I debated whether to head out on the town or go to bed. After wiping everything down, I turned off the bar lights and went to my room to shower and think it through. I'd emerged from the bathroom wrapped in a towel when the window curtain was quietly pushed aside, and a barefoot decorated with red painted nails appeared over the sill. It was followed by its shapely owner dressed in the skimpiest of nighties, long blonde hair flowing halfway down her back.

She turned to face me. Her ice-blue eyes smouldered with desire.

It was Bettina.

"Decision made," I said.

"Vot?"

"I was popping out for a drink, but now you're here, it seems churlish."

"Sorry?"

"Hi, Bettina, I said, dropping my towel on the floor. "How can I help?"

Bettina lifted the nightie over her head and threw it on the towel. We hesitantly moved towards each other and hugged.

"I haf to besser mein Englisch," she said, lying on the bed.

"Perfect," I said, panting. "I have a dictionary in the bedside drawer."

"You are a gut teacher, nein?"

"Sometimes my conjugations miss the mark, but I vill try my best."

For three nights, Bettina visited for more intensive lessons. When I kissed her farewell early on her last morning, I was amazed at how much her English had improved. There must be something in this pillow talk, I thought. I'll have to give it a go to improve my Spanish.

I only learned a couple of German words.

Nochmal bitte.

Again, please.

CHAPTER 21

DARTS LESSON

"I've been dusting this thing for a couple of weeks now," said Irena in Spanish, standing in the Fontainebleau patio doorway, feather duster poised in hand and inspecting the dartboard. "What is it exactly?"

Our new cleaning lady, Irena, kept the place spotless and was incredibly quick. She'd worn a shabby black dress for the first few days until her uniform was ready. A tradition among the many widows in Nerja whose men had been carted off by Franco's goons and never seen again. She was only forty with a trim figure but appeared older with greying hair. I loved it when she occasionally smiled. Such a tiny change to her usually sad expression radiated warmth and happiness. She had the appearance of a person with a painful life, but we didn't know her well enough to inquire. Mainly because she spoke with a broad Andaluz accent, which omitted 's' and pronounced 'c' and 'z' as 'th', making it even harder to identify what she said. I didn't understand her often, including now, but I guessed she was inquiring about the dartboard.

I consulted the dictionary parked permanently by the till and found the word for darts. I extracted a container of three from the till, went over to join her, and opened the dart board.

"Dardos," I said, stood at the throwline, aimed, and put three consecutive arrows into the treble twenty—one of the benefits of my misspent youth. I pulled out one at a time, with each said, *sesenta puntos, en total ciento ochenta*. I wrote the total on the chalkboard, presented her the darts, and nodded.

"Mi turno?" she said.

I nodded again, pointing at the throwline marked on the floor. She stood square on to the board and made to throw. I stopped her and showed again how to stand and aim. She grimaced but understood, then threw all three into the board, scoring seventeen. I added her score to the board and wrote down the target of 501. We continued playing, and by the time I had finished on a bullseye, she had scored a respectable two hundred, taken a chip out of the wall, and blunted one of the darts.

"*Explíca a Bar Bilbainos*," I said. "*Ellos puede pasar aquí para practicar y después un torneo.*"

Amazingly, she understood my execrable explanation, asking the bar to come and practice before we arranged a match. "*Si, si. Voy a hablar con Pepe, el jefe.*"

I replaced the darts in the till. Irena carried on cleaning, often asking questions. I couldn't understand a word and just shrugged. Thankfully, I was saved by La Rubia, who sat down for his morning break with a coffee and a toasted bread roll smeared with grated tomato and olive oil.

"What is she asking me?" I said.

They babbled rapidly, often at the same time. I was amazed communication had taken place.

"She love your Dad's car," said La Rubia. "Particular large boot and back seat. Plenty of room to transport vegetables from Campo. She wish she could borrow it for delivering to family. At moment, it take ages walking there and back and with cleaning here she no longer have time."

"Does she have a driving license?"

"No."

"Then I can't see my Dad allowing that. Doesn't she have teenage children?"

"Yes."

"Then suggest they deliver to her family."

After another rapid exchange, La Rubia said, "They tired. Many schoolworks. She also ask if you have girlfriend?"

"Why does she want to know?"

"She have daughter, nearly sixteen, big boobies. She also love car and want rich boy. If you interested, she arrange meetings."

How the hell should I reply, I thought. I don't want to hurt her feelings, but I also don't want to be involved with staff beyond a professional relationship. It's a recipe for disaster.

"Please say. I am sure her beautiful daughter would be an amazing girlfriend, but I need one who can speak English. Also, like her, I am always working and do not have time to give a girl the attention she deserves."

"Good answer," said La Rubia. "I explain her." Irena listened and said a few words. "She understand," said La Rubia. "She hope you not object to her asking."

"*Todo bien*," I said.

She shrugged.

A gesture confirming we understood each other and had no hard feelings—at least, I hoped so.

Later, a thought struck me as I lay in bed wondering what Bettina was doing back in Germany. What if I hadn't recently enjoyed several nights of passion, and Irena's daughter turned out to be an absolute corker? Might I have rejected her mother's offer so readily? And a Spanish girl would force me to learn their language much quicker than the occasional exchange with Irena.

CHAPTER 22

ON THE OCHE

After La Rubia's failed attempts, Irena must have pushed hard with Pepe from Bar Bilbainos because the following day, four gentlemen arrived at the Fontainebleau and approached me in the bar shortly after we had cleared the breakfast things. "*Soy Miguel. Estamos aquí para practicar dardos,*" announced the veteran on crutches. His lack of teeth made him hard to understand but the rest of him was lean and wiry.

"*Buenos días,*" I said, holding up the palm of my hand to signify wait. "*Momento.*"

"Can you spare a minute," I said to La Rubia, who came out of the kitchen drying his hands. I approached the front of the bar and introduced myself, shaking hands with each.

"Soy Robert," I repeated. I was stretching my Spanish now, but this was just what I wanted, learning by doing.

The others were Pepe, the owner of Bar Bilbainos, a short, stocky man in his fifties with long, dark, greying hair and a drooping moustache. Fran was a short, cheeky fellow in his early thirties with chiselled features, dark curly hair, and a muscular frame. Jorge was mid-forties, lanky, almost bald, and had a steel grip. He had a piece of straw stuck to his shirt sleeve.

Irena chose that moment to start cleaning the bar, so we briefly paused while they all gabbled among themselves. They seemed amiable and keen to get on, so I fetched the darts from the till, stood on the throwing line and rattled three into the treble twenty. I chalked up 180, pulled out the darts, and offered them to our new friends.

Fran stepped forward, aimed, threw, and hit the board with all three. I chalked up his score. Pepe and Jorge did the same. I explained that starting and finishing with a double and that the winner was the first to 501. La Rubia translated. After half an hour, they were reasonably competent, and Miguel announced he wanted a go.

Jorge took his crutches. Pepe and Fran held him up while he aimed and threw. He also rattled three into the treble twenty. I applauded. Pepe gabbled something, and they all laughed.

"He was an expert grenade chucker in war," said La Rubia. "They laughed because Miguel said the darts would be good to throw at the Guardia Civil backsides."

They departed happily and agreed to fix a date for a match against the Fontainebleau.

I was amazed when Irena popped in that evening to confirm when. She brought a chubby but pretty teenager with her. "*Ella es mi hija,* Natalia," she said.

"*Hola*, Natalia," I said, relieved she wasn't my type.

"*Hola*, Robert," she said quietly, blushing.

The darts match was to be for the following Wednesday evening. I made a poster in English and Spanish and had it copied. After work, Irena went around town handing them out and sticking them up in prominent places.

From the chitchat I overheard behind the bar, the buzz around the migrant community was expectant. This was the first event between locals and foreigners and was becoming a big deal in a town renowned for nothing happening.

After dinner on the appointed Wednesday, I rearranged tables and seating to point toward the dartboard and, in a humble attempt to save lives from wayward arrows, fixed ropes between the toilet passage and bar and the open patio doors. La Rubia's job was to control the ropes while games were in play. Dorn and Jimmy were behind the bar; the kitchen was closed.

The other two hotel team members were Mike from Bar 23 and Mick Jingles. David Rowcroft was the referee and scorer.

"It's nearly nine o'clock," said Jimmy, pouring a large vodka and orange for David. "Are they coming or not?"

"In true Spanish fashion, they'll be here when they are here," I said, sitting on a stool at the bar sipping a pint, the go-to beverage for darts players. Beer was reputed to relax the throwing arm and enhance accuracy. Professionals swore sufficient beer consumption guaranteed a protruding belly large enough to anchor the body while allowing the arm to swing freely.

There was a commotion at the bar entrance.

Pepe stood at the patio door with his team, plus a hoard of supporters talking loudly in Spanish. La Rubia moved back the safety rope, and they crowded into the bar and demanded drinks.

I spotted several girls. One pretty lady with fair hair caught my eye as she passed and smiled.

"Service," called Jimmy at the top of his voice.

I joined my parents behind the bar to accommodate the initial rush. All the seats were soon taken, many with wives and girlfriends sitting on partners' laps while the remainder stood where they could and peered at the dartboard expectantly as if waiting for it to light up.

"David," I said. "We should explain what is about to happen so our Spanish guests can follow progress with some understanding."

"Fine," said David, taking a large drink. He moved over to the board and clapped his hands.

Nobody took any notice. Dorn tapped a spoon against a glass, and the din died down.

"Ladies and gentlemen," said David in Spanish, sweating profusely, his hands shaking. He pointed at the dartboard. "Today is a landmark occasion. Last month in Munich, Germany beat Holland in the World Football Cup. Because they are useless at football tonight, England competes in their only remaining talented sport. The inaugural darts match between Spain and England will occur tonight in The Fontainebleau."

He gave a brief explanation about how play proceeded and the scoring system.

"Can the first two players step forward? Please tell me your names so I can inform everyone. Be silent while the players concentrate. Any noise can put them off their aim, and as scorer, I am standing in a precarious position. Drinks will only be served in between rounds."

Fran and I presented ourselves. David tossed a coin, and Fran was first to go. David held up his hand, and the noise volume faded, almost. Fran aimed and was about to let loose with his first arrow.

"What about the air conditioning?" said a Spanish lady from the back, fluttering her fan madly.

"It's on full already," said David. "Wait, Fran. Can those near windows please open them?"

The windows were duly opened. They made not a scrap of difference.

Everyone was sweating, and body odours began circulating. Jackets and wraps were discarded, and sleeves were rolled up. Cigarette smoke added a misty ambience.

Fran aimed once again and waited until the noise abated slightly. He flexed his forearm and wrist several times and let it rip. The dart flew straight and true into the double five.

His supporters went wild.

I stepped forward and settled into my stance. I waited like Fran for the noise to abate. When it hadn't, I shrugged and swung my arm. I missed the double to a massive boo from the English supporters and a cheer from the Spanish. Somehow, I couldn't find my normal rhythm, and much to the surprise of everyone, Fran won easily.

Mike and Pepe stepped forward.

Pepe was trying for his opening double when Mike finished with a bull.

It was one game each.

Mick Jingles waited at the oche, impatiently tapping his foot waiting for his opponent.

"Who is your third player?" David asked the

Spanish team, deep in conversation by the bar door.

"Me," said Miguel. "I will play."

"But you can't stand on crutches and throw simultaneously," said David.

"We will hold him up," said Fran. "Ok?"

"I'll have to discuss it with the other team," said David, heading over to our team and standing at the board.

"You're not going to believe this," said David. "But they want Miguel, the old war hero on crutches, to be their player. He needs someone to hold him up, ok?"

We regarded Miguel, who calmly returned our gaze and smiled.

"He's probably their star player," said Mick.

"He is," I said.

"Bring him on," said Mick.

David introduced the players. When Miguel's name was announced, the Spaniards were politely supportive but puzzled. Miguel shuffled forward and stopped at the throw line. He passed his crutches to Pepe and leaned on Fran's shoulder with his left arm. Fran held his waist. Miguel took aim but lost his balance at the last minute and threw the dart.

It sailed through the air straight into the back of David's hand as he was wiping the chalkboard.

"Ouch," yelled David.

"Ooo," said everyone, sharing his pain. It went deadly silent. You could cut the mood with a knife. David scrutinised the offending object. It had only penetrated a little, but blood had begun to flow and dripped on the floor. David grabbed the flights to pull it out.

"Wait," shouted his wife Kay as she pushed through the crowd, extracting a packet of tissues from her handbag. She removed his hand from the dart, surrounded the entry point with the absorbent paper, and pulled the dart out. Blood flowed into the tissue.

"Vodka, quick," shouted Kay, holding the tissue to the wound, "And a plaster."

Dorn grabbed a packet of plasters from the first-aid kit by the till while Jimmy poured a shot of Vodka. Dorn rushed around the bar and held up the glass.

Kay dipped another tissue into the vodka and wiped the wound clean to another wince from David. Dorn prepared the plaster and, as soon as Kay had dried the wound, slapped it over the top and stuck it down. Then, for luck, added another plaster.

They watched the plaster for a moment.

The blood had stopped flowing.

David held it up for all to see.

There was a loud cheer from both sides.

David grabbed the remaining vodka and held it over the wound just in case it continued to shed blood. Satisfied the plasters were working, he held up the glass, inspected the clear liquid, and downed it in one.

"Medicinal purposes," he said, some colour returning to his pallid cheeks. "Shall we continue?"

Miguel seemed distraught. "I am so sorry," he said. "Does this mean a red card?"

"What do we think?" I asked.

"Get on with it," said Mick Jingles. "Otherwise, we'll be here all night."

"I agree," said Mike. "If he's so bad, we should win easily."

"Don't be so sure," I said. "Let him continue."

"You may carry on," said David, moving well away from the scoreboard. "But try and hit the target, please."

Miguel reset his stance with his holders and threw his first dart into the double twenty. The Spanish went berserk. Miguel won by a whisker.

"First round to Bar Bilbainos by two games to one," announced David.

The hotel narrowly won the second round. In the third, Miguel and I were the decider for the match. I returned to my usual form, hammering treble twenty with each dart.

"One hundred and eighty," shouted David. "Leaving me with one hundred and seventy for a nine-dart finish.

Miguel was tiring, and his initial accuracy waned as I finished with two treble twenties and a bull.

"The Fontainebleau wins the match," announced David.

Everyone cheered but was desperate to escape the fearsome temperatures as they stampeded into the fresh night air. As the crowd pushed by me, some shaking my hand, others offering congratulations, the pretty girl with fair hair from earlier stopped before me and smiled. Several of her female friends stood at her back, nudging each other and grinning.

"What a great night," she said in Spanish. "My friends and I enjoyed it tremendously."

"Soy Robert," I said, holding out my hand and having failed to understand less than half of what she said. It was all I could think of on the spur of the moment to avoid behaving like a complete moron.

"*Encantada*, Robert," she said taking mine firmly, "*Soy Vicky. ¿Quiero aprender a jugar a los dardos, me enseñas?*"

"*Por supuesto*," I said, hoping she had asked me to teach her darts.

"*Bien,*" said Vicky. "*Vendré una tarde.*"

"Say, *espero que*, idiot," whispered Mick, creeping beside me. "You look forward to it."

"*Espero que,*" I exclaimed.

"*Entonces, nos vemos,*" said Vicky. She let go of my hand, blew me a subtle kiss, and left with her friends.

"Who was she?" said Mick.

"Vicky," I said.

"Wow," said Mick. "She's nice."

CHAPTER 23

THREE HAIRS IN A FOUNTAIN

Most of Club 18-30's latest group were only eighteen. Sweet, innocent things on the verge of adulthood; lacking in self-confidence, capable in English but, unlike many of the previous groups, useless at Spanish. They wanted to spend the day waterskiing on Burriana Beach, followed by a group paella at Ayo's. I had agreed to take time off and translate for them. My motive had nothing to do with customer service; one of them looked just like Bettina, and my dictionary was ready for some more action.

Early the following day, I was straightening cutlery with my usual precise attention to detail at the breakfast tables when I heard a commotion on the patio. "Eek," came a female voice followed by several more equally loud shrieks of laughter.

I went to see what was afoot.

The patio was jammed with a dozen half-naked girls in their underwear trying to wash out shampoo from their hair in the fountain water.

"*Scheiße*," said a young blond from the German group. "*Es gibt nicht genug Wasser.*"

"Vass, er, what is the problem," I said, trying not to ogle the mass of shapely young curves on display.

"Ze showers in our rooms haf run out of water," said one, giggling. "In the middle of vashing our hairs. We cannot go to ze beach with shampoos in our hairs, ze saltz vill make alles kaput."

Soapsuds were spilling over the fountain's edge, making disturbing gurgling sounds. Hair and soap were not included in the filter design criteria. The waterspout shot in the air about two meters, there was a bang, and the water stopped flowing altogether.

"Zis is a disaster," said another girl. "Vot are ve going to do?"

"Attention, gals," said a posh elderly lady appearing in her dressing gown from her room. Her ageing husband, in matching white shorts, shirt, and Panama hat, also appeared, excited at the display on show. "I ran a bath before the water was cut off. You can use our room."

"I'll show you up, ladies," said the old man, fumbling desperately in his pocket for the key.

"Humphrey," commanded the old lady. "You can't be here with these girls; give me the key. You will wait in the bar and no gin."

Seeing a solution had presented itself, I returned to the bar to find Humphrey tapping his fingers on the counter, checking out the patio nervously. "Give me a large gin," he said, handing over a hundred peseta note. "Make it quick."

I served him straight away, and with a relieved expression, he gulped most of it down.

"Humphrey," shrieked the old lady entering the bar,

followed by the scantily clad Germans. "I said no gin."

Humphrey ignored her, emptied his glass, and placed it on the bar. He grinned at me like a naughty schoolboy, then turned to face the wrath of his loving wife.

If looks could kill, he should have died on the spot.

"Barman," continued the old lady, glaring at her husband. "We need a plumber straight away. The water supply in all the hotel has been cut off."

I tested the bar tap, and she was right. There was no water. Based on previous attempts to find a plumber before nine in the morning, it would take a while to track one down.

"Sorry, ma'am," I said in my humblest tones. "Spanish plumbers don't quite grasp the urgency required at times. If you can't wait for a shower, I suggest you head to the beach and use the public ones."

"But we haff not ze breakfast," said one of the girls.

"Then take what you want from the buffet," I said. "Wrap it in a serviette and eat it on the vay to the beach."

The girls didn't hesitate. Within seconds, there wasn't a bread roll or pastry in sight, and minutes later, they trooped off to the beach, munching happily dressed in bikinis with towels wrapped around their heads.

"See you at Ayo's later," they shouted.

"When I find a plumber," I said.

The plumber arrived mid-morning and discovered the ballcock in the tank had rusted and jammed, cutting off the supply. We were up and running within an hour, so I handed over to Dad, changed into beach gear, grabbed my bag, and headed off to Burriana.

The sugar cane plantation still abutted the sand on

Playa Burriana. Colourful fishing vessels, in various conditions of maintenance, lined the shore. Several middle-aged fishermen sat between the boats mending nets in preparation for another night on the water. They used bright lamps, hoping to attract a bountiful catch of sea bass and sardines. A giant rusty hand winch was anchored into the sand near the sugar cane and used to haul the heavy craft clear of the water line.

Francisco Ortega Olalla–Ayo, a legendary local character renowned for his marathon running and informative guided tours around Nerja caves, started selling drinks on the beaches in the 1960s. As sunbathing grew popular, he opened the first Chiringuito in 1969, a flimsy temporary structure on sand covered with cane panels for shade. As the business expanded, the kitchen became too small, so he moved outside and cooked a giant paella over an open fire. His outdoor cooking demonstrations rapidly grew into a huge tourist attraction.

One Saturday night, earlier that summer, I took my sound system and lighting to Ayo's and lit up Burriana until dawn. It could have been the first music festival on a beach in Spain because nobody had experienced anything like it. The equipment wasn't available back then, at least not in Nerja.

I found the group lying on sunbeds in front of Ayo's, said 'Hola' to everyone, waved to Ken Taylor and his son Chris, who were beavering away with paddle boats and water skiers, stripped off my shirt, and lay down next to them.

As the sun warmed my pale body, it reminded me that this was my first time on the beach for ages, yet I had always loved stretching out and enjoying the rays. It was relaxing and soporific. When Tracy was here, we were on the beach every day, playing beach tennis, volleyball or paddling along the shore, holding hands and exchanging lustful glances.

I watched a father building a sandcastle wall within reach of the surf and trembled with joy when a wave knocked over his endeavours and drenched his children. Their laughter was carefree and infectious, and I couldn't resist giggling with them. Then Chris took a group out on the banana boat and ensured they all fell off by turning quickly. Again, I laughed along. It was so peaceful and relaxing. Why didn't I come here more often? Because I worked seven days a week. How could I?

Somehow, I should make time to enjoy Nerja's beautiful facilities.

"*Es ist zwei Uhr, Mittagessen*," yelled one of the group.

"*Endlich*," shouted another.

I understood that it was time for lunch at last.

Ayo lived with his family next to Fontainebleau, so we often exchanged greetings. He had long dark hair tied back into a ponytail, a round, handsome face, and an athletic body. He and Antonio, his bearded assistant, had just started a new giant paella. We nodded at each other. "*Un grupo de alemanes*," I said.

"The assistant looks like von of our footballers," said one of the boys.

"Because of that, they call him Antonio Breitner," I said.

"Does he speak German?" said Blondie.

"Probably not," I said.

Ayo smiled at them. He smiled at any pretty girl with blond hair, especially if they were German or Swedish. His reputation with the ladies was well known.

"Robert, you must explain vot he is doing," said one

of the blond beauties.

How could I refuse such a pleading expression?

"I'll do my best," I said, but I soon struggled with no idea how to cook paella. Thankfully, Ayo quickly realised the situation and nodded at Antonio, who looked most uncomfortable. It was well known that on windy days, he stuttered. Today wasn't too bad but public speaking affected him. In faltering Spanglish, he stuttered over the ingredients, especially saying paella. We all felt for him but understood his commentary, which he'd changed to rely more on visual pointing and actions than words.

The girls were fascinated; several took notes.

Half an hour later, we sat at a table, and Ayo served us a plate each.

"Vot should wi drink mit paella?" said a young man.

"Sangria, of course," I said. "Look, the barman is mixing some now." They turned to watch a young man throw ice into a glass jug. He added sliced lemons, oranges, and peaches, then poured orange juice, red wine, and a splash of brandy and topped it up with Casero, a local brand of lemonade.

It tasted sweet and refreshing, and after the second glass, they were giggling.

"How do wi know if zis ist a gut paella?" said blondie.

"Moist but not runny," I said. "You should be able to identify the taste of the individual ingredients, and the rice should have a toasted crust at the bottom. Shall we try?"

It was delicious.

I checked around the table to gauge their reaction. Nobody said a word as they savoured their first mouthful. Their faces said it all. They were extremely happy Germans.

But it didn't last long.

When we arrived back at the hotel, I relieved Dad from behind the bar, and Blondie rushed to see me with a furious expression.

"Vi cannot open our doors?" she said.

I went up with her to see what the problem was thinking. Would this ever end? I tried to insert the key, but the keyhole was blocked. Some bugger had glued the locks.

"Well, this one isn't about Spanish craftsmanship," I said.

Blondie didn't appear amused.

Some German boys who were observing the scene were smirking like crazy, while some other girls had the same problem with their rooms.

"The German sense of humour?" I suggested.

"Ve don't haf a sense of humour," Blondie replied.

"I'll see what I've got in the toolbox."

I went downstairs and found some solvent. It eventually softened the glue and enabled the key to go in. I did the same with the other rooms.

We never discovered the culprit.

Dad, though, was angrier at the clogged fountain.

He would have to pay to get it repaired and repainted.

It took over a week.

During this, not one shapely leg appeared through my window.

CHAPTER 24

FLIRTING WITH DARTS

As the season was ending, we weren't busy, so the Harris family decided to have a game of darts and invited me to join them. I'd have to keep them waiting while I served customers, but they had no problem. After such a long break in Nerja, they were well chilled and accustomed to the local pace.

It was getting late for most Brits, and we were halfway through reaching 501 in our final game when I heard several Spanish women enter the bar, all chatting at once in the usual volume, loud. This was a first. Spanish visitors are usually there to sell us something or to satisfy their curiosity. Whether it was the Rolls parked outside, our list of fancy cocktails, the music, or simply because we were foreign. But I hadn't expected a hen party. I saw one of the women waving at me. It was Vicky, the pretty lady with shoulder-length fair hair from the darts match. I'd been wondering if she would return.

I shook her hand, and she introduced me to some

of her friends. I instantly forgot their names. Vicky was taller than most Spanish girls and had a slender figure. Her warm smile was most endearing, and her eyes were brown, sparkling, and beguiling.

"Dardos?" said Vicky.

"You want to learn?" I said.

"*Por supuesto*," said Vicky.

"Take a seat; we finish the game, then I'll teach you," I said.

"Amazing how your Spanish has perked up, Robert," said George as I returned to the board and took my turn. There's nothing like an incentive to teach the ladies the finer points of our national sport. We are off back home tomorrow, so give us the bill, and we'll leave you to it."

"Thanks, George," I said, grateful for his sensitivity as the Harris clan headed to bed. George gave me a suggestive backward glance as he left the bar.

Sharing an empty bar with a group of beautiful Spanish women was unusual. If they understood English, I could impress them with my terrible jokes, but as none of us could speak anything other than each other's language, I would be wasting my time. My solution was to combine my limited Spanish vocabulary with sign language.

I poured them a shandy each, picked up the darts, aimed, and missed. My usual triple twenty gambits deserting me. Nerves? Don't be ridiculous. I thought. And threw again. I hit a double-twenty and double-five. Hesitating slightly, I handed Vicky the darts. She stood on the throw line and took aim with a severe expression mimicking me. She spun around to see how her mates were reacting and then threw. They laughed as the first dart dug out a plaster chip from the wall below the board. She shifted her stance to compensate and let one rip straight down the passageway to the toilets. By now, she was laughing so much that she couldn't do anything with the third.

And so, the first darts lesson continued.

After half an hour or so, we were all exhausted from laughing, and the wall around the dartboard looked the worst for wear, as were my darts. I suggested we sit down around a table. I topped everybody up, and we attempted a conversation.

Astonishingly, we made some progress, and what I found fascinating was they were as interested in learning English as I was in Spanish. For example, Maria, who wore one of the shortest skirts I have ever seen and had shapely legs to go with it, pointed at things around the bar. I said what it was in English, and they in Spanish. I was then to say it in Spanish while they repeated it in English.

This was more fun than darts, as fits of giggles accompanied the mispronunciations on everybody's part. We agreed we had to keep repeating the word until everybody pronounced it correctly.

I had a considerable problem rolling my 'r's. For example, the word for jar is jarra. No matter how often I tried wrapping my tongue around the double letter, it continued to sound like an 'r'. They had a problem with 's' always trying to put an 'e' in front of it, so school was escool.

"As new words dried up, Maria changed the theme and said, "*¿Qué errores vergonzosos has cometido?*"

Thankfully, the dictionary was by the till, and we translated it into what were my embarrassing mistakes.

There were plenty. On the tamer side, in the early days, when in the La Torna apartment, Jim's kids had asked for baked beans, so on my way to Antonio's, the corner shop referred to as Ultramarinos, on Castilla Perez, I thought I'd inquire. I always carried an English-Spanish dictionary and looked it up. There was no direct translation, so I combined individual words that might describe them. White beans were *alubias*, baked was *horneado*, tomato sauce was, *salsa de tomate*. Logically, *alubias horneados con salsa tomate* ought to do the trick. Easy, or so I presumed. The shop was fitted with long and narrow racks, so I wandered back and forth along the aisles but saw nothing resembling the kids' favourite.

Then I spotted Antonio. He had experience with the growing number of inept foreigners, so I asked, "*¿Tienes alubias horneados con salsa de tomate?*" I watched his face. He was bemused, paused for thought, and asked me to follow him. He grabbed a glass jar off the shelf containing large white beans in a clear liquid and gave it to me. I studied the Spanish text carefully, which didn't help. I held the jar to the light and concluded they didn't resemble baked beans. Jim Junior and Samantha would never go for whatever these were. I handed the jar back to Antonio, shaking my head, having no idea what the contents of the jar were or what to do with them.

"*Conocemos alubias blancas, pero nunca hemos oído hablar de alubias horneados con salsa tomate. ¿Qué son?*" asked Vicky.

"*¿Conoces a Heinz?*" I said.

They shook their heads.

That was a typical example of humour lost in translation.

On another occasion, I needed eggs, so asked Antonio's young daughter, "*¿Tienes huevos?*" I'll never forget the embarrassed expression on her face.

The girls howled.

Only later did I learn I'd inquired if she had balls.

The correct request should have been, "*¿Hay huevos?*"

I was buying baguettes freshly baked in a natural wood-burning oven when another Brit who didn't speak a word asked for sliced bread. The girl had no idea what he meant, so I stepped forward and said, "*¿Hay Bimbo?*" a famous brand of sliced white bread. The English guy regarded me strangely and said, I wanted bread, not a dollybird and walked out."

The girls failed to get this entirely and just shook their heads.

"Do you want to know my most embarrassing moment," I said, yawning.

They nodded furiously.

"On my first day in Spain, I ordered a Sandwich de polla."

The girls fell off their chairs and had to go to the restrooms to recover.

Polla is slang for a male appendage. Pollo means chicken. Unaccustomed to gender-free language, I discovered the importance of using the correct definitive article with its appropriate ending, only to be horrified by the enormous quantity of irregularities such as *buenos días or el problema*.

"We have one like that," said Vicky when they returned from the ladies.

"I work in the cinema," said Maria. "We were showing a James Bond film with English subtitles. The seats are not comfortable, so we hire out *cojines* cushions. Two English ladies requested *cojones*. Everyone in our office howled. They had requested to sit on their balls."

As the night wore on, I noticed that none of the other girls attempted to flirt with me. Whenever I asked a question, they deferred to Vicky, and eventually, I understood what was going on. They were her chaperones and there to opine what they thought of me.

After midnight, they were still full of energy, but I was flagging and needed to be up for breakfast. Vicky noticed and announced they should go. Immediately, they asked for the bill and insisted on paying for my two beers.

These evenings became regular events, but Vicky wasn't always with the same group. Over the remaining weeks, I was introduced to many more friends and relatives, including her sister and brother.

Whenever we shook hands and said goodbye, I keenly anticipated our next meeting. I longed to escort her home and even take her out, but she maintained her decorum other than occasional lingering looks and the touch of my arm. Despite our communication difficulties, we became good friends. By the warm vibes I received from her friends, I could only assume they approved, but I did wonder where this was going.

As the low season progressed and the number of hostel guests reduced, I had more free time. I could have hit the town or struck up a relationship with one of the many available girls at Narixa, but I was drawn to Vicky. We would probably have moved on a stage if she was English. As much as I wanted to be alone with her, I resigned myself to the fact that things were different here, and I would have to be patient.

With the prospect of long and lonely winter months ahead, I thought one morning, as I showered, I should probably do something to move things along. However, the last time I had similar thoughts, I'd been too fast on the draw, which had embarrassing consequences. One night, when entering another disco in the town, I spotted a shapely body with long hair and a slender waist, wearing yellow flared trousers, sitting on a bar stool with their back to me. I watched and waited, hoping the person would turn around. As they stood to dance, I was shocked to see that the shapely figure was Pepe, who owned a local gay bar.

I didn't want to repeat that experience, so getting physical with Vicky would have to wait until she showed her hand.

I yearned to.

But did she?"

CHAPTER 25

CHAPERONES REQUIRED

"Hola Vicky," I said one morning, bumping into her on the way to the greengrocer. She was about to enter a single-floor house just down Calle Pintada from the corner of Alejandro Bueno, less than one hundred metres from the Fontainebleau. Dressed in tight jeans and a hugging red blouse, I couldn't help but regard her more closely than I should have. "Is this where you live?"

"Checking up on me already?" she said with a cheeky grin.

"Of course," I said in English. "Start as you mean to carry on."

"Perdon?" she said, frowning.

"Never mind," I said.

"Where are you going?" she said.

"Our chef needs potatoes. Fancy a coffee?"

"When?"

"Five minutes?"

"I'll check with my Mum."

"We're only going for a coffee?"

"I appreciate it is difficult for you to understand, but neighbours and friends will see us together in public. They gossip, which could be misinterpreted by my parents. Things will be different when we can grab the occasional private moment together but, in the meantime, I must uphold appearances."

"This means I need to meet your parents?"

"Yes, but it works both ways. My parents will also need to meet yours."

"That could be interesting," I said. "Your parents speak English?"

"No."

"Do you speak English?"

"You know I don't."

"So, no misunderstandings."

"This could be fun."

"Sounds like the perfect combination for a long and happy life together."

"Ha, not yet, but we seem to be communicating despite our lack of language skills. You make me laugh and like me, no?"

"I do," I said, nodding. "I can't wait to kiss you, but I must be patient."

"Yes, but not too patient; in Spain, we marry young and have many babies. Lots of my friends are already married, but I don't have a boyfriend."

"You do now," I said, reaching out and caressing her arm.

She clasped my hand, stroked it, and gazed into my eyes. "We finally agreed. All that remains is to convince my parents."

"Problem?"

"My mother is ok. She likes your hotel, especially

the car, but I'm unsure about my father."

"You discuss me already?"

"Of course. My instincts tell me we would be good together and I could help you in the hotel, but you must win their approval before we can continue, or my life won't be worth living. Oh, and don't forget the rest of my relatives and friends; you must impress them, too."

"I thought I had done."

"There are more?"

"How many?"

"About sixty?"

"Wow," I said. "My mini car too small, have to buy coach."

She giggled.

"Then I buy potatoes and have coffee in Plaza Cantarero."

"If Mum is free, I will be there. If not, another time?"

Our touch lingered as we admired each other.

"*Bueno, hasta lluego*," said Vicky and closed the door.

Our little chat encouraged me as I waited in line to pay—coffee with my dream lady at last, but what a palaver to arrange a date. Ten minutes later, three shoppers remained before me, exchanging family updates with the elderly lady manning the cash drawer. She weighed each item on some antique scales, wrote down the prices of each item on a scrap of paper, and added up the total—Spanish bookkeeping at its finest. We should try it, I thought, fascinated by the ultimate in tax avoidance schemes. Fifteen minutes later, I arrived breathlessly at the crowded café. To find Vicky sitting at a table with an older version of herself and a slender, middle-aged man with a deadly serious expression.

"Sorry, late," I said. "Queue in fruteria."

"*De nada*," said Vicky. "We've just sat down."

The man stood and proffered his hand. I took it and gave it my best.

"This is José, my father," said Vicky. "And Francisca, my mother."

Francisca held out her hand, appraising me thoroughly. I shook it gently, wondering if I'd passed muster.

"Please meet you," I said as I parked the potatoes under the table and sat in the spare chair. "Coffee?"

I placed their orders when the waiter eventually arrived and glanced at Vicky.

I had no idea what to say.

"Please forgive," I said, turning to her parents. "For not applying to see your daughter. English ways are not habitual to your culture."

José looked at me blankly, turned to Vicky, and I think he said.

"I didn't understand a word. Are you sure you like this man?"

"*Si, papa.*"

"José grimaced, looked at me, and said, "Let me define our rules. You may see Vicky, but unless you go to a restaurant or cinema, she must be accompanied by friends or family. Don't buy her alcoholic drinks, and make sure you bring her home on the dot of midnight. More importantly, you cannot touch intimately until we are happy your intentions are honourable. Do you understand?"

"Of course," I said. "Wondering what I'd agreed to."

Francisca and José exchanged glances and nodded.

"Then you may pay the bill," said José.
"That, I did understand.

CHAPTER 26

LUNCH WITH THE IN-LAWS

I had no idea what to expect, but on the positive side, after our coffee with Vicky's parents, I received an invitation to join her family for a *Matanza* at their campo for Sunday lunch, but on one condition. It was forbidden to bring wine or gifts, but they would be delighted to meet my parents.

Dad was grumpy about driving the Rolls down a long dusty track, but we didn't have much choice as their farm was at the end of the Camino de Rio Seco riverbed leading down to Playazo beach.

Vicky was waiting for us at their gate with several children, her sister Paqui, and her husband Antonio, who ran the farm. He indicated where we should park among several beat-up vehicles and mopeds.

The kids were gorgeous but had been playing in the sand. Their feet and clothing were covered in it. Naturally, they were curious about the car and, with the usual confidence of Spanish children, jumped in as soon as we had climbed out.

I could see my father's renowned apoplexy rising quickly to the surface, so I joined the kids and pointed out all the gadgets.

Then Vicky shouted, 'Lunch is served'.

They were out in a flash and running for the house.

We followed Antonio onto the property surrounded by unkempt prickly pear and were surprised to find some two acres of land planted with fruits and vegetables in neat rows. Toward the back was a small bungalow with outhouses on either side and a large terrace to the front shaded with vines and bamboo. The kids washed their hands at an outdoor sink and then rushed to sit at a long timber table under the shade. There was no tablecloth, but table settings were in place with glasses of different sizes and terracotta jugs of water along the centre.

And twenty other people.

We were introduced to Vicky's immediate family one by one.

None of them spoke English.

This promised to be a quiet lunch.

It wasn't, but not because of the lack of communication.

"Do you understand what *Matanza* means," said Vicky as we sat in the middle of the table. My parents were ushered off to the top end, where they sat silently, smiling at anyone who looked in their direction. My mother was dressed totally over the top compared to the others in working clothes, and we soon understood why.

"*Matanza* means we slaughtered our fattest pig just before you arrived. We butchered it and have barbecued some of the tender cuts for lunch," said Vicky. "We share the remainder of the carcass among the family but save the blood and guts and mix it up in a giant bowl. After lunch, we will sit around this table chatting and stuffing the intestines with the mixture to make *morcilla*, black pudding. We hang it to dry in the outhouse and, when ready, share it with the rest of the family. We'd love for you to help."

I failed to understand every word but got the gist and explained it to my parents. My mother was horrified, gesturing about her lovely dress.

Vicky's mother, Francisca, was well prepared. She brought out a colourful housecoat and offered it to my mother.

After a few moments of peering at it in horror, Mum twigged what it was for and stood. Vicky's mother helped her with it. It was a turning moment. After more smiles, Jose delivered a plate piled with cubes of burnt pork.

"I bet you can't singe the meat as well as my Dad," said Vicky.

"Vicky," said her mother grinning. "Your father is a wonderful grill expert."

"Perhaps he and Robert can make a team," said Vicky. "Burnt burgers and crucified chicken."

"Next time, I bring La Rubia," I said, struggling to contribute. He can translate and show you how English roast beef."

"English roast beef?" said Francisca. "I have heard of it but never tried it."

"It my favourite," said Dorn. "With Yorkshire Pudding."

The Spaniards were astounded as I explained the traditional accompaniment.

"Puddin' with meat?" said Vicky. "Sounds disgusting."

"Believe me, it good," I said. "Wait you try before deciding bad."

"Fair point," said José, nodding favourably in my direction.

"What you grow in Campo?" said Dorn.

I was amazed. This must have been my mother's longest-ever tirade in Spanish.

"It's a large plot," said José. "Besides raising pigs, goats, chickens, and rabbits, we grow most fruits and vegetables."

"Do you sell any?" I said.

"The family takes most of it," said Vicky. "But we always have too much."

"Perhaps we buy direct?" I said.

"Good idea," said José, wiping his mouth.

The hot afternoon drifted by with a couple of glasses of wine accompanied by their own goat' cheese and home-baked bread. While the food was exquisite, I most enjoyed the friendly buzz of conversation around the table. I failed to understand most of it but tried to join in when I could. Vicky would then explain what I tried to say, and many questions would be fired back and forth by her cousins, uncles, aunts, and grandparents. I respected that they made no judgments and showed genuine interest in learning about our traditions and then telling us about theirs. I could sense their love as they exchanged banter, feelings and opinions. This vast but close family lived and worked with each other daily; their joy in being together was unmistakable. What a fantastic support mechanism to have around, I thought, you need never feel alone. Then, the *morcilla* production line began.

The women cleared the dishes while the men carried a giant metal tub full of almost black blood, which sloshed over the edges as they heaved it onto the long table. Swimming in the liquid were lumps of meat and fat, the consistency of slightly runny porridge. Piles of intestines cut to twenty-centimetre lengths were passed around the table, and everybody, including the children, took a few for themselves. Even my father seemed to approach the forthcoming tasks with enthusiasm. Francisca gave us a rapid demonstration of tying off one end before spooning the blood mixture into the open end and packing it tight by squeezing the outer casing. When full, the top was tied off, and the children took the finished items to hang on a washing line in one of the outhouses. It was tedious work made fun by everybody mucking in. The hot afternoon flew by, and as the sun began to set, my parents decided to call it a day, and I had to open the bar.

José and Francisca shook hands with my parents, said their farewells, and we headed for the front gate. Vicky held my hand. I smiled lovingly at her, and she glanced down demurely.

"How we do?" I said.

"No idea," she said.

"Should I be worried?"

"I'll let you know, but what concerns me more is how little we understand each other when we need to discuss serious issues."

"Does this mean you want stop?"

"No," said Vicky, shaking her head vehemently and squeezing my hand more tightly.

"I happy keep trying," I said.

"Me too, but for how long?"

"As long as it takes."

For the first time, she hugged me and watched as

we drove away.

As we crawled along the bumpy track, I was amazed that Dad wasn't grumbling about the dust thickening on his precious paintwork.

"What a lovely family," said Mum. "That was one of my most rewarding experiences since living in Spain."

"I agree," said Dad. "Imagine my fellow bookies back in Staines trying to get their heads around *morcilla* stuffing as a therapeutical after-lunch activity."

"They will probably have to redo all mine," I said. I loved every moment, but how could that be? Why was it such a memorable afternoon?"

"It's a combination of a beautiful place, a leisurely pace and kind, friendly people," said Mum. "Despite the lack of verbal communication, I felt welcome and comfortable in their presence. There wasn't a hint of resentment or pressure, and they made no extra effort to impress us. They were happy in their skin and treated us like we were part of their family."

"And that is precisely how I felt, "I said.

CHAPTER 27

CHRISTMAS

Undeterred by the communication struggles with Vicky and her family, our relationship continued to blossom through autumn and winter. Slowly, our understanding of each other improved, but as soon as the conversation turned to more complex issues, we were both lost. She, when trying to explain them in simple terms, and I, in grasping the point.

I still failed to accept why I couldn't take Vicky away for a weekend or stay out beyond midnight without a host of family trotting along in proximity. I had several heated and frustrating arguments with her father, who was determined to keep a tight rein on his unwed daughter.

"Will you marry me?" I said to the mirror in my bathroom while brushing my teeth the following day. "Will you, marry me? Will you marry, me? *¿Te quieres casar conmigo?*"

I had no idea which was the most romantic way to say it. I pondered but was worried about using the wrong word. *Casar*, to marry, and *Casa*, house sound similar, especially with my dodgy pronunciation. I didn't want her to think I asked her to share my house. Her parents would disapprove of cohabiting until after a church wedding.

But the real question was, am I ready to make such a life-changing decision at twenty-one? It meant a long-term commitment to one-person, potential parenthood, and no more illicit nights out with demanding guests.

I'm flattered such a beautiful girl is so interested in me, but is she only seeing the Rolls and the hotel? In other words, most Spanish men are unlikely to offer such a route to a wealthier lifestyle. Yet these long and lonely winter nights would have been unbearable without her vibrant and enjoyable company.

The entertainment program was working a treat, and the bar was full most nights of the week. However, as Dad is saving to pay the builder, not much finds its way into my bank account. How could I afford a wedding? And with the final payment due to Emilio de Miguel on the first of February, Dad can't either. The brain turmoil continued through the night, and I woke on Christmas morning feeling worse than with a hangover.

I had breakfast with our sole guest, David Wilks. I often envied his independent and responsibility-free lifestyle, which included travelling, writing, and not worrying about anything other than his next chapter. He seemed happy being alone for Christmas, but I invited him to have lunch with us.

My parents arrived to join my sisters and their respective families in the hotel. We unloaded the presents from the Rolls and arranged them around the tree. The bar had more lights and decorations than the rest of the town.

My sisters started straight away.

"How is your romance?" said Diane.

"When are you getting married?" said Gloria.

"I haven't asked her yet. She might refuse me."

"No, she won't, son," said Dorn. "I can see the twinkle in her eye."

"What twinkle?

"Women know these things," said Dorn. "Believe me, she is ready for asking."

We spent the morning preparing for lunch, singing along to carols, deterring the kids from ripping the crackers to shreds and chatting about the usual family nonsense. We were merry after a couple of sherries when Vicky arrived, and the translating began again. The alcohol helped, and Vicky was soon practising her limited English.

Lunch was drawn out with roast turkey, all the trimmings, and plenty of wine.

Traditionally, my father made a speech after we were stuffed with Christmas pudding. When my mother tapped her glass, this year was no exception.

Dad stood, raised his glass, and toasted the family.

Usually, he was relaxed, cigar in one hand, gin and tonic in the other, and entertained us with amusing family anecdotes. But for the first time in my life, I saw him downtrodden and distraught. He regarded us with a pained expression and said, "I'm sorry to be so negative, especially at this joyous time of year, but this business venture in Spain has been the worst experience in my life. We, er I, have failed miserably and are now stuck between a rock and a hard place. We cannot sell until we have paid the final instalment to the builder, which is due next month, and as it stands, we cannot make the payment. Therefore, we have only one choice. We have to sell the Rolls."

He sat down, shoulders shuddering.

CHAPTER 28

ENGAGING PURSUITS

Christmas Day never recovered after Dad's sobering admission of failure. We all did our best to cheer him up, but only when my mother dragged him back up to their villa could the rest of us relax, and the fun begin. We pulled the crackers, chuckled at the rubbish jokes, solved the puzzles in two seconds, donned our party hats, and danced the evening away.

"How will your father sell the car?" said Vicky as I escorted her home to beat the ever-looming Cinderella deadline. "There are no Rolls Royce garages in Andalucía, especially for one with the steering wheel on the wrong side."

"We will call the dealer where we purchased it in London in the New Year and see what they advise," I said. "What did you think of your first English Christmas?"

"It was wonderful," she said, pulling away from me and twirling in the middle of the road. "And completely different to ours."

She danced her way to me and jumped into my arms.

Thankfully, I managed to catch her. She wriggled to the ground, pushed me up against the apartment block wall, and kissed me passionately. It was now or never. I eased her away from me and dropped to one knee.

"*¿Te quieres casar conmigo?* Will you marry me?"

She threw her arms around me and said in English, "Oh yes, please. When?"

"As soon as we can afford it. I have enough to buy you a ring. I thought I'd ask George Harris, the jeweller guy from London who often stays with us, to make one. What do you fancy?"

"Anything will do," she said. "As long as there is a sliver of diamond in there somewhere. Listen, can we not announce anything until we know a date? Then my parents will know you are serious and will present fewer objections."

"Ok, my love. George is due in February; I'll speak with him."

Maybe my smug grin had conveyed my victorious excitement to him, but her father peered at me most suspiciously as Vicky disappeared into the house with a skip and a wave. Finally, it wouldn't be long before I could be alone with his daughter. Perhaps he could sense the inevitable on the horizon when he could no longer keep her locked up in his fortress.

I ought to tell my parents about my impending nuptial intentions but wondered, after Dad's miserable announcement the previous day, if now was the right time. When my parents arrived at the hotel the following day, he surprised me with his usual jolly and confident disposition. Having decided to sell, it was as if a weight had been lifted from his shoulders. With the proceeds, we could move forward or, in this case, survive until the first guests arrive in April.

"You seem pleased with yourself," said Mum as she sat behind the lobby desk. "Vicky, say yes?"

I could barely contain myself.

"She did," I said. But we are keeping it a secret until I can buy a ring and set a date."

"Why?" said Dad. "You should be shouting it from the rooftops."

"Out of respect for her parents," I said. "She feels a ring and an exact date demonstrates my commitment and will minimise any family objections. She is, after all, breaking tradition and marrying one of those bloody foreigners."

"Not just any bloody foreigner," said Dad. "One heavily invested in their country."

"Makes no difference," I said. "We all look the same no matter the size of our wallet."

"Fair enough, we'll keep it quiet until you're ready," said Mum. "And when we've sold the car, we'll have a bit left to contribute to the wedding."

"Fantastic," I said, hugging them both. "How do you propose to sell the car?"

"I'll call Jack Barclay in London after New Year," said Dad. "We'll see what they advise."

CHAPTER 29

FAREWELL OLD FRIEND

"Robert," said David Wilks one morning in early January as I passed his table in the bar after breakfast. "I wonder if you could do me a favour?

"How can I help?"

"I've finished the first draft of my book and need someone to test-read it and tell me what they think."

"My spelling and grammar are atrocious," I said.

"I don't need you to correct the English; just read the story and tell me if you enjoyed it."

"I can do that."

"Great, thanks. I'll have a final read-through and deliver it to you this evening. And please tell me the truth. Trying to be nice won't teach me anything. I need a brutal appraisal and constructive criticism."

"I can only do my best," I said, passing him his crutches from their usual slot behind the bar.

"That's good enough for me," said David, hobbling to his room.

"Good morning," said a smartly dressed man in a

tweed jacket and military tie approaching me as I watched David swinging back to his room on his crutches. "Name is Hustler. Captain Hustler. I'm from Jack Barclay's in London. Is that the Rolls parked in the alley?"

"Just a minute," I said. "I'll fetch my father. He'll take you for a spin. I should warn you that he delights in telling the car's history, so be prepared."

"Just what I want to hear," said Hustler.

What an unfortunate name for a car salesman. I thought as I went to collect my parents from the storeroom.

We left Mum in charge of the bar, went outside, and stood gazing at the car as if it were a revered God. Hustler inspected the bodywork respectfully, almost bowing, occasionally wiping an imaginary speck from the gleaming bodywork. After thoroughly examining the engine and boot, accompanied by nods and hums from Hustler, I climbed into the back, and Dad headed toward the main road.

"I've owned this little beauty for nearly nine years," said Dad as we crossed the bridge over the river. After the recent rain, the usually dry riverbed was swirling with muddy water. "She's one of only six special long wheelbase, custom coach-built editions in the world? When I purchased her in 1966, I couldn't believe my luck when the previous owner, Sir Robert Ian Bellinger, The Lord Mayor of London, who bought it new in 1961, decided to leave his numberplate AFC 27 on the car. He was also the president of Arsenal Football Club, and the number represents their first appearance in the final of the Football Association Cup in 1927 against Cardiff. They lost 1-0."

I'd heard the story hundreds of times but still

cherished hearing him talk so lovingly about what had been a significant part of his life. Hustler nodded but didn't comment.

Twenty minutes later, after a round trip to the recently started Torrox-Costa Centro International apartment blocks on the beach, we pulled back into the cul de sac by the hotel. Dad turned off the engine and turned toward Hustler. "What do you think?"

"It's a perfect example of a well-maintained Rolls Royce," he said. "Anybody would be proud to own it."

"But?" I said.

"Thanks to the oil crisis and Wilson fleecing the rich, not many are buying new luxury cars anymore," said Hustler. "However, it means fewer cars are being manufactured, so second-hand has become much in demand among the nouveau riche, such as pop stars and football players. This car's bottom book price is worth more than its new cost. However, because of the costs of me having to drive it back, I am only authorised to offer you ten thousand pounds, providing you accept a banker's draft, and I drive it away today with all the relevant papers."

"I was expecting a lot more," said Dad.

"Sorry, sir, but that is my final offer," said Hustler.

"Then I reluctantly accept," said Dad.

We went inside, where Dad dug out the papers from the lobby filing cabinet and handed them over. Hustler extracted a draft from his jacket, filled in the amount and gave it to Dad.

I gave Hustler the keys, and we went outside to watch him drive away.

I was sad to see the car disappear down the street. My mind flashed back to many fond memories, the earliest of which was being driven to a private school when I was twelve.

We'd often travelled across France and Spain. Most journeys were incident-free, but once, on a Spanish main road, we hit a deep pothole, which caused the engine to misfire massively. When we stopped at a small repair garage, the local mechanics couldn't believe their eyes when we drove in. After further inspection, a spark plug lead had jumped off and caused the malfunction.

On another trip, we were about to disembark the car deck of the cross-channel ferry at Le Havre. Just as we were rearranging the luggage in the boot, the whole vehicle lurched forward about a metre, causing me to fall flat on my face and the others to jump. A lorry parked next to us had moved forward to vacate the ship and caught the bottom lip of the open left-hand door. We breathed a sigh of relief when we realised what had happened.

In London, my parents had invited me, my sister and her husband Fred to the Talk of the Town, a top London nightclub. My father stopped outside, and the club valet opened the doors. After we climbed out, Dad discreetly handed him a tip, indicating he should park the vehicle—a regular custom in those days. The Rolls was driven away. Then Fred moved forward in his Vauxhall, expecting the same treatment. As he got out of the car, put his hand in his pocket and made a similar gesture, the valet took one look at the car and said: "Piss off. Park it yourself."

"You're going to miss it, Dad," I said.

I anticipated some tears, but as the car disappeared around the corner at the end of the street, he turned to me and said calmly and bright-eyed, "Do you think Vicky can help purchase a new car?"

"Why her?" I said.

"They won't rip her off like they would me."

"What were you thinking of?"

"There's a local Renault garage in the town, so I wouldn't have to drive to Málaga every time it needs servicing."

"You want a Renault?"

"Not really, but it's the most practical solution and will give us enough to pay the builder and a wedding."

"Wait," I said. "You're paying for the wedding?"

"Not the ring, but your suit, cars, reception, and honeymoon are on me."

"Well, thanks, Dad, that's very kind. What's the catch?"

"You've worked for hardly any pay for nearly a year now. Without your help, we would be even worse off. Take it as a token of thanks."

Usually, emotions were kept under wraps in the Edwards family. Stiff upper lip and all that, but as we hugged, I wondered if I'd ever see the Rolls again.

CHAPTER 30

A MILLSTONE LIFTED

The final payment of one million pesetas to Emilio, the builder, was due on the first day of February 1975. Thanks to selling the Rolls and clearing the check from Jack Barclay, we had the money to repay the bank loan, settle the debt on time, and finally become the sole owners of The Fontainebleau.

But it still didn't solve our main problem. Attracting enough bookings for the coming summer. While Wings and Club 18-30 had confirmed they would book with us again, we had not received confirmation of how many and when.

Long-term bookings like David Wilks were rare, and passing trade was slow. We had no money to advertise or print brochures to approach other Tour companies. Dad believed everything would be fine with our existing deals, but I wasn't so sure. However, with no spare cash, we just had to hope Wings would deliver.

Another complication was that Franco was in and

out of hospital. Every time another health scare was announced, most of the population prayed he wouldn't be coming out alive. I could sense the collective sigh of disappointment when he was released, taken back home alive, and almost kicking.

Everybody was aware that Franco's death could be the turning point for the future of Spain. The big question was whether they would stay as they were and continue to be judged as a pariah state by most of the world or attempt to revert to some form of democracy. In the meantime, many tour companies, such as Wings, were sitting on the fence, not wishing to commit to contractual obligations with hotels in Spain until the last minute. During this long winter, we still had to pay La Rubia and Irena irrespective if we had customers. It was worrying.

As the end of January approached, my parents and I avoided mentioning the apparent pressure caused by our situation. Here we were, about to own a hotel outright, but in a country with an uncertain future. It felt like being rich while playing Monopoly.

To escape this debilitating issue, I buried myself in David Wilks's manuscript as I sat behind the bar, waiting for the first clients of the day. At least it made me chuckle.

Having lived in the Fontainebleau with its many oddball guests and characters, it was apparent where David had drawn his inspiration. It was a fictional story about starting a business in Spain.

I felt weird reading about certain similarities, but he invented some amusing scenarios about a mobility-impaired Canadian living in Spain. I couldn't find fault with it and easily imagined it as a holiday read in airport bookshops. I happily told David that. He was delighted, and I enjoyed helping him wrap it up, taking it to the Post Office, and sending it off to his literary agent in Toronto.

The big day arrived.

I ripped January off the wall calendar from Pepe Garcia, the local printer, to reveal the first of February.

We'd arranged for Tosspot, our useless English-speaking lawyer from Málaga, to attend the meeting with Emilio. While we were prepared to pay the total sum in cash, we wanted to negotiate a reduction to contribute to the extra costs incurred because of his delays and poor workmanship. We had invoices for everything: electrics, tiles falling off bathroom walls, no damp course, which was causing us mould problems on the lower floor, and poor drainage on the patio.

Unsurprisingly, Emilio arrived bang on time to collect his money, and we sat around a bar table with Tosspot arguing our case. I failed to understand everything that they were gabbing back and forth, but I impressed myself with how much I did.

Tosspot relentlessly pressured Emilio about his unacceptable delays, cost overruns, and shoddy workmanship, threatening to denounce him. This could mean having his business license revoked. Emilio was unhappy but reluctantly agreed to reduce the final payment by half a million pesetas. It failed to cover our additional expenditure, but it was something. We stood and shook hands. Dad and Emilio signed a letter of agreement. Subject to confirming everything at the notary and modifying the *escritura,* deeds, the Fontainebleau was ours.

We cracked open a bottle of Freixenet champagne and celebrated our newfound status as owners of a hostel in Spain. However, after the lawyer and Emilio departed, the reality settled in. Had we made the right decision or taken a leap in the dark? One thing was sure: Dad wouldn't spend another penny until it broke even. Until then, we would have to carry on as usual.

My main concern was the potential impact on my future and getting married. How long would we have to live in Fontainebleau? When could we afford a house or have children? Irrespective of my long-dreamed-for luxury car, my forthcoming new life demanded a more significant income. Yet, I couldn't see how or when I would start making a decent living to afford it.

CHAPTER 31

LAST MINUTE DOUBTS

The only date available for the wedding on the church calendar had been mid-July. I was so pleased the priest had agreed to marry us I stupidly forgot to think about the implications of a summer wedding. Vicky was hectic making most of the arrangements as the hotel was full, and I had no free time to help, but tragedy struck the week before our nuptials. Vicky's brother was knocked off his moped and killed. The family were devastated. I suggested we delay the wedding, which they agreed to.

We had to rearrange everything hastily, but a week later, the big day dawned.

I was terrified.

"Good morning, Dad," I said as I cleared the final breakfast table. "Ready for it?"

"Yep, suit pressed, shirt and tie selected, but I wish you had arranged an earlier date when the weather was cooler. The middle of July has to be the worst time ever for a wedding in Spain."

"I agree, but we are where we are."

"Are you sure Vicky's family is up to this? It's only a few days since the funeral. They must feel devastated. I would be."

"They are but remain determined life shall go on."

"A funeral and a wedding in one week are a bit much, and with Vicky leaving the house today, they will have lost two of their three kids at the same time. It will take a huge amount of readjustment."

"As her father told me months ago, the advantage of having large families is that you are never alone. Someone will visit every hour of the day to share their grief."

"Fair point. Your mother and I will pop in next week. We won't be able to chat much, but it's the thought that counts."

"Kind of you; they will appreciate it. You know what your role is?"

"Not much as I understand it. How do you feel?"

"To be frank, I've had some last-minute nerves. I was convinced I was too young to be wandering up the aisle, but I had a long chat with Tony and Elizabeth, the young couple staying with us for a month. We've had a few nights out with Vicky, and they got to know her quite well. I was persuaded she doted on me and was barmy even to consider not marrying her."

"I agree. Listen, son, I had the same doubts before marrying your mother. Every groom does but look at us now. It's been a wonderful life, and I'd have been a fool to have her left in the lurch. Vicky is a lovely girl; you're fortunate she wants to marry you. Your mother and I are convinced she'll be a good wife, mother, and asset to the business. How did you persuade the priest to marry you in the Catholic church?"

"Vicky arranged that. All I had to do was produce my Anglican Baptism Certificate to prove I was associated with religion and sign a waiver to raise any children in the Catholic way. I've also had to attend a few sessions with the priest."

"Bet it was interesting."

"Didn't understand a thing, but I pretended."

"Good lad. It's a load of nonsense, really, but I sympathise the church provides a haven away from the stress of living under a brutal dictator. It's not surprising so many locals attend."

"Dad, they don't have a choice. While Franco remains a figurehead, the parliament is managed by professionals who are members of Opus Dei, a deeply religious group of men who strive to sanctify ordinary life. While it's not the law to attend church, from a political standpoint, it's mandatory. Franco's doctrine is based on the premise that you're with me or against me; not going is considered antiregime.

"The delicacies of Spanish politics are way beyond my understanding. Franco is back out of the hospital but under close medical supervision. If he lives or dies, I couldn't care. My sole interest is our business surviving."

"It's more likely to succeed when he's dead and Prince Juan Carlos has taken over as King. If, as expected, he continues with the Opus Dei regime running Parliament, I suspect nothing will change, and we plod on as we are. However, if he surprises everyone with a move to democracy and allows other political parties, tourism could explode. Then we will desperately need a bigger bar."

"Here we go again, speculating on matters you have no control over. Now forget about bloody Franco and concentrate on the most important day of your life. Go and spruce yourself up. We'll meet in the lobby midday, and I'll drive us down to the church. What about the hire car?"

"They're delivering it to Meson Toledano on Castilla Perez at six this evening. We'll head off to the UK when the reception is finished."

CHAPTER 32

THE WEDDING

Dad dropped Mum and me by the church and searched for a parking spot near the restaurant. Some sixty or so smartly dressed Spaniards stood under the shade of the huge Norfolk pine tree in front of the church, chatting quietly. They were Vicky's family and friends. With the recent death fresh in their minds, the mood was subdued. We moved among them, shaking hands and exchanging words before finding the thirty-odd English-speaking guests by the church door.

It was shortly before midday when someone indicated Vicky was due to arrive. It was the signal for me to enter the church. Catholic tradition states that the groom cannot see the bride on their wedding day until she stands by him before the altar. The guests followed me in, and while they took their seats, a horse-drawn carriage pulled up in front of the church.

Spanish weddings do not have a best man or bridesmaids. Vicky's mother and sister fussed over her veil, long white dress, and orange blossom bouquet.

Vicky took her father's arm, walked up the aisle accompanied by the traditional wedding march, and joined me before the altar. My mother stood to my left, her father to her right.

My tailormade midnight blue velvet suit with flared trousers and matching bow tie were typical al la mode for the mid-seventies. However, the material was more appropriate for weddings in the Arctic. In the sweltering July heat of Spain, I melted or was it my nerves. My white carnation was already wilting, and putting my hand into my inside pocket to fish out the rings was a sticky affair.

Five minutes later, or so it seemed, Vicky and I were on the church steps, crowds waving and photographers snapping. In reality, the church service lasted an hour. I understood little and remembered practically zilch but was informed later that I responded as requested without disgracing myself. Having been pelted with rice from all the onlookers, as is the custom in Spain as opposed to confetti, we were photographed in various poses and groups on the Balcón. It had to be the most photogenic location in the Costa del Sol. When the photographer was done, we climbed onto the carriage for the short ride to Meson Toledano.

Vicki wore her engagement ring on her left hand, but our wedding rings were on the right. Orange blossom was the traditional Spanish wedding flower, a custom arriving in Spain from the East during the Crusades. The white petals represent purity, and since orange trees flower and bear fruit simultaneously, they represent happiness and fulfilment.

Castor and his brother owned the restaurant. They were originally from Toledo, but Castor had worked in London, where, coincidentally, Dad had met him several times at one of London's top nightclubs.

After a splendid meal, the celebrations began.

Mike from Narixa did the DJ honours. Apart from Frank Sinatra for my Dad, he played contemporary pop, including *Love Will Keep Us Together* by Captain and Teniel.

Vicky and I twirled around the floor. I was confused when male guests cut in after a few minutes, waving money at Vicky. She brushed my concerns aside, telling me it was a tradition to pay for her favour—some would later bid for her garter. The money would go towards our new life together. I declined offers for cuttings of my precious bowtie, not understanding that I would receive a small envelope in return.

I hadn't told a soul about delivering the hire car to the restaurant. Still, somehow, our wily English invitees had located the Seat and embellished it according to British customs. A 'Just Married' placard penned in red lipstick filled the back window, balloons of inflated condoms were tied to the radio antenna, and colourful streamers knotted to the rear bumper with tin cans attached. A rotting fish was taped to the top of the exhaust. Everybody gathered outside around the vehicle to send us off with a loud cheer and outrageous clatter.

The Spanish are accustomed to celebrating noisily. After a wedding, the guests drive around the town in a convoy, beeping horns and shouting *viva los novios* out of open windows. Onlookers wave and wish them luck. When we rattled by, they stopped and stared with open mouths, unsure whether to offer congratulations or condolences.

We returned to the Fontainebleau as man and wife for some final photos, removed the car's appendages, and changed for our long journey north for our two-month honeymoon in England.

CHAPTER 33

FROM HONEYMOON TO FLOOD

Talk about baptism by fire. Mr. and Mrs. Edwards, or so I had anticipated, turned out not to be the case after exchanging vows and signing umpteen registers. Vicky continued with the Spanish tradition of using her two surnames just as before the wedding. Our children would share her family name of Jimena with mine. I discovered this when registering at our first hotel in Northern Spain, and insisted she was not Mrs Edwards. What's in a name? I thought and gave her the hotel pen to sign for herself as we followed the porter nervously to our room.

I must have done something right, as she was most attentive during breakfast the following day, ensuring I had enough to eat and fetching me another coffee when my cup was empty. I thought I could soon become accustomed to this as we drove to Calais.

This was my first trip back to the UK, and after nearly two years of driving on Spanish roads, I was confused momentarily as we drove off the ferry at

Dover with the steering wheel now on the wrong side of the road. I was too busy concentrating on my driving to notice Vicky had her eyes tight shut as I negotiated her first-ever roundabout.

As we approached the outskirts of London, we were driving through a town centre, and Vicky remarked on a carpet store she had seen. Having not noticed it, I looked over my shoulder, puzzled by what she had seen, only to discover she had confused rolls of carpet with the brushes of an automatic car wash. I laughed. They hadn't seen them in Nerja yet.

It was also a culture shock for Vicky. She had to speak English but quickly adjusted and soon managed basic conversations with the family and when shopping.

We enjoyed a welcoming party at my sister Gloria's house, along with her husband Fred and family. Then, Vicky noticed the relevance of carpets in a British home.

"Could you live here?" I said after a few weeks.

"It's different," she said. "But I miss my family, so it couldn't be for long."

"You've only been away for a month or so."

"This is where we differ, Robert. My family is an integral part of my life. We share everything all day, every day. Especially since my brother died, it is something you must learn to accept."

"I have no problem with it. Do you want to call them?"

"Yes, but we don't have a phone."

"We could speak to my parents, and they could take a message."

"Thank you, my mother would appreciate it."

Happy that I'd done my good deed for the day, I

asked Gloria to use their phone.

"Sure," she said. "It's in the hall; you'll need coins. Sorry, but it was the only way I could stop the kids bankrupting us."

As I picked up the handset and loaded the money, it reminded me of our Dad's phone fetish. Perhaps it runs in the family? At least it wasn't locked.

At the end of September, we returned to Spain, relaxed and happy with a boot full of the latest hits. As we sped by Barcelona, I noticed that even more hotels had gone up since I passed this way. Somebody thinks hotels in Spain are a good thing, I thought. Surely, we must be in the right business.

On our return to Nerja, we moved into a larger room on the second floor as husband and wife. Vicky started working in the hostel, putting her hand to every task. She was a great addition to our tiny team.

"Settling in ok, Vicky?" said Mum as she joined us for breakfast in the bar.

"My room bigger than home, thanks, Mother-in-law. I have more spaces in cupboard for my clotheses."

"Excellent, think of the Fontainebleau as your home now. Do tell me about your honeymoon."

"Many new experiences," said Vicky, blushing.

"I should think," said Dorn, laughing. "But where did you go, and how was meeting the family?"

"My first trip out of Spain, my first voyage on ferry, on double bus, and underground train. Carnaby Street fantastic. Robert buy me nice tops. Family very nice, you have many grandchildren."

"I miss them. Hopefully, they will come to visit this year. What about you? Do you want to have children?"

"Oh yes."

"Wonderful. What did you think of Paris?"

"Dirty like Barcelona. We pass near Eiffel Tower but not stop. Robert drive all way through France in one go. Why he no like stopping?"

"Yes, Robert. Why?" said Dorn.

"In a hurry," I said. "Once I start, I want to try and beat my previous record. How are we doing?"

"We've been full all summer with Germans Club 18-30 and Wings Tours. Bookings are good until early November. After that, we are in trouble. I can't stop worrying if we will make enough over the summer to keep us going through the winter. We're low on cash."

"Dad won't expand the bar?"

"He wants to, but we just don't have the money, and after his last experience with a Spanish bank, he refuses to borrow another peseta."

"I understand. Any more problems with the police?"

"We see Cienfuegos often but only when passing by or watching for furtive activities in Bar Bilbainos. The news about Franco's health isn't good; we hear a big cheer from them every time there's another scare."

There was a knock on the door, and in came a sheepish Irena. She had something in her hand. "Excuse me, please," she said in Spanish, holding a broken bathroom wall tile. "This fell off when cleaning."

"Robert, can you check it out," said Dorn.

I followed Irena up to the top floor and into the bathroom. Most of the Fontainebleau bathrooms were tiny. The toilet was behind the door, preventing entry when being used. The bath was only a metre long and fit for children or showers. The sink was an afterthought crammed into the far end in front of a mirrored wall. A towel rack was mounted on the wall opposite the bath. It was fine for one person at a time.

"Ye gods," I said upon seeing Irena's concern. Most of the tiles on the inner wall above the bath had buckled and bowed outward. How they all hadn't fallen into the tub with the first one was a mystery.

"Is anyone using the room?" I asked.

"Tonight, no, but tomorrow, more Germans are arriving."

"Can you call the builder? If he can't come immediately, I must repair this."

"Ok," said Irena, scuttling off downstairs.

Joaquim, our friendly builder, arrived. Given that the tiles were out of stock, he would have to carefully remove each tile, one by one, soak them in an oil drum full of water, and then refit them.

This was the third room in as many months. The original cement had dried out, breaking the bond between the tile and the wall, yet another of Emilio's shortcuts. The builders used glue in the previous two rooms as a makeshift repair. An oil drum, a trowel, a bag of cement and Joachim's telephone number were always on hand in the storeroom for future maintenance.

The shower tube was also on its last legs; if not replaced, it could have flooded the bathroom.

Just as we had finished, the heavens opened.

Giant flashes of lightning lit up the black sky, and thunder clapped so loudly overhead that the building shook. This happened regularly during October, so it wasn't a surprise.

The outcome, though, was completely unexpected.

We had always wondered why we had rising dampness in the bedrooms downstairs. And how the bougainvillaea planted in a flower bed beneath the stairs had raced ahead of its cousins in the corner beds of the patio and quickly reached the roof. We later discovered that the wastewater downpipes from six bathrooms had never been connected to the main sewage drain. They emptied directly into the foundations of the building. Underneath the fountain were four small drains to allow rainwater to flow into the sewers. But this thunderstorm was the mother of all storms. The drains couldn't cope and flooded the patio, bar, lobby, and rooms. David Wilks paddled into the bar barefoot with his trousers rolled up to the knee. He leaned his crutches against the dartboard.

"I didn't request a room with a pool," he said. "I trust you won't be charging me extra."

"Let me ease the pain with a beer on the house," I said, paddling barefoot with my trousers rolled up. "I've called the plumber, but every house will be suffering from similar problems. All we can do is ride out the storm and hope the waters recede before inundating the whole ground floor. Meanwhile, I'll sweep as much water as possible through the lobby and into the street."

"It will be a long night," said David, savouring his beer. "Wait, there goes one of my crutches floating into the lobby?"

I splashed through the ankle-high water but missed the crutch as it sailed through the front door.

"Oh no," screamed David. "There goes the other one."

By the time I had recovered them both, I was drenched. But as I brought them back, the plumber arrived, and the rain ceased as suddenly as it had started.

"The drains are blocked," the plumber announced

when he arrived five hours later.

"*No me digas*. You don't say."

He attacked the tiles under the fountain with a hammer and chisel, only to confirm that the drains were going nowhere. This demanded digging up part of the patio in search of the main drain to connect the downpipes from the bathrooms. It would also go some way to alleviate the rising damp problem by allowing us to rent the ground floor rooms out in winter. Before that, we had provided guests with a small two-bar heater, which, combined with the dampness, offered a remedy to those clients requesting a sauna in their room.

The complaints during the next few days were unbearable.

My father wished he had retained more from the last payment to the builder.

It certainly wasn't the best time to repeat my expansion wishes.

CHAPTER 34

FRANCO DIES

"Finally," shouted La Rubia, leaning against the kitchen door, hands covered in flour. "He's dead." It was the twentieth of November 1975. Franco had died early that morning at La Paz Hospital in Madrid. A string of heart attacks over the last five weeks had finished him off. He was eighty-two.

The hostel bar had been packed every morning with eager patrons starved of English news and desperate to hear the latest bulletin on Franco's health via La Rubia's newspaper. All nationalities were united by their lack of Spanish. It never ceased to amaze me how many foreigners had chosen to live in Spain despite the lack of language and the potential hazards of dictatorship. Did they leave their brains behind at the airport, or was there something about the country that was so appealing it overpowered its sinister politics?

Now Franco was gone, deceased, stiff as a dead parrot; we were desperate to know what might happen next. Could we stay, or would we be forced to return to our homelands and face whatever demons we had escaped from?

As Prince Carlos announced what would happen next, I opened the bottles of Freixenet Champagne I'd been guarding vigilantly for this potentially life-changing occasion. When everyone was served, La Rubia raised his glass. "To freedom," he said.

Most foreigners in the bar were from Europe and accustomed to freedom. Our latest war to achieve it had incurred the deaths of millions not so many years previously. Many who had participated were still alive or had lost loved ones on the battlefield or in death camps. We respected freedom and could relate to the excitement expressed by our hosts. We politely and quietly raised our glasses and joined La Rubia—each of us reflecting on the price paid by our forebears. Bar Bilbainos, however, was not so restrained. They were ecstatic and danced in the street, screaming, *"Libertad, Libertad, Libertad."*

"What if Cienfuegos is watching?" I asked. "Surely, he won't tolerate such flagrant disrespect to the regime."

"Believe me," said La Rubia. "Until they resolve what happens next in Madrid, we won't see hide nor hair of him or any Nationalists."

"Period of transition," said Charles. "What did Juan Carlos mean by that?"

"The Principe be crowned Head of State exactly as Franco say," said La Rubia. "He also ask for peace and forgiveness between all sides, factions and divided families while solution for future is discussed with all personas interested. Transition take as long as needs and will address concerns of all citizens."

"It sounds positive but vague," said Charles

yawning.

"*Poco a poco*," said La Rubia. "Little by little. They don't want to upset extremists, so rather than announcing grand plan, they build consensus that change is better than staying same. Otherwise, Spain continue as pariah state and remain isolated from rest of world. Military also need agree. They muy difícil."

"The prince will have his work cut out," said Charles. "If he seriously wants all to contribute, he has to consider the wishes of the Basques, Catalans, Unions, Socialists, and Communists, all of whom are considered by the military and nationalist movement as persona non grata."

"Nobody say it easy," said La Rubia.

"At least the prince seems to be implying he is interested in change," I said.

"While Arias continue as prime minister, nothing happen and we stay same," said La Rubia.

"Possibly," said Dad. "And don't forget, while Arias remains in power, the fascists could be back at any moment."

It was the most astute statement he had ever made about Spanish politics.

"How long do you anticipate Madrid will take to decide which way to go?" said Dorn.

"To avoid mass chaos, it need be quick," said La Rubia. "I think they announce something next week but then it take another year to agree the transition detail."

"This could be the turning point of our business," said Dad. "Hopefully, democracy will prevail, but we could be in serious trouble if it doesn't."

"Not much we can do about it," I said.

"We could pray," said Charles.

"I usually find alcohol more effective," said Rowcroft, joining Charles at the bar.

CHAPTER 35

WHAT NEXT?

"If Spain does revert to a democratic monarchy," I said, cuddling Vicky as we lay in bed sharing a cigarette early on the day after Franco had passed. "It will surely be a boost to tourism. Visitors need no longer fear the Guardia, hotel investors will pile in, and airlines will extend their flight schedules."

"I'm not so sure," said Vicky. "My father told me the last democratic republic was chaos. All the different factions clashed with each other, so nothing was ever done; the economy was shot, unemployment rife, and many starved. If we are to go that route, it must be a modern democracy like other European countries."

"And you could join the European Union," I said. "What I'm trying to say, my love, is this hostel could be perfectly poised to make a killing. Think full hostel year-round. We could buy a house and move out of this poky room."

"Really," said Vicky, excited. "You mean it?"

"Of course."

"And we could try for a baby?"

Vicky's face lit up.

"There's only one minor stumbling block," I said.

"Your father," said Vicky.

"In one. The big question is, what do we do if Spain does move to democracy and Dad still refuses to expand the bar?"

"We continue to live in this room?"

"I suppose so."

"Is that so bad? We have each other, a roof over our heads, a job to feed us and provide a small income, plus a few tips. I've had it worse."

"But I haven't. For the future I am aiming for, we need a larger and more regular income stream. In England, I could earn a lot more money, and we could purchase a property quickly. Whereas here, if we don't expand the bar, our income will remain the same, and we will never be able to save up the deposit for a house."

"What could you do in England?"

"Drive a cab, restart my music business, and you could teach Spanish."

"I will support whatever you decide."

"You don't mind leaving Spain?"

"Permanently, no, but it will be an adventure for a while, and I can improve my English."

"What about your parents, won't they object? You guys are so close you see each other ten times daily."

"We will miss each other dreadfully, but they will accept if they know I'll return. What about yours, won't you miss them?"

"Not really; I grew accustomed to living my own life when they sent me away to school."

"I remember how horrified I was when you told me.

No Spanish parent ever sends their children away, and I can tell you now that I won't agree to send our kids anywhere."

"Well, we'll see. I did acclimatise to not being at home, and some aspects of the school probably toughened me up."

"Have you considered working elsewhere, for example, in Real Estate for Charles and Jean?"

"Yes, but being an employee doesn't suit me."

"You work for your Dad."

"True, however, I run the bar as I want, and he lets me because he knows my DJ gear brings in extra cash. I'm a partner in our family business. If I worked for others, it would only be to earn money; I'd be bored to tears within hours."

"I understand completely. My father is the same. Our campo is his heart and soul."

"There you go. So, let's agree to wait until we know which way Spain is going," I said. "If my father won't expand the bar, we go to England."

"Fine," said Vicky, snuggling closer. "I agree we wait; however, until then, lack of money and grand political plans shouldn't interfere with having a baby; it's the one thing we control."

"When do we start?"

CHAPTER 36

MORE DICTIONARIES REQUIRED

I expected a significant change when Franco died, but life carried on pretty much as before. The only visible difference was that there were no secret police and fewer Guardia officers on the street. After so many years of brutal repression, Spaniards were still suspicious of authority and continued to keep their mouths firmly shut with habits unchanged.

As winter turned to Spring, we were worried about the lack of bookings. Tour Operators told us they held back their marketing until Spain had a definitive political solution.

"It's been a long winter," said Jimmy, coming into the patio where I was cleaning the fountain to celebrate the first group's arrival. "But we scraped through."

"It's great, Dad," I said. "Something to do at last. The question is, are you ready to dip into your wallet."

"Cheeky bugger," said Jimmy. "But no, not yet. It's good to see some new faces again, albeit in smaller numbers."

"And some old," said Dorn, taking Dad's arm. "Bettina is back."

"She must have enjoyed her previous stay," I said, blushing. "When was it?"

"According to the file, it's two years now," said Dorn. "I don't need to remind you about being a married man, do I?"

"No, Mum. Anyway, I expect Bettina has moved on."

"I don't think so," said Dorn. "She's sharing with another extremely gorgeous girl."

"Then, I'll inform her about my status change as soon as we bump into each other," I said.

"Please," said Dorn. "We don't want any misunderstandings. Oh, and Robert, next month, we have a capacity problem. We need another room."

"Vicky and I could find an apartment," I said. "Assuming the budget will stretch."

"There's one available on Pintada," said Jimmy. "Opposite Kronox and above the small supermarket. I've made a viewing appointment for you this evening. If you approve, move in next week. It will give us time to repaint your room and replace the bathroom tiles."

"I see you've thought of everything," I said. "Vicky and I will be happy to be out of here. Two of us in one room is becoming a bit tight."

"We did wonder," said Dorn. "We're only looking out for your best interest."

"Of course you are, dearest parents, nothing to do with cheap labour."

We loved the apartment, which was less than a ten-minute walk from the Fontainebleau and agreed to move in as soon as possible.

After a busy evening in the bar, Vicky and I

adjourned to bed for our last night in the hostel. Shortly after midnight, we had just entered our room when an ear-piercing scream reverberated around the patio.

"Lock the door," I said, slipping back into my jeans. "Who knows what is going on?"

I ran barefoot downstairs only to bump into a scantily dressed young girl sprinting in the opposite direction. She was concentrating on negotiating the steps and failed to see me. As gently as possible, I held out my arms and placed them on her shoulders to stop and reassure her she was safe. She screamed and looked at me, but I only saw a mass of beautiful, long blond hair covering her face.

"Robert, Zank godt," she said as she threw her arms around me.

I put my arms loosely around her and patted her shoulder, wondering who it was. I recognised her perfume.

"Bettina?" I asked. "Vot er, what is happening?"

"I wanted to surprise you. You nefer said you changed rooms."

"I expect Mr and Mrs Robinson were a tad surprised."

"I didn't stay to find out," said Bettina. "When she screamed, it was enough. I make big mistake, nein. What shall I do?"

"Let's keep it a secret, just the Robinson's affair."

"Vot?"

"Forget it."

"Ja, you are here now," said Bettina. "Take me to your new room, please; my English needs more improvement."

"Er Bettina, slight problem. My wife might not be

so enamoured to see you."

"You are married?"

"Yes."

"Oh dear, I go now."

Bettina, embarrassed, put her hand up to my cheek and stroked my beard. "Your vife is lucky lady. Congratulations."

She gave me a smouldering look and continued her sprint up the stairs.

"What was all the fuss?" said Vicky as she let me back into our room.

"Nothing much. A guest was confused about her room. It's resolved."

"Which guest?"

"Did I ever tell you about dictionaries?"

CHAPTER 37

HAPPY MOTORING

I don't know what it is about the British obsession with vehicles. When the Spanish chat among themselves in cafes or bars, they talk mainly about family or football, whereas we talk about anything on two or four wheels.

After we sold Dad's Rolls, he followed Rowcroft's advice and bought a brand new bright yellow Renault 12 Familiar from a main dealer in Málaga. The servicing, however, would be done by a local mechanic proficient in Renaults because they were what most people purchased.

Cars were still a rarity in Spain; people couldn't afford them and walked everywhere. The roads were full of slow-moving surprises such as mopeds converted into agricultural trailers. When out in the Rolls, we often had to stop to let an ox cart trundle by or wait for a herd of goats chewing the verges to munch their way past.

While farmers could keep an old machine going forever, the general population was ignorant of mechanical things, especially if they were brand new. Buying a new car in the early seventies was a sign of opulence and 'coming up in the world'.

Word had leaked out that a neighbour was buying a new car and had gone to the main Seat Dealer in Malaga to collect it. Neighbours appeared outside Manolo's hostel on the corner of Calle Pintada and Alejandro Bueno in eager anticipation of his arrival. Minutes later, a bright white and sparkling new Seat appeared slowly down Calle Pintada. It turned into Calle Alejandro Bueno and stopped immediately in front of Manolo's bar. Everybody crowded around excitedly. He proudly stepped out of the car; everybody clapped and applauded his new acquisition. I was watching from a distance and slowly walked up to the thronging crowd, and noticed a smell of burning. In my limited Spanish, together with some sign language, I indicated that the car seemed a little 'hot'. Other locals, more knowledgeable about cars, also informed Manolo that something seemed to be burning. Manolo immediately replied, "Ah yes, that's because it's new. The salesman told me the car must be run in during the first few hundred kilometres, so I have carefully driven it from Málaga to Nerja in first gear." He wasn't called *El Cateto* for nothing.

Trafico, the Road Traffic Authority, demanded Dad attend a test in Málaga to prove his driving capabilities. I went with him to translate. The test was on a quiet country road in El Palo on the city's eastern fringes. We arrived at what resembled an old military base in good time to find several other foreigners waiting outside a dilapidated Nissen hut to face the same ordeal.

"Did I tell you I never took a driving test?" said Dad.

"Then how did you qualify for a licence?"

"I drove a staff car during the war, which was considered enough," said Dad as the examiner strode toward them, clipboard in hand. "Now I'm petrified of screwing up."

"You'll be fine," I said as we climbed out to greet the diminutive officious man with greasy hair who stunk of garlic and body odour. "Drive like you normally do."

Dad presented his English driving license, which was subjected to intense scrutiny. The original was in English, but we had brought an officially stamped translation, which cost an arm and a leg. Eventually, the examiner nodded and invited Jimmy to take the wheel. I sat in the back.

"*Vamos*," said the examiner.

"Drive, Dad," I said.

Jimmy set off confidently as always, but with one minor difference: He was on the wrong side of the road.

"Dad, we're in Spain, not Britain," I said as calmly as he could. "Drive on the right."

Jimmy glanced nervously at the examiner but continued on the left.

"*Para el coche*," said the examiner.

"Stop the car, Dad."

Jimmy checked his mirror, signalled, pulled onto the side of the road, and stopped as a car sped by in the other direction, blowing its horn with a loud, long blast. Dad was as white as a sheet.

The examiner, clearly annoyed, rattled off a string of Spanish.

Jimmy looked helplessly in the mirror at me.

"*Lo siento,*" I said. *"Mi padre está muy nervioso."*

"Dad, I've apologised," I said. "He prefers that while in Spain, driving on the right like everybody else is advisable. Now begin again."

This time, Jimmy drove on the correct side.

After a short journey of about ten minutes, we arrived back at the start point. The examiner hesitated for a moment, his pen hovering. Eventually, he ticked and signed the form and presented it to Dad with a wry smile.

Afterwards, we had lunch on the beach at the iconic Málaga beach restaurant, Chiringuito El Tintero, where the waiters wandered between the tables carrying plates and shouting. "I have prawns, or I have lobster." To order, diners raise their hands at the passing waiter. We waved at the man to pay, shouting, "*¡Y yo cobro!*" I collect the money. He counted how many plates were in front of us and added them on the paper tablecloth. Payment is cash only.

It had been quite a while since I sold our mini, so when I went home, I said. "I've saved up enough tips this summer and think we should buy a car,"

The season had ended, and another long winter with not much to do meant we had time to enjoy the delights of Nerja and the surrounding area.

"To commute to work?"

"Hardly, it would take us longer to find a parking place than walk. No, I loved our little countryside trips out in the mini. Didn't you?"

"I did, but then we were single. I recall fending off your wandering paws most of the time."

"Won't have to now."

"Make sure it's not another mini."

"I've seen a second-hand Renault Dauphine for sale from one of our neighbours; the back seat is enormous; well, it's bigger than a mini. It's getting on, but you won't believe the price. The guy only wants one hundred pesetas."

"That's cheap. Are you sure it's mechanically sound?"

"I took it for a little drive around the block. It's old, but it goes.

"Sounds a bargain."

A simple receipt was signed and exchanged, but the paperwork and insurance required weeks of back-and-forth between various offices. Eventually, the car was mine. I parked it outside our apartment and washed it to celebrate, which didn't improve its appearance. The months of accumulated dust and mud were holding it together. When the washing revealed a rusting heap, I splashed the filthy water back over it. When done, I stood back and admired my handiwork.

I was in the bar one day, and Juan, one of our regular Spanish customers, called in. He'd heard I'd bought this old relic and said he'd wanted it, but I'd beaten him to it. "Anyway," he said. "If you think about selling, let me know."

"I don't recall the Frigiliana Road being so steep in the mini," said Vicky a few weeks later as the old banger struggled around another hairpin bend. Air whistling through the hole in the floor under her feet."

"What do you expect for a hundred pesetas, a Ferrari."

"Bit of a come down after the Rolls."

"Er, yes, but a lot cheaper to run."

"Then make sure you only buy gas one litre at a time. Otherwise, the tank contents will be worth more than the car, and frankly, I don't feel comfortable with the engine in the rear. Every time we go downhill, it vibrates dangerously; I think it will join me in the front."

"Fingers crossed it gets us home."

After a delightful lunch at a tapas bar in the pretty mountain village, we returned home. As we turned into the top of Calle Pintada, there was a loud bang. The car lurched to a halt, and the front bumper fell off and hit the tarmac.

We regarded each other with raised eyebrows.

"At least home is nearby," I said.

"How embarrassing. I'll walk. You sort it."

I watched my wife walk away more quickly than I had ever seen her move, then tentatively opened the engine compartment.

Oil had sprayed everywhere, and there was a large hole in the side of the engine. As I stood there scratching my head, the drivers accumulating behind me began losing patience. Horns started blowing louder than the town band, with similar discordance. Not being mechanically minded, I wondered what was wrong as I closed the boot, or was it bonnet?

I stuffed the bumper in the back seat, climbed behind the wheel, and turned the key, praying for a miracle. Nothing happened. Fortunately, Calle Pintada sloped down to the **Balcón**, so I freewheeled to park outside our apartment.

I paused before heading to the apartment and looked back up Calle Pintada to see a thin black line in the middle of the road. It was my oil.

The following morning, I was behind the bar. We'd finished serving breakfast, and I was preparing for the lunchtime trade.

I looked up, and Juan walked in. He needed a little anis booster before working in the campo on his moped.

How convenient, I thought.

Buenos dias, Juan, "I said.

"Off to work, are you."

"Yes, but the moped is a problem. I can't transport produce from the campo. I need a car," he said.

"Ah, I might be able to help," I said.

His face briefly lit up.

"Still interested in my car," I asked.

"Well, yes."

"It's just that Vicky preferred something a little more luxurious. She's been spoilt by the Rolls. So, I might sell it. But it's developed a little problem." I said.

"Well, I'm sure we can fix it," Juan said.

"Let's meet this afternoon opposite Kronox, where the car is parked," I said.

I was waiting by the car at the agreed time, and Juan appeared with an excited look on his face.

He'll never buy it now, I thought, opening the engine compartment.

Juan peered at everything, which was beautifully oiled throughout.

"Caramba," shrieked Juan.

"Well, yes, a tiny hole appeared from somewhere."

"I'll have to find a replacement engine," said Juan. "But I still need a car, so how about fifty pesetas."

This has to be the best car deal ever. I thought. Several weeks motoring for fifty pesetas.

Not wishing to appear too keen, I hesitantly accepted his generous proposal, and we shook hands.

Rowcroft would have been proud of me.

"Fixed it?" said Vicky as I entered the kitchen where

she was fixing supper.

"Permanently," I said, flicking the coin in the air and catching it.

"Wow, super salesman," said Vicky. "Perhaps you're in the wrong profession?"

"I don't see myself as a second-hand car dealer."

"What a relief. I don't think I'm ready to be the wife of such a high-standing young man just yet."

The car had gone when I peered out the window the following day.

I smirked and showered, knowing my old wreck was in good hands.

When we arrived at work, we found David Wilks chatting light-heartedly with my parents, his suitcase in front of the lobby desk.

"David is leaving us," said Mum.

"I've had a letter from my agent," said David. "They have a publisher for my book and need my input for the final edit. Regretfully, Robert, this is goodbye."

Vicky gave him a hug and a traditional kiss on each cheek. I shook hands.

"Thank you all so much for looking after me and helping me find the inspiration for my book. I'd still be looking at a blank page without you guys."

A taxi pulled up outside. We helped David into the back seat, then stood and waved as he departed.

The vision of his floating crutches flooded back to me.

CHAPTER 38

WE'RE LEAVING ON A JET PLANE

The lack of hostel guests was causing us a huge problem, and we struggled to make ends meet. We assumed everyone was sitting on the fence waiting for Madrid to announce anything, and then finally, halfway through summer, it came.

"Have you heard the news?" I said as Rowcroft walked toward the hostel bar.

"Hang on," said Rowcroft, stretching and yawning. "I'm not worth a damn in the morning until I've had at least one drink."

"Coming right up," I said.

"Thanks," said Rowcroft as I placed his first of the day before him. He stared at it with intense longing, raised the glass to his lips with trembling hands, gulped it down, and banged his glass in front of me. I refilled it, and he repeated the process, then nodded with an appreciative grin, "Now I'm ready to be enlightened by the day's headlines."

"Today, the first of July 1976, Carlos Arias Navarro

has resigned as Prime Minister. In two days, King Juan Carlos will appoint Adolfo Suárez as his replacement. He will be sworn in on the fifth and form a government by the eighth. Their purpose is to preside over the country's governance, oversee the formation of new political parties, and lead the way to democracy. When ready, a date will be announced for when free and open elections will be held in which all citizens over the age of eighteen can participate."

"Really," said Rowcroft. "But we all know Spain. It could take years. Did they mention a date for this supposed first general election?"

"The date will be set sometime next year," I said. "Do you know what this means?"

"Forgive my scepticism, but Nerja announced last year that it would build a golf course. Just because intentions have been announced doesn't mean anything will happen."

"I know, but you cannot deny they are setting out their stall for democracy. If they return to their word, they will become a global laughingstock. I doubt they would make their announcement without having thought this through."

"I can't disagree, but we can only wait and see. The question is, will this news change your father's mind about extending the bar?"

"I doubt it."

"Then what will you do?"

"I must consider our future. We are thinking about having children. Without the extra income, we won't be able to afford it."

"Then I say again, what will you do?"

"I'll talk it over with Dad, and if we can't agree on an actual date, we will go to England until he comes round."

"What makes you think you can make a go of it over there? With the winter of discontent and strikes everywhere, unemployment is rife."

"I know, but I'm sure something will come up. In Spain, as we have discussed before, foreigners only have a choice in tourism or real estate. I can drive a cab in London, and Vicky can teach Spanish."

"Sounds like a plan," said Rowcroft.

"Perfect timing," I said as my parents entered the bar.

"I'm off," said Rowland, downing his drink and hurrying out the door.

"Talking about me?" said Dad."

"No," I said as my parents took a table for breakfast. "About me and Vicky. We need to talk, Dad."

"Sorry, son," said Jimmy. "The answer to yet another request to expand the bar is still no. Franco's death and the possibility of a tourist boom in Spain make no difference to our current finances. The hostel is only half full, and another long winter looms ahead of us. With the return of David Wilks to Canada, we have lost our only permanent resident, and income will be practically zero until April. We must wait at least another year before I can spend capital without incurring dollar premium, or early withdrawal penalties. In my position, you would do the same."

"I understand, Dad, but I'm a married man now. Vicky and I dream of a house and family, which means more income. I can't sit around here wasting another year; we must get on. Either expand the bar soon, or we will be forced to make other arrangements."

"It's difficult, son, but don't take this personally.

Your mother and I would love to say yes, but we must be solvent enough to relax and enjoy our retirement. Sorry, but you and Vicky should do what you must."

"Then, sorry, Dad, Mum, we will go to England. We'll leave as soon as Vicky says her goodbyes, and I've sorted plane tickets."

"What will you do?" said Dorn, sniffing.

"I'll drive a cab and restart my music business. Vicky will teach Spanish."

"Is she prepared to leave Spain?" said Dorn, taking her handkerchief out of her bag. "Her family will be devastated."

"Listen, neither of us wants to go, but stagnating here waiting for you to dig your hands in your pocket would be unbearable. Like my brother, Mum, I must take control of my destiny."

"I can see you've thought this through from your perspective," said Jimmy. "Have you considered that you are abandoning us? We can't afford to employ someone to replace you, so will have to do your work. We came here to retire, not sweat behind a bar, and who knows how to work all that music stuff? I hope that makes you feel happy."

"No, Dad, only sadness. England might be fine for earning money, but Spain has my soul. I'll return as soon as I can earn a respectable income."

"You know where the airport is," said Jimmy.

CHAPTER 39

BACK WHERE WE BELONG

Vicky had been right. I had found returning to England difficult, but she loved it. Our first daughter, Syreeta, was born in Ashford Hospital and was everything we had dreamed of. She was a gorgeous little girl whose every gurgle stirred the cockles of our hearts, irrespective of the sleepless nights and stinking nappies.

Despite our acrimonious parting, my brother Jim had kindly loaned me the money to purchase a second-hand car, and I signed up with Heathrow Cars, ferrying people back and forth to the airport.

Sadly, Vicky's family couldn't afford the trip to see their first grandchild, so we sent a photo every so often.

The long hours on the road with the cab provided enough to save the deposit for a terraced house in Cove, near Farnborough in Hampshire. Finally, we were on the property ladder.

Our communication skills improved. Vicky and I spoke English and Spanish to our daughter whilst the two of us got by in Spanglish.

After a life in the sun, I found living in England depressing. I realised I had spent most of my time polishing glasses, wiping surfaces, and lending false sympathy to drunken ramblings. However, knowing that just outside were spectacular mountains, the blue Mediterranean and clear sunny skies almost every day promoted a positive attitude toward life. Even after thirty-five years of dictatorship, the Spaniards enjoyed their lives. The flat countryside and bad weather in England added nothing to my sense of well-being. Now I understood why tourists from all over northern Europe fell in love with Spain. It brought a touch of joy into their tedious pursuit of money.

Listening every day to my passengers freshly returned from their wonderful holiday in Benidorm or Barcelona only reminded me what I was missing. As we drew closer to their front doors, I could almost see their euphoria disappear out the cab window as the doom of everyday life drew closer. I knew exactly how they felt. I never stopped pining for when I could return to Nerja with a future in front of me. Meanwhile, I went through the motions.

We visited my sisters regularly, which relieved the monotonous daily routine, but even they could see I resembled a fish out of water. On our occasional visit to a pub, I talked with Vicky in Spanish to deter the locals from asking what car I drove or what I did for a living.

I called Mum regularly, and she updated me on how the hostel was doing. "Fine," she would reply, but Dad finds it tiring behind the bar, and frankly, we are both yearning for retirement. When I inquired about money to expand the bar, the answer remained no.

Occasionally, Mum arranged for Vicky's parents to chat at the hostel, but these conversations were always emotional, especially when little Syreeta graced them with a gurgle.

Nearly a year after we had left Nerja, we had a call from Dad. It was the first time we had communicated since we left.

"We need to talk," said Dad.

"I'm here," I said.

"No, face to face," said Dad. "Book us into a hotel near you for next weekend. Somewhere nice if there is one."

I booked them into the Ely Hotel in Blackwater, built in the 1860s with the proceeds of a bet put on a horse of that name in the Ascot Gold Cup and sounded just right for a man of Dad's background. We drove over and met them for lunch.

Syreeta dominated the first half an hour in the bar, but after ordering, Dad said, "That's it. We can now access our capital with impunity and are ready to retire. Will you come back and run the hostel?"

My heart soared, but I wasn't agreeing until the picture was clear.

"I can change the bar?"

"Listen," said Dad. "Come back to Spain, talk with your friend, Manolo Cuenca, the interior designer, get some quotes, and if the price is right, I'll pay for it. Then you can pay me a token rent and run the business as yours. Mum and I will probably be one of your biggest clients, but we will be there to socialise with all the friends we have made, not interfere with how you do things."

"You do know I'm going to charge you for your drinks," I said." I learned that from you."

I rattled off the excellent news to Vicky in Spanish.

She jumped up, ran around to my Dad, and hugged him, then my Mum.

We ordered champagne and drank way too much. We ended up staying overnight. The following day, we quit our jobs, sold the minicab, put the house up for rent and booked our flights back home to where we belong.

We landed in June 1977, the day after the first free and fair elections since before the Civil War. After forty-one years, democracy had returned to Spain. At the end of a quiet summer, we closed in early October and let the builders loose. Manolo Cuenca had done a great job redesigning the new layout, and we entrusted him to complete the conversion. Most of the punitive cost overruns and delays incurred in 1974 were because we trusted supposed professionals and left them to it. Not this time. Manolo had agreed to oversee all suppliers and contractors. We had to be open for the following Easter and the arrival of the first groups from Wings. If I had to shovel cement or plaster to ensure we were ready in time, I would and did.

Thankfully, it was done by Valentine's Day. The family walked around with Manolo, checking the work.

We had knocked down two rooms on the ground floor to make way for the new bar. David Wilks' was one of them. The toilets remained where they were, but we moved the kitchen and storeroom back to where the rooms were and extended the bar to provide more space for the breakfast buffet and a proper Italian coffee machine. Vicky had insisted.

We kept the traditional Spanish style for décor and

used the same timber for the bar support and counter. I now had an intelligently designed niche for my sound equipment, and the speakers were correctly mounted on the upper walls of the bar with the cables hidden in channels chiselled out of the plaster.

The kitchen was the same style, a little larger, but not much. It would still be La Rubia's domain, but at least two people could enter without having to dance around each other. The latest model microwave with an integral grill meant we could simultaneously speed up crispy hot croissant delivery without running the oven.

"I love the backward clock," said Dad as we crept around the new bar, now twice as big as the old one. "If late drinkers can't work out what the time is, they'll say sod it, let's have another one."

"Where did you find the clock?" said Vicky, hugging little Syreeta, who burped as she kicked her legs.

"How cute," said Dorn, gazing at her.

"David Wilks sent it from Canada as a thank-you for our hospitality," I said. "He dedicated his book to the hostel."

"He finished it?" said Dad.

"Bestseller, apparently," I said.

"Do we know what it's about?"

"About the trials and tribulations of setting up a business in Spain," I said.

"How appropriate," said Dad. "Our happy and efficient disposition must have made an impression."

"Canadians seem to like it," I said.

"Has he sent a copy?" said Dad.

"Signed copies arrived with the clock," I said. "Have a read. It might sound familiar."

"Probably too near the truth for my liking," said

Dad. "What happened to Jim's racing posters?"

"Still there," I said. "We beefed up the air-conditioning. They are above the false ceiling we installed to hide the ductwork. And we included your bottle club idea."

"What?" said Vicky.

"With a longer bar and more shelving, Dad suggested we build some bottle-sized boxes. He stole the idea from the sixty's nightclub scene in London. Each box has its key. Regular customers buy a bottle of their favourite spirit at a discounted price and have access to it each time they drop in. We provide mixers and a bucket of ice; they serve themselves. At the end of each session, we return their bottle to its box and charge them for the mixers. Hopefully, they will brag about it in other bars by saying, oh, I have my bottle at the Fontainebleau. We'll have to put one up for you, Dad. What will it be, Gordons or Larios?"

"Since you're charging me, Larios, it's cheaper."

"How is the new apartment, Vicky?" said Dorn.

"It's a bit cramped with Syreeta and her paraphernalia," said Vicky. "But it will do until we can find a house to buy."

"Did you profit from your house in Cove?" said Dad.

"We are renting it out for now. The rent pays the mortgage."

"Keeping your options open?" said Dad.

"No. House price inflation in the UK is rampant; it's a good investment."

"Wow, at last, a chip off the old block."

"Amazing, what a difference it makes when you're in charge."

"Proud of you, son," said Dad, turning to Mum and

putting his arm around her waist. "Well, my dear, the new bar should make an enormous difference to the takings, especially in winter. I think we can finally say, let's retire."

"About bloody time," said Mum.

CHAPTER 40

A FRESH APPROACH

The new bar was an instant success. It attracted more locals, including many Spaniards curious to learn our secrets. With the increased income stream, I decided to sell our UK house and look for a property in Nerja.

Paco Rico, a reputable Nerja developer builder, showed us around a completed three-bedroomed house in La Hacienda just below Pueblo Andaluz with incredible views over Playa Burriana. It had been built for the German restauranteur Udo Heimer and his family. We loved the design and asked him to do the same for us. We made a reasonable profit on our UK house so that I could put down a hefty deposit. But with the painful memories of delays and bankrupt builders, I used a Nerja lawyer to ask all the right questions before I paid anything. He assured me the legality and planning permissions were in order and that the builder's financial situation was acceptable. I paid up but held my breath, hoping it wouldn't take as long to complete as the Fontainebleau.

With Dad no longer involved in the day-to-day running of the Fontainebleau, I was free to explore new avenues to move the business forward. Although the rent we agreed to pay him was far less than it should have been, it still had to be paid even though the winters remained long and quiet. Now, Spain had decided to join the rest of the democratic world. The future was bright, but somehow, we must attract clients all year round to exploit this exciting potential.

I failed to understand why people ignored the low season. The best time of year weatherwise for me was November through March. The average daily temperature was over twenty degrees, with no crowds and cheaper flights. We'd celebrated several Christmas Days on my parents' terrace in our shorts, so why would tourists prefer to stay home and freeze their backsides? Perhaps things were about to change.

During our absence from Nerja and while hovering over builders during the refurbishment project, the rest of the town had moved on. There was more competition for accommodation. Visitors could choose to rent or buy a rapidly growing number of beachside apartments and villas. Urbanisation Capistrano was under construction on the eastern fringes, and locals converted town centre properties into hostels and rental apartments. I put a lot of this frenzied activity down to imitating the success of The Fontainebleau. We had been among the pioneers and taken risks any sensible businessmen would avoid. But now Franco was gone, they set out to do the same.

The Hotel Monica, a vast five hundred-odd bedroom, fully air-conditioned holiday factory, had recently opened directly on Torrecilla beach. Customers came from all over Europe, paid an all-in price, and didn't venture far from the hotel. The hotel's marketing thrust was outright scaremongering—a fortnight in the sun with a pool, no language or dietary problems and no crime. The idea of battling for sunbeds to spend the day on packed terraces with no room to swim in the chlorinated water was horrendous, but thousands went for it. They also offered live entertainment every night and day trips to nearby cities and attractions such as the Alhambra Palace in Granada. It forced me to re-evaluate our offer.

We had no pool, and there was no cooling besides the bar. Our tiny patio hardly caught the sun and had room for up to ten sunbeds. We were half a mile from the nearest beach but near the shops, Tuesday market, and a growing selection of restaurants and bars.

Our most appealing asset was that we were a small family-run business offering personal attention, English food, and a bus stop around the corner for the more adventurous who enjoyed finding their way. Our room costs were also less expensive, and I remain convinced that our romantic musical evenings in an intimate atmosphere played a massive role in attracting repeat customers.

I had only just turned twenty-four, and while I could manage a hostel, pull a pint, and operate a music system, I had no business development skills and few travel contacts other than those I'd met at Wings and Club 18-30. Consequently, I wasn't a qualified marketeer and had no budget to promote our business. All I could do was build relationships with those who did bring people to Nerja and try to piggyback on their success.

The first phase of Capistrano Village was started by

Ken Brabant, a Canadian whose goal was to attract his fellow citizens here, or snowbirds as he called them, to escape their arctic winters. The construction of the five hundred-odd villas and townhouses built in the style of a typical Andalusian white village was well underway. However, the Canadians were not buying as many properties as envisaged, so they expanded their marketing to the UK.

One day, Graham Maynard and Bernard Reilly, members of the Capistrano sales team, sat on bar stools and introduced themselves. Graham was a tall, well-built, charming man with longish dark hair, a chiselled face, and grey eyes. Bernard, his colleague, was a burly, dark-haired, vivid character. Both were in their early thirties. Graham was a gifted personality. He was good-looking and entertaining and could charm the hind legs off a donkey. Within minutes of taking a bar stool, he would have anybody who cared to listen in fits of laughter.

Graham and Bernard began popping in during the week for a drink and a chat with anyone who cared to listen. The Fontainebleau was a warm sanctuary where they could escape the ever-watchful eyes of their customers and boss and maybe meet a potential buyer. Slowly, we became good friends and joined the Lions Club.

Although what was mainly a charity had been here for a while, it had recently started to play a more significant role in the town's increasing number of businesses. Being a member added credibility to us as foreigners and increased our acceptance among the Spanish members. Instead of treating us as competition, they recognised we needed each other. We brought the tourists, and they provided the facilities.

One day, when we were quiet, Graham explained how their sales system worked.

"We advertise inspection trips all over Britain," said Graham. "Interested buyers pay to come here on a Friday at their own expense on what they perceive is a cheap weekend deal. We meet them at the airport and bring them to Nerja by bus. They are accommodated in a Capistrano property, and we entertain them at our own Caves Bar. On Saturday, we bombard them with sales presentations and viewings until they pay a deposit for an off-plan property. After taking their money, we give them lunch at Ayo's and don't let them out of our sight until they fly home on Sunday."

"If we let them wander on their own," said Bernard. "They may be distracted by another property, or some other agent will sink their claws into them."

"You could bring them here," I said. "You might find having an English-speaking bar with English food is appealing to your buyers as a change from Spanish."

"Could you organise a Flamenco evening?" asked Bernard.

"Of course," I said.

"Good idea," said Graham. "But you'll have to keep other agents out. I don't want them poaching our clients."

"Charles Bishton is the only one to worry about," I said.

"Charles is fine," said Graham. "We've signed him up as an approved agent. But no others or we'll forget about the Flamenco."

"Fine by me," I said.

Despite my attempts to fend off other agents, more Spaniards started using us, especially those seeking to meet potential property buyers and offer their building and related services.

"They call me the fisherman," said a thick-set middle-aged Spaniard approaching the bar wearing an open-necked shirt and baggy jeans. "Or, if you prefer, Miguel."

"Pleased to meet you, Miguel," I said, shaking hands. "I'm Robert. For what do you fish, *boquerones* – anchovies?"

"Properties," said Miguel.

"And why would that interest me?" I asked.

"Most property purchasing dreams start in places such as your hostel. Two weeks of relaxing and drinking on our exotic beaches is a powerful seduction process. Many don't want to return home; some do something about it. You would be amazed how easy it is to sell them a property, especially when they are dirt cheap compared to UK prices. Should anyone inquire, contact me, and I'll fish around for whatever they fancy."

"Do you have an office?"

"Not necessary. I move around the local bars, talking to people. When I hear somebody wants to sell, I discuss it with them."

"Do you know of many for sale?"

"When you add up the plots of land, fincas, ruined cortijos, and single-floor family homes to be converted into apartment blocks or townhouses, it is more than two hundred."

"Don't local people buy them?"

"Rarely, we have no money, whereas you *guiris* – foreigners buy almost anything."

"Food for thought," I said as Miguel knocked back his drink and reached into his pocket.

I shook my head and said, "On the house."

Miguel nodded. We shook hands, and he left.

This is good, I thought. I do not know where this might go, but our hostel is potentially becoming a magnet for property buyers, sellers and associated services.

Wings had expanded their brochure for our area. They had more flights and hotels, so they appointed a permanent representative. Ann was an attractive blond English lady who had married a Nerja shopkeeper and introduced herself to me in the bar. It turned out she lived just around the corner. Her job was to liaise with hotels, meet the people at the airport and bus them to their hotel. Instead of the entire bus coming to us on a Friday to collect the departing group and deliver the news, they were dropped off in smaller numbers throughout the week. Almost every day became a changeover day; it was less stressful than before when we all had to share duties cleaning, changing bedding, and signing in fifty-odd people at once. It also meant we could handle things ourselves rather than pay for an army of cleaners.

Ann also suggested we offer various day trips or activities for their customers who wanted to do more than sit on a beach all day.

Now I had to think.

CHAPTER 41

EASTER FLAMES

I was surprised by how many of the group and other guests wanted to accompany Vicky and me to watch the Easter procession on Thursday evening while my parents managed the bar. Perhaps we should make more of Holy Week, I thought, as nearly thirty of us stationed ourselves just after nine pm on the Balcón at the top of the passage leading down to Playa El Salon. It was a balmy evening with a gentle breeze as we absorbed the stage. It was dimly illuminated by candles and a few streetlights, which, when combined with incense and cigarette smoke from almost every adult, created a misty ambience usually associated with an Alfred Hitchcock horror film.

The crowds were three deep around us, chatting quietly. Many of the women were dressed in black dresses with long sleeves. Some balconies overlooking the Balcón had their railings decorated with red fabric and a gold cross. Traditionally, Easter is the most significant of religious festivals in Spain, far more so than Christmas. Celebrating the end of a purposeful life is more meaningful than its uncertain beginning. To prepare, property owners whitewashed their facades, painted the black wrought iron window bars, and spring-cleaned the green window blinds. Those who didn't were ostracised for at least a week.

Knowing that the band would deafen our voices when the action kicked off, Vicky explained what they were about to see to the group.

"Do you know what a cofradia is?" she asked.

"No," said some, others shaking their heads.

"It's a brotherhood or group of men who pledge allegiance to each other and their saints. Every town and village in Spain has at least one. In Nerja, we have three, founded during the seventeenth and eighteenth centuries. They carry their thrones around the street in a procession exclusively for them and their members. They also wear unique clothing and have a variety of badges of office. The boss is the *hermano mayor*, a senior brother. Tonight is the turn of Cofradia Nuestro Padre Jesús Nazareno y María Santísima de los Dolores. Their members wear white robes and purple headwear, depending on their status. The first throne represents Jesús carrying the cross toward Mount Calvary in Jerusalem. The second is María Santísima trailing after him, weeping. Both thrones are extremely heavy and difficult to manoeuvre, and it is a great privilege to be one of the *costaleros*, the guys who carry them. They practice turning corners and negotiating steps for weeks in advance. They sway side to side and shuffle slowly forward as one. Their progress is controlled by a senior member who rings a handbell. You'll see how big and cumbersome each throne is as it emerges from the church.

"The people wearing robes, masks, and conical hats carrying large candles are penitents, referred to as Nazarenos. The mask allows them to pay penance without revealing their identities. The cone symbolises rising toward heaven and brings the penitent closer to God. The shape resembles the cypress trees we plant in cemeteries to symbolically raise the dead upward rather than down to hell. Depending on their seniority in the brotherhood, some members carry an ornate staff, others' candles. Look, the church doors are opening."

The crowd noise faded away as the first throne crawled down the steps and took up its position to head off around the crowd-lined main streets of the town. Every citizen was watching from somewhere.

The brotherhood band was forming up dressed in bright blue uniforms, their spotless brass instruments reflecting streetlights and candles. When the band was ready, a bell rang, the thrones were heaved back onto solid shoulders, and the band started playing a loud and raucous dirge, the drummers setting the pace for the *costaleros*. Many of those on the Balcón fell behind the procession as it headed up Calle Cristo. Having absorbed everything, we returned to the Fontainebleau to relieve my parents behind the bar.

I'd been pouring drinks for half an hour when Ted Bartlett approached. I went to top him up.

"Sorry, Robert," said Ted. "I don't want to be alarmist, but the patio is smoky. Has La Rubia burned the cottage pie?"

I checked the kitchen, but all was as usual.

I left the bar to Vicky and rushed into the patio. Smoke was everywhere and thickening by the second, but I couldn't see where it came from. I climbed the stairs to the first-floor gallery and walked around but spotted nothing. I ran up to the second floor, where the smoke appeared thickest, and concluded it was coming from one of the rooms, but which one?

This is not good, I thought as the smoke started choking me. If I couldn't see the source of the fire, perhaps I could sense it. I climbed the metal ladder leading to the flat roof, where I removed my shoes and padded about in my socks to establish where the heat was coming from. The hottest spot was above room 205. I rushed downstairs to fetch a spare key.

By this time, guests were milling around on the patio, coughing, spitting and shouting instructions on how to remedy the situation, most of which were unhelpful.

"Call the fire brigade." Someone suggested.

"Good idea," I mumbled, grabbing a fire extinguisher from the toilet passageway and rushing upstairs again. "We will have burned down by the time they arrive from Velez-Málaga."

I paused outside room 205 and hesitated. I delved back to my experience while undergoing a training course with the school's Duke of Edinburgh Award program. Doesn't oxygen feed a fire? I slowly and deliberately opened the door, terrified the cool night air from the patio blowing into a hot room might fan the flames. The smoke was extremely dense, and it was impossible to see around the interior.

Once the door was fully open, I sprayed the entire contents of the fire extinguisher in all directions because I couldn't see any flames. I opened the window, and gradually, the smoke dissipated, revealing that everything in the room was smouldering. The walls were black, some plaster had fallen, the double mattress wholly burnt, and the place was a wreck. On further inspection, the remnants of a cigarette end lay in the ashtray on the remnants of the bedside table. The end must have fallen onto the mattress and started the fire.

As the smoke cleared, some guests came up to see what all the fuss was about, all rendering their own expert opinions of the cause.

"I spotted the occupants leave only a few minutes before the fire started," shouted someone above the melee. "They are an American couple. One of them must have been smoking, left a cigarette burning, and then went out."

Extraordinary powers of deduction, I thought.

"At least the fire is extinguished," I said. "And we can do nothing more until the morning."

We retired to the bar to continue the scientific debate about the cause.

"First the flood, and now this," said Ted Bartlett. "I hope your insurance policy is up to date."

"Oh my god, what's happened? There's smoke everywhere," said the American couple when they returned two hours later.

"No thanks to you," I said.

"What do you mean?" said the man approaching the bar.

"You left a lighted cigarette in the ashtray. The whole place could have gone up." I said.

They rushed upstairs and returned moments later.

"Jeez," she said. "All our things are destroyed. We've lost everything."

"They are replaceable," I said. "But I've lost a complete room, which will need replastering and redecorating. Plus, smoke has penetrated the adjoining rooms via the air ducts in each bathroom."

The following day, Vicky called the insurance company, which sent a rep to inspect. Substantial collateral smoke damage had been caused to other rooms. Several rooms had to be completely repainted, and all the furnishings in room 205 had to be replaced. Thankfully, the insurance company paid, but the premium increased.

The American couple left immediately with nothing more than the clothes they stood in, followed by the arrival of the Guardia Civil to prepare their official report.

The general smell of smoke hung around for several days until the painters and decorators had completed their work. As it was early in the season, we were just over half full, so the guests on the top floor were relocated to the one below. There were complaints, but we soldiered on.

CHAPTER 42

SAN ISIDRO

Working with Tour Operators was usually a well-organised relationship. One morning in early May, I was surprised when Ann, the Wings Rep, popped in to tell us there had been confusion over the numbers in the group arriving later that day. At the last minute, a family of three decided to bring their elder daughter, who wanted a room to herself, but the office failed to notify us.

"Do you have a free room?" asked Ann.

"We don't," said Vicky, checking the reservation diary. "Can't you put them in another of your hotels?"

"Impossible," said Ann. "With San Isidro approaching, they are full. What about the nearby hostels?"

"I can try," said Vicky. "But they are likely to have the same problem."

"If that is the case, the two children will have to share," said Ann, which proved to be the only solution.

The airport bus arrived on time, and after

processing those with rooms, Ann undid a button on her blouse and, with her best smile, approached the family in question. Mr Davenport was a big, hard-looking man dressed smartly in a grey suit and open-necked white shirt. By his dripping forehead, he suffered in the heat.

"Sorry to keep you until last, Mr. Davenport," said Ann, firing her sparkling, white-toothed smile and revealing cleavage. "But we have a problem. Our booking department informs me you added your daughter's reservation at the last minute. Regretfully, this information has not reached the hostel management. They only have two rooms available so the children will have to share. To compensate, we will refund you in full for the cost of one room and give you a voucher for a day trip."

"I'm not sharing with dork-face," said the daughter, a frumpy mid-teenage girl with acne wearing a flowery patterned dress. Long blond golden hair and ice-blue eyes were her best feature. She glared at her skinny and nerdy thirteen-year-old brother, buried in a Spiderman Comic and oblivious to the conversation.

"We'll work it out," said Mrs Davenport in a contrived posh voice, edging her husband aside and holding her hand for the room keys. She was dressed in a lime green twin set and silk pink blouse. Her permed platinum hair was swept back from a somewhat oversized forehead. Bottle-green tortoiseshell framed spectacles were perched on the end of her nose, and she had an enormous engagement ring. "Meanwhile, we are happy to accept your offer."

"Mummy, I am not sleeping in the same room as a boy," screamed the daughter, stamping her feet.

"He's your baby brother," Mrs Davenport said with

an astounded expression. You shared a room with him for years; why on earth are you having a meltdown?"

"I made it crystal clear I would only come if I had my room."

"You must learn to be flexible, dearest," said Mrs. Davenport. "Circumstances have a habit of changing at the last minute."

"Then so can you," said the daughter. "I will share with you; it can sleep with Daddy."

"He snores," said the son, sticking his head out from behind his comic.

"Tell you what," said Mrs. Davenport. "Shall we go and see the rooms and discuss who shares with who in private? Hubert, lead the way."

"Yes, dear," said Mr. Davenport, torn between ogling Ann or the beer taps at the bar. He turned to Ann and added. "I'm sure we'll find a solution, so please arrange the refund. What time does the bar open?"

"At eleven am," said Vicky. "And seven this evening when there is a free drink at the welcome reception. It's a good opportunity to meet fellow travellers."

"Hubert," said Mrs. Davenport, looking daggers at her husband. "We agreed, no alcohol until the evenings."

"Of course, dear. I was only inquiring."

The Davenports headed to their rooms, squabbling as they climbed the stairs." I don't think I'd seen such miserable people all my time in the Fontainebleau.

Fifteen holidaymakers attended the drinks party. Most of them were happy, except the Davenports.

After the usual speech, I added.

"You have timed your holiday perfectly. Next week

is San Isidro, a truly colourful and entertaining Romeria, unlike anything you would have experienced. My wife Vicky and her family have entered a float into the procession and invite you to join them for a small fee to cover costs. We will provide the appropriate clothing accessories, but you must put your names down tonight.

"How much?" asked Mrs Davenport.

"One thousand pesetas," I said. "About seven pounds per head paid tonight."

"What is a Romeria?" asked Mr Davenport.

"Good question," I said. "It evolves from processions of pilgrims going to Rome. Sprigs of the aromatic herb Romero or rosemary were stuck in travellers' hats to ward off evil spirits and robbers, hence the name. Romerias are famous all over Spain, none more so than El Rocio, held at the end of May in Sevilla Province. Hundreds of thousands of pilgrims walk, ride horses, or tow caravans through Doñana National Park to El Rocio, a village purposely built just for this festival with several hundred houses, a cathedral, and a hotel. The streets are made of sand so horses can be tethered outside owners' properties.

"The pilgrims take several days to reach the village. Every night, they stop and celebrate with BBQs, Flamenco, and flasks of sherry. It is a remarkable and spiritual occasion. Nerja's procession is minuscule by comparison but still attracts six thousand. It kicks off at the church around midday and ends two kilometres away on top of a hill overlooking the coast road, where a hermitage has been built to accommodate the Saint's effigy for the duration. Now, who would like to participate?"

"Is sherry included?" asked Mr Davenport.

"Food and drinks are included

"What are the clothing accessories?" asked Mrs Davenport.

"Gentlemen wear white shirts, jeans, red bandannas around the neck, and Córdoba hats. Spanish ladies wear traditional dresses with polka dots and their hair tied back with a red rose above the ear. We will provide the bandannas and hats and can recommend a few shops if anybody wishes to buy other festival clothing such as a dress."

"I want one," said Davenport's daughter."

"We will see, Matilda," said her mother.

"Duh," said the son.

It was mid-morning on the fifteenth of May when eleven guests entered the lobby wearing their festival clothing. After several days of sunbathing, the Davenports were transformed into happy holidaymakers and were chatting with George and Cheryl Harris. Mother and daughter had splashed out on Spanish dresses and were stunningly attractive with a red rose above their ears. Father and son had also entered into the spirit of the occasion, but the father looked decidedly uncomfortable in tight jeans.

Vicky headed out onto Calle Pintada; I brought up the rear. As we approached the town centre, we heard the loud whoosh of a rocket followed by an explosion. On the Balcón, we paused to watch the official town fireworks igniter, dressed in his uniform of a battered straw hat, torn baggy trousers, and grubby T-shirt, send yet more rockets aloft into a clear blue sky. The noise echoed around the countryside, summoning the surrounding populace to join the festivities.

While the church bells tolled, spent rocket sticks headed earthward with luck to land harmlessly. It wasn't always so. One year, a fishing boat on Calahonda Beach caught fire; on another, the mayor's laundry drying on his roof terrace.

We joined Vicky's family outside the church and introduced everybody. We waited amid a crowd buzzing with anticipation, nearly all dressed in Romeria attire. The wealthier wore tight-fitting suits of striped, grey trousers, waistcoats with black bolero jackets, and boots.

Regardless of shape, age, or dimensions, figure-hugging Spanish dresses transformed the wearer into gorgeous, elegant women who carried themselves gracefully. They were a pleasure to behold. Most men were doing a lot of beholding.

Cute children ran about everywhere, wearing mini versions of whatever festival clothing their parents wore and endearing themselves to everyone by drenching them with water pistols. Few complained; they soon dried off in the sun.

The church doors opened.

The small San Isidro effigy was mounted on a portable throne resting on the sturdy shoulders of six *costaleros*. The men, selected from the religious brotherhoods, swayed in unison as they shuffled down the church steps and over to the lead oxcart elegantly decorated with palm fronds and dangling loaves of bread.

The effigy was a wooden statue, a metre and a half tall, with a golden halo mounted over his head, wearing a long brown cloak, green clothing, and beige boots. A carving of a pair of oxen yoked together, pulling a plough, was at his feet. The throne was placed reverently onto the cart while a group of women danced, swirled, and twirled in unison in front of the church to shouts from the crowd, "*Viva, San Isidro, Viva"* Long Live, San Isidro.

Once the Saint was secured onto the cart, a uniformed horseman carrying San Isidro's intricately woven green-and-purple banner led the procession past the church toward Plaza Cavana.

The remainder of the participants were waiting in the wasteland north of the cinema. They fed into the procession, tailing the oxcarts. As each cart departed from the church, family members watching the activities climbed aboard or walked behind. Our combined group of over twenty was too many to ride on the last oxcart, occupied by Vicky's mother, her aunt, and an array of younger children.

Following us were nearly a hundred finely groomed and well-muscled horses of every breed, followed by mules, donkeys, and a tiny Shetland pony. Some exquisitely dressed riders were accompanied by beautiful girlfriends perched on the horses' hindquarters behind the saddle and holding onto the rider tightly. They were most decorous. Spectators photographed them intensively as the procession crawled by.

Behind the horses was an array of carriages. They varied from stylish and gleaming four-seaters drawn by three elegant matching pairs of horses to battered single-seaters pulled by Dobbin, the bedraggled mule, a stubborn grey beast needing constant prodding with a whip.

Up next were rusting tractors towing large trailers carrying up to twenty people. They were highly decorated with flowers, palm fronds, polka dots, and shields representing their club or association. One was equipped with a generator. It powered a fridge, a fan and the latest audio system blaring popular Latin music. On one rig, a chef stood dressed in kitchen whites, flamboyantly carving a leg of *serrano ham*. Each piece cut was added ceremoniously to a nearby plate with shouts of "Ole."

Beer, *fino*, and *Tinto Verano* flowed, but not excessively; this was a family occasion. When the procession paused to give the animals a rest, those behind the carts and trailers danced the Sevillana together, receiving much appreciation from the spectators. It is a rhythmical and joyful dance with partners facing each other, arms raised with much twirling and exchanging positions. It is infectious to anybody watching. Children begin learning when they can walk and move with fluidity, grace and confidence. I was utterly useless, but some group members followed Vicky's instructions. It was a disaster, but the fun was in trying. I noticed Matilda watching avidly as they danced.

Finally, the charabancs—a mixed array of new, old, and wrecked vehicles clad with an occasional palm frond, the odd polka dot painted on cardboard, and masses of soccer club scarves. Here were the town's youngsters enjoying themselves. Their music was so loud the speakers were vibrating, but they were having fun, and their behaviour, although boisterous, was inoffensive.

Vicky's father led the oxen on foot with a stick in hand, cap on head, and a red bandanna around his neck. Her sister walked alongside, providing him with drinks and a cloth to keep his shoes clean. It was almost impossible to tread carefully—the joys of processions with live animals. It was even worse further back, where over a hundred horses had added to the oxen's outpourings.

San Isidro was born Isidro de Merlo y Quintana sometime in the Twelfth Century. His miracles with never-ending sacks of corn and bottomless pots of stew had endeared him to the poor and needy. In recognition of his talents, he was beatified nearly five hundred years later in May 1619, hence the loaves of bread hanging from his processional oxcart.

Few festival-goers were bothered or even aware of the saint's achievements. Today was mainly an excuse for another grand social occasion—one of half a dozen throughout the year. Since Franco's death, religion had been fading throughout Spain. Yet, the traditional religious festivals were more popular than ever because they presented one of the few opportunities for the hard-working, mainly agricultural community to meet up with old friends and discuss mutual problems.

We trundled slowly up Calle Granada, stopping at fifteen-minute intervals to rest the animals from the uphill haul. Vicky's family cart was covered by a U-shaped awning covered in polka dots and palm fronds. The large wheels were woven with flowers. I took these opportunities to refresh the sherry glasses of my guests and encourage conversation with Vicky's family. Their lack of Spanish reminded me of my communication hardships in the early days, so I wandered back and forth, translating what I thought they would find interesting.

They were loving every moment.

In the next pause, Raul, one of Vicky's teenage cousins, invited Matilda to dance a Sevillana. He was a tall, thin boy with glasses and was extremely patient with her. With a combination of signs, demonstration and words of encouragement from Vicky, she made some progress.

The procession progressed over the Rio Chillar bridge, turned up the Frigiliana Road, and, after a few hundred meters, left onto a farm track that led to the hill topped by the hermitage. The track up to the top was rutted and steep, so passengers on carts dismounted and walked up behind in clouds of dust, some pushing.

The carts were parked in the shade of pine trees, the oxen unyoked and left with water and hay while we carried our picnic boxes and folding chairs to a vantage point where we could enjoy the folk music and dancing events after lunch. There were also dressage competitions to discover the finest equestrians.

It was a beautiful, warm, and sunny afternoon. To the south, the Mediterranean sparkled, and the mountains to the north and west provided a sense of horizon. We sat in the shade, chatting and people-watching. At such events, one sees the Spanish at their best: carefree, relaxed, and happy families talking and laughing at the antics of cute children. I enjoyed this about Spain—outdoor pleasure not spoiled by a handful of idiots who couldn't hold their drink.

Halfway through the afternoon, Mrs Davenport approached me with a concerned expression. "I can't see my children anywhere," she said.

"Follow me," I said.

I took her to the young people's dancing area, where the music blasted so loud it was impossible to speak. I stopped and pointed.

In the middle of some hundred teenagers, her daughter and son danced the Sevillana with Vicky's cousins. Besides their typical English looks, their dancing was so good that you would have thought they were Spanish.

Mrs Davenport rushed off to bring her husband.

They watched their children proudly.

Matilda then danced with her brother, their expressions happy and loving as they glanced at each other.

I could see the parents' eyes watering. They exchanged looks, put their arms around each other, and kissed tenderly. They seemed so nervous; it was probably their first in years.

Was this the magic that brought people back to the Fontainebleau year after year?

People started leaving around six. I gathered our group, and we walked back to the hostel.

CHAPTER 43

PROPERTY MATTERS

That summer, the three of us and Syreeta's nanny, the reliable Mercedes, moved into our brand-new home in La Hacienda precisely as scheduled. It was a terraced house with terracotta roof tiles in a rectangular complex surrounding a central garden and swimming pool. On our first morning, we stood on the terrace, arms wrapped around each other. The kaleidoscopic sunrise over the beach below and the twittering birds rendering their dawn chorus were mesmerising. The fiery orange ball crawled out of the sea, illuminating a sparkling pathway over the turquoise water aimed at our house.

There were now several makeshift merenderos on the beach, and fishermen were working on their nets, having just landed their catch after a night on the water.

Early bathers paddled hand in hand where the Mediterranean kissed the shore. Photographers snapped away from behind palm trees. The sugar cane plantation still terminated at the edge of the sand, and the plant leaves fluttered in the gentle breeze.

It was enchanting.

"We did it," I said.

It was a surreal experience walking along empty streets to work, unlocking the front entrance, and letting ourselves into the Fontainebleau. After all those years cooped up in the bar, a tiny bedroom or apartment without hardly ever leaving the building, it was an absolute pleasure to enjoy the beauty of our town. I began to appreciate it all over again.

Nobody was up as we prepared the breakfast buffet.

Most of the current group from Wings were as good as gold, and we were thankful for a stress-free fortnight. Only one couple had problems with there being too many Spanish people everywhere.

While Wings and Club 18-30 eventually sent us more guests for longer, I remained desperately worried about what we would do for income after the end of October. Somehow, we had to find the money for the house insurance and mortgage on top of the hostel rent and staff, irrespective of our income.

As Dad would say, think positively, and a solution will appear.

I looked up at the ceiling and projected all the positivity I could muster.

"What are you doing?" asked Vicky.

"Seeking divine intervention."

"With your religious track record?"

"Every little helps."

We finished our preparations, and when La Rubia arrived, we had breakfast together, sitting on bar stools so as not to dirty a table.

"I'm worried," said La Rubia.

"Why?" I asked.

"The fire set me thinking. What do I do if there is disaster and you not here?"

"Phone us," I said. "Didn't you know it's the modern way to communicate?"

"With what?" said La Rubia. "The lobby phone is locked when you are not here."

"We'll give you a spare key," said Vicky.

The first breakfast guests started trickling down. By the time the last coffee was poured, and we had cleared the tables, the usual early birds had begun propping up the bar for their first infusions.

"I've just finished reading David Wilks's book," said Rowcroft as I served his vodka and orange. "It was beautifully written, and I concede to the odd chuckle or two."

"I enjoyed the distinctive Canadian flavour," I said.

"I don't recall lumberjacks being mentioned," said Charles.

"You mean the 'eh' and 'sorry' references," said Rowcroft.

"That and his frustration about trying to track down their national delicacy wherever he travelled," said Charles.

"You mean that Poutine crap," said Rowcroft.

"La Rubia had a bash at making some for David," I said. "He said it reminded him of dog vomit."

"What was it again?" asked Charles.

"French fries with cheese curds and brown gravy," I said. "It's a delicacy originating in Quebec during the 1950s."

"I can't see real French people being taken by it," said Rowcroft.

"It's even worse than cottage pie," piped up La

Rubia from the kitchen.

"Wow, a compliment for fine British gastronomy," said Charles. "Listen, I need to be about my business."

"Me too," said Rowcroft. "I'm sure there was something important I had to do."

We were busy for lunch as usual, and toward the end of the session, a tall man with a familiar face in his mid-forties with freckles and curly fair hair approached me as I was adding up a bill.

"Hi, Robert; sorry to disturb you.

"Hi Bob, you're back again." Bob Richmond was a car dealer from Southampton. They initially stayed with us but rented apartments on subsequent visits.

"After much debate, we've finally decided to buy a property. We like the look and location of La Hacienda. I heard you live there?"

"That's right, we moved in a few days ago."

"Would you mind showing us around?"

"You'd like to see my house?"

"If it's not too much trouble. We adore the views over Burriana."

"Of course, if you hang on until the lunch trade has quietened, I'll take you myself. Can I serve you with anything?"

"Thanks, a couple of shandies, please."

"I'll give you a nod when I'm ready."

We closed the bar and headed home with Bob and his wife Marianne, a bubbly, dark-haired woman a few years younger than her husband.

"As you can see," I said as we stood together on our terrace; the house is well-designed and built with a spectacular view over your favourite beach. What do you think?"

"Just what we dreamed of," said Marianne.

"Two others are for sale and ready for occupancy. Would you like me to introduce you to the builder and help with translations?"

"We'd love it," said Bob. "But we want to be quick. We are returning home at the end of the week and want everything confirmed before we go. Would that be possible?"

"I don't see why not," I said. I'll call Paco to meet us here this evening, and we can show you the two properties and let you decide which one you want."

"Perfect," said Bob.

That evening, we met Paco Rico, a short, balding man in his mid-thirties, in the house next door to ours, and it all went like clockwork. Bob signed a purchase contract and handed over a check for the deposit.

Three weeks later, Paco came into the bar one evening. He reached into his pocket, extracted his chequebook, scribbled on one, ripped it out, and handed it over.

I glanced at it, but it was too distant to see the detail.

"For Señor Richmond's house," said Paco.

"Not necessary," I said. "But thanks, can I offer you a drink."

"Another time, I'm meeting my wife. See you."

I read the cheque—half a million pesetas. I whistled. Over sixteen thousand gin and tonics at thirty pesetas each, I thought.

I'm in the wrong business.

After we had cleared the tables after dinner, I cranked up the volume on the sound system and put on *Sweet Caroline* by Neil Diamond. It never failed to encourage dancing and out-of-tune singing. About an hour later, Irena beckoned me to the lobby door; she looked harassed.

I changed the album to *Night Fever* by the Bee Gees and left them to strut their disco stuff as I edged through the dancers to the lobby. Irena pulled me outside the main entrance, where I found Pepe, the owner of Bar Bilbainos, propping up a huge but happy man in his fifties dressed in a light-blue shirt and black pants. He looked as if he would collapse at any moment.

"His name is Luis," said Irena. "He's paralytic and tried to drive his taxi back to Málaga."

"We had to stop him," said Pepe.

"How can I help?" I said as Luis sang to himself.

"Do you have a spare room we can put him in? Then he can drive back in the morning."

"I was in two minds. We had a spare room. But for someone in his condition, I was reticent. However. It was the neighbourly thing to do."

"We have a room on the first floor above the bar," I said. "I expect he won't mind the music. What brought this on?"

"After he dropped some clients here," said Irena. "He bumped into Marco, an old pal who had moved to Nerja from his neighbourhood in Málaga. They hadn't seen each other for years, so they took a brief tapas tour. It evolved into a grander affair than they envisaged. If you're worried about a mess, I will clean the room for free."

"Ok," I said. "Can you take him up to Room 109 and settle him down with a bucket nearby?"

They nodded.

I fished out the key from the lobby desk and handed it over.

Thankfully, the music masked the drunken singing as Pepe and Irena staggered up the stairs with Luis between them.

On their way out about twenty minutes later, they signalled Luis was asleep.

I nodded, waved, and they left.

CHAPTER 44

FROM FARCE TO FLAMENCO

Vicky and I were recovering from a late night at home celebrating our new house with friends Pepin and Mari, Eduardo and Mercedes, also known as 'Mataperra,' 'Mosca,' and Conchi. While Vicky served drinks, Pepin inquired if there were any decent films on our first-ever TV.

"Here's the paper, take a look," I said.

While they checked the listings, I went to the sideboard cupboard, removed a videotape and popped it into our brand-new Betamax video player. I pressed the play button and waited.

"*¿Que es eso, qué canal es ese?*" asked Pepin, as they looked in astonishment.

"*¡Dios mio!*" they shouted as a porn movie started to play on the TV. In those days, hardly anyone possessed a video recorder, let alone an X-rated film.

After a few more beers, we were rolling about, laughing at the antics on screen.

"Impossible, shouted one, trying to ape an unusual position.

"I was still chuckling when someone repeatedly banged on the front door and pressed the doorbell simultaneously. Who the hell is that at eight-thirty in the morning? I thought. I rushed downstairs and opened the door to find El Rubio breathing hard and shouting in Spanglish. "Robert, Robert, you come now. Big problema."

"What's happened?" I asked.

"Flood. Big flood in bar," said La Rubia. I grabbed my stuff, and we rushed out of the house, jumped on my moped and sped in the wrong direction along one-way streets to the Fontainebleau.

We entered the bar and were confronted by water dripping through the ceiling, filling breakfast cups, juice glasses, and cereal containers lined up for breakfast. On the patio, a mini-Niagara Falls cascaded from the first-floor landing. The source had to be in one of the bedrooms immediately above the bar. We grabbed spare keys and rushed upstairs to see water gushing out from room 109. I opened the door and entered. The bathroom door was ajar, and water flooded the entire bedroom floor. I gingerly pushed open the door and stopped in astonishment,

Luis was asleep in the bath, completely zonked out and oblivious to the overflowing water. He was fully clothed with shoes on, lying with his back covering the bath taps. Consequently, we couldn't turn the water off. La Rubia and I heaved him upright to gain access to the taps, only to find there weren't any. He had fallen heavily and sheered them clean off the wall.

Luis started to come around, dazed and confused but shocked to find himself fully clothed and soaking wet.

"Where am I?" he mumbled.

I rushed downstairs and closed the entire water system down.

When I returned, together with La Rubia, we heaved Luis out of the bath, out of his clothes and onto the bed so he could dry out and recover.

When we returned to the bar, water was seeping into the toilets and kitchen. I looked at the clock, and it was nine a.m.

Time for breakfast.

Nothing was prepared, given the circumstances.

Astonished guests gasped as they surveyed the dripping scene and inquired how long breakfast might be.

By now, the water had stopped flowing, and we set up a buffet table in the dry section of the patio for a standing-only breakfast while the water dripped relentlessly. I scratched my head, wondering how we would dry out and clean up in time for the Capistrano Flamenco show this evening.

There was extensive damage to the ground floor rooms, room 109, and adjoining rooms. Water had seeped upwards into the plaster on the walls and sideways to the rooms next door. Furniture in the bar had also been affected, so we had damp sofas.

The rest of the day was spent chasing a plumber and drying out Room 106, the landing, patio, and bar.

When Irena arrived for work, she went up to talk with Luis. Her screaming tirade was way too fast for me to understand, but the outcome was that she popped out and came back with some of Pepe's dry clothes from Bar Bilbainos. Luis came down later looking the worst for wear and extremely sheepish in overly tight trousers, whose bottoms flapped six inches above his feet. He apologised profusely but made no effort to help or compensate us for his sins. He slipped out the door, never to be seen again.

As the day progressed and we slowly started winning the drying race, I became more nervous about my next concern: Would the Flamenco group turn up on time? When Graham and Bernard arrived with twelve inspection trippers just after seven, they still hadn't arrived. We always served our meals early to suit English biorhythms, so we wheeled out the fish and chips at seven-thirty and let our first Flamenco evening begin.

Even though the air conditioning was on full blast, the bar and patio still smelled damp, but at least everything was dry.

Thankfully, Mick Jingles had offered to play during the meal. He had been strolling between tables, playing well-known Spanish numbers to the many couples sharing a romantic evening over their beautifully presented English cuisine. He finished up at the bar, bowed, and walked out through the patio to appreciative applause.

The dancers still hadn't arrived.

I was now a complete wreck.

Graham and Bernard flitted from table to table, checking on the inspection trippers and making sure glasses were topped up and everyone was happy. After the meal, they helped clear the tables and rearranged the chairs into a cinema format for the first-ever Flamenco Show at the Fontainebleau.

I heaved a sigh of relief as the dancers arrived while people took their seats. The conversation rumbled on, cigarettes were lit, and a smoky haze filled the bar.

People chatted as they waited and waited.

I was about to explode.

Then, about a microsecond before my fuse was about to blow, three women in red and black Spanish dresses walked in via the patio from the storeroom where they had been changing. Two guitarists, including Mick Jingles, followed them in black pants and red shirts. Another man joined them, carrying a wooden box. Five chairs were lined up in the corner between the lobby and the front window. The chairs stood on a thick timber panel covering the floor tiles on which the dancers would perform. The man with the box placed it on the panel and sat on it; the remainder sat on the chairs and waited. The timber protected the tiles from stamping feet and provided the appropriate quality acoustic effects for the dancers.

I did have a prepared speech briefly describing Flamenco and its history, but had no time for it. Instead, I announced through the microphone, "Welcome to our first Wings Tours group of the year, regular customers and those joining us from El Capistrano Village. Tonight, we have a special treat. Appearing for the first time at the Fontainebleau, from Vélez-Málaga, is Cecilia Fargo and her Flamenco Spectacular."

Cecilia, a tall, slender woman in her mid-thirties with jet-black air pinned back into a bob with a red rose, appeared at the patio door. She wore a bright red Flamenco dress with a trailing ruffle. Heads turned as she walked to the corner, her dress swishing and metal-studded shoes clicking on the tiles. She took her pose on the stage. One arm raised, head down, and one toe pointing at the floor. For a moment, total silence engulfed the bar.

A single guitar chord shattered the stillness.

The dancer leaned forward slightly from the waist, her weight favouring her left leg. Both arms raised above her head formed a heart shape as the guitarist continued strumming the introduction. She glanced at the audience through dark brown eyes set in a striking face with well-defined cheekbones. She smiled fleetingly before setting her jaw in a serious mask of concentration.

The lead guitarist upped his tempo and volume, joined by Mick strumming in the background. The fluid rhythm of the traditional Spanish instrument echoed around the bar as dexterous fingers with long fingernails reinforced with glue flew over the frets and strings. The man on the box tapped its front between his legs; he provided the percussion.

The musicians paused. Cecilia breathed in deeply, her pert breasts rising under her sleeveless gown. She raised a thigh, stamped her heels three times, bent one knee, pointed her foot at the floor, and tapped it once with her toe. The wooden floor amplified the raucous sound, highlighting the difference between the heel's robust stomp and the toe's more delicate tap. The music restarted.

Cecilia began to twirl, moving her arms, wrists, and hands, then stamping in beautifully coordinated elegant movements. The harmonious combination of guitar, clapping, and foot-stamping generated a thunderous noise bouncing around the far corners of the bar. It reached out to the inner musicians in the audience, who tapped their feet or fingers more or less in time.

While the music created the ambience, Cecilia captured everyone's hearts. Her accentuated hip and body movement drew the eye to her curvaceous femininity. Her waving hands and arms emphasised her hips, waist, breasts, and swan-like neck, while her sparkling eyes engaged the spectators with smouldering, intense glances.

The audience was enthralled by the speed of Cecilia's foot stamping. Her heels and toes thundered against the floorboards, which at times created a sound reminding me of the drum rolls at the Queen's Trooping of the Colour birthday parades. Then she spun out of the stamping into a series of elegant pirouettes, lifting her skirt, exposing bare athletic legs. She swept the ruffled train of her dress up in the air with one leg while spinning around on the other.

This was Flamenco surpassing its finest, blood-stirring, erotic, and captivating.

When the number finished to the audience's roar of *olé*, Cecilia stood centre stage with arms by her sides, head bowed, waiting, and breathing hard.

A tall, handsome man with long dark hair and a superb physique joined her from the patio. He was dressed in tight black pants and a frilly white shirt and carried two pairs of castañuelas or palillos, also known as castanets or clackers. He handed her one set of the traditional percussion instruments.

They faced the audience, bowed, turned toward each other, raised their arms, and simultaneously clicked castanets. Then the pair weaved around each other, turning, arms undulating, foot-stamping, and castanets clacking in a fast-moving fandango. But this display was far more than a dance. Their hip movements and admiring glances toward each other, as they moved around the stage, were subtle, but no one could miss the raw sexual chemistry exuding between them even though they never touched.

The evening's entertainment progressed to its climax with another final spine-tingling number. The performers joined hands and bowed to a well-deserved standing ovation. An encore was inevitable.

After the performers had departed, I started playing records while Graham, Bernard, and Vicky pushed the made space for dancing.

"Brilliant," said Graham as he ordered more drinks. "Where did you find them?"

"Mick Jingles tracked them down in Vélez-Málaga," I said. "There is a large gypsy population living in the town centre where there are many Flamenco bars. It was a question of who was available."

"Then we need to make this a regular event for our buyers," said Graham. "I'm already hearing positive comments about how great it would be to have the Fontainebleau down the road from their Spanish property."

I heaved a sigh of relief and gulped down a rum.

CHAPTER 45

WHEN IRISH EYES ARE SMILING

The Kerrigan brothers owned a travel agency in Dublin. Entirely coincidentally, they were frequent visitors to Nerja and were among the growing number of regular Irish bar customers. After a few visits, they declared us their go-to place in Nerja and promised to send guests. At the time, I took it with a pinch of salt, putting it down to whiskey-fuelled bravado. As it had been a while since I had heard from them, I'd forgotten their assurances.

I was pleasantly surprised when the phone rang.

"Hi Robert, it's Brian Kerrigan. Do you remember our last conversation about me sending some punters?"

"Hi Brian, of course I remember, but was it a while ago?"

"To be honest, I'd probably had one over the eight, but I hope it's not too short notice, but the O'Leary family will be arriving in three days."

"Great, thanks, Brian. A double room?"

"Good heavens, no. There are thousands of them. They own a hotel in Dublin, a chain of fifteen butcher's shops, and about a million children. They only require six rooms this time, but next time, who knows, maybe more."

"Sounds like my sort of client," I said.

"Indeed, but they can be demanding, so be on your toes."

"After fending off the secret police for years, they can't be that bad."

"Don't say I didn't warn you."

"What time are they due?"

"Around noon, ok?"

"Perfect."

Three taxis arrived at twelve on the appointed day. The cab drivers unloaded their enormous suitcases into the lobby while two burly men with ruddy complexions, freckles, and fair hair carried several large duffle bags.

"Sean O'Leary," said the largest in his mid-forties. "Where do you want this meat?"

"Sorry," I said, suitably perplexed while I sorted the room keys.

"I have prime-quality vacuum-packed Irish meat that needs to be kept cool. Do your rooms have fridges?"

"They don't, I'm afraid."

Sean was rapidly losing his rag.

"Do they have cooking facilities?"

"This a hostel, not an aparthotel," I said.

"Could you store them in your kitchen?"

"No chance. Our fridges are jampacked."

"Then we're fucked," said Sean. "All this way for nothing. Right, back to the airport; we might get this meat back in Dublin before it crawls there itself. Are the taxis here?"

One of the twelve in their party peered out the door. "Nope," they said.

"Then order us some taxis and make it quick," said Sean.

"If you tell me what you need," I said. "I'll try to find a solution."

"We need a fridge and somewhere to cook, plus double rooms for this lot."

"Would an apartment nearby be okay? The others could stay in the hostel and meet for meals."

"That's not what we booked, but yes, and a wee drink might help," said Sean.

"Then may I suggest you take a seat in the bar? Drinks are on the house while I organise something. Meanwhile, work out among yourselves who will sleep where?"

"Didn't those bloody Kerrigan morons tell you what we wanted?" asked Sean.

"Six double rooms are all they said."

"Fucking eejit," said Sean, his wife, trying to restrain him with a hand on his arm. "I'll chop his legs off. Can you get him on the phone?"

"I'll try," I said, dialling the number. When Brian answered, I handed over the handset.

It was not a pleasant conversation concluding with "fucking useless travel agents, I'll sue you when we return."

Thankfully, Irena saved the day.

There was an apartment available in her block.

I took Sean and his wife across the road.

"Don't mind him," said his pretty redhead wife. "I'm Eire. His bark is worse than his bite."

"Not when he needs to be," said Sean, scowling. "And this is disgraceful; we won't return here again."

"I'm sorry you feel that way," I said. "However, I'm providing exactly what the Kerrigan's requested. Wings Tours and Club 18-30 have used us for years; we seldom have complaints. Hopefully, you'll change your mind after a few days and some of our finest Cottage Pie."

The apartment on the second floor had an impressive balcony and a spacious kitchen-diner. The décor was traditional Spanish, with timber cupboards and floral armchairs. It was clean and had a massive dining table.

I regarded Sean. He was looking at his wife.

"Grand," said Eire.

Once they had settled into their assortment of rooms, the O'Leary family came into the bar for a drink to calm their nerves. They seemed concerned about Sean's happiness and were accustomed to deferring to him.

Sean continued to grumble. I continued to apologise and blame the Kerrigan's. The prognosis for their two-week stay was ominous. But I hadn't considered the Nerja effect.

Three days later, after copious sangrias on the beach, they relaxed and began to enjoy themselves. The Kerrigan affair seemed forgotten.

Sean and Eire entered the bar the following lunchtime with a huge bag.

"Prime Irish beef steaks," said Sean. "You'll find them an improvement on Cottage Pies."

They were delicious.

Thanks to the O'Leary clan, bar takings went through the roof, yet they were never intoxicated. The rest of the family was much more relaxed than Sean and soon forgot about the initial accommodation problem as the charms of Nerja's constant sunshine and intimate beaches went to work.

"Property expensive here," said Sean one night the following week.

"A lot cheaper than Dublin," I said. "What would you be needing?"

"Three beds and a sea view."

"How does brand new and er with fridge sound?" I said.

"Perfect," said Sean, laughing.

"There's one a short walk away," I said. "The price is between three and four million pesetas depending on plot size."

"Really?" said Sean. "In Dublin, you can't buy a garage for that, even with a view of the duck pond. When can I see it?"

Here we go again, I thought.

"I'll take you there in the morning."

After breakfast, Sean, his wife, and the other ten O'Leary family members crowded onto our terrace. I didn't bother to mention the crystal blue waters and azure sky. Nature spoke for me. They were keen to commit before returning home, so they signed up within hours for a large three-bedroom apartment on the top floor in the block at the back of La Hacienda with a view over the pool, gardens, and Burriana beach.

"You'll need to pay some sort of deposit," I said.

"I don't have a Spanish account," said Sean. "I'll phone my bank and instruct them to organise a transfer. Could I send it to your account, Robert? And you give it to the builder,"

"Mine?" I said, astonished as Sean would kill me for

ballsing up his holiday a week before. What a turnaround. Now, he wants to send me money.

The transfer was sent. The O'Leary's completed their holiday and returned to Ireland. A few days later, he called me to confirm safe receipt, and I forwarded it to Paco.

A year later, when the apartment was completed, the O'Leary clan came over to furnish it and move in. Their first celebration was to throw a party to which we were invited. For years afterwards, various family members regularly met in the Fontainebleau bar, cementing a warm friendship after what had started as a disaster. But my second commission cheque from Paco of another half a million pesetas changed my perspective on hostel management.

Maybe there was another more lucrative way of earning money in Spain.

CHAPTER 46

THE BRIDGE

The Lions Club held a garden party at a detached villa on the edge of El Capistrano belonging to Sydney Wolleck, a committee member and regular at Fontainebleau. He was a short, rotund man in his late sixties, having recently retired from his family-run camping site business in south England.

A thunderstorm drenched the area overnight, turning many country tracks into quagmires. As always, the sun prevailed, and we proceeded with a vast buffet, BBQ, music, and dancing as planned.

Dark clouds massed over the Sierra toward late afternoon, and another rainstorm appeared imminent. I had to leave anyway to collect friends from the airport. During our year in the UK in Cove, Geoff, Jacky, and their two children were neighbours. They were also butchers.

I set off around six as the heavens erupted. The streets were awash by the time I crossed the only bridge in Nerja on the way to Torrox Costa, where there was a long queue of traffic.

I dashed out of the car to take a quick look toward Punta Lara, only to see the usual trickle of a stream raging across the main road in torrents.

My new green Citroen GS had a fancy suspension. Perhaps it could get me through the torrent blocking the road. Why not? I thought and overtook the stationary line of cars to much hooting and jeering. I stopped before the water, gauged the depth and scratched my head. Would it or not? I set the highest position, waited while the car rose smoothly, engaged first gear and slowly drove into the river, keeping everything crossed. I crawled out the other side unscathed, stopped and looked back to see a crowd of onlookers standing by their cars, probably hoping I would sail down the river and onto the beach. They roared and gave me various hand signs, some favourable, others not.

I returned the suspension to normal and drove on. I didn't go far. At Calaceite, a kilometre further, the hillside had slipped down and blocked the road. There was just enough room to navigate past the block, except the swirling stream of sliding mud looked particularly nasty. I rode my luck and managed to drive through on the middle setting.

This obstacle course continued to Málaga airport, and it took me over three hours to arrive. During this time, the rain was constant, the thunder continuous, and the lightning flashed so often that it lit up the sky.

There was only one terminal. It was built during the sixties to a typically dull Franco specification, with grey cladding, single glazing, low ceilings, and poor air conditioning that, even in winter, couldn't cope with the combination of body heat and sunshine. There was talk of a second terminal, but like many grand Spanish infrastructure projects, it would take over a decade to become a reality.

I parked the car, which had now changed colour from green to a fine blend of beige and brown, and walked into the terminal, where I bumped into Ann, our Wings rep.

"Robert," she gasped. "Have you heard the news? The bridge over the river at Nerja is down."

"I'm not surprised. How on earth are we going to get back," I asked.

"I have clients for Rincon and Torre del Mar before the Fontainebleau, so I have no choice but to take the usual route and pray they have fixed the bridge, but you could go via Granada."

"But that will take hours."

"There are no alternatives, but at least you should get through."

The plane bringing my friends had been diverted to Seville, but thankfully, the delayed Wings flight arrived minutes before the airport was temporarily closed. I had no choice but to wait, so I offered my services to Ann.

We stood by the railing outside the only exit door from the customs hall. It was a prominent position and easily visible. The brand-new mechanical arrivals board to the side clicked every minute or so with updated flight status. It was the first time I had seen such new technology, and I was staggered by how many different airports were flying into Malaga.

I counted the number of meeters and greeters, including taxi drivers, private individuals, and tour company representatives holding up signs. There were at least thirty.

"In summer, there are over a hundred," said Ann. "It's unbearable, and we all complain bitterly about the lack of air conditioning. It's hardly welcoming to our visitors."

"The Brits won't notice," I said. "Their first reaction will be Yippee, it's hot."

"Not today."

"And that, of course, will be our fault."

"Welcome to the world of group travel."

"How long before they are through?"

"They landed two hours late, but the luggage will take a while. I anticipate another thirty minutes. Why don't you get a coffee?"

"Do you want one?"

"No, I'm okay. I must keep my liquids down, as the bus has no toilets. And I will be busy answering questions; I dare not leave the group even for a minute."

"Good advice, I'll skip it. What are their usual questions?"

"Sadly, some people have no sense of direction and are completely disoriented. I must treat them like children, but it's okay because they are too scared to wander off. The worst are those who think they know it all and ignore my instructions. I try categorising them as incapable or competent as they approach me."

"How?"

"When they start coming through, you'll know immediately."

"How can I help?"

"Take them to the marshalling point by the exit. Show them the toilets and where to change money. Once comfortable, they must wait until we have everyone and can summon the bus."

"Your office told me there are twelve in this group?"

"Yes, and I can confirm they all boarded at Luton, but I have twenty-seven for other hotels."

"Do you ever lose any?"

"No, but if their luggage goes astray like Hancock, it can take ages for them to register at the lost luggage window, and they keep everybody waiting. Tempers can fray if they have small children or are elderly and need to sit down. These are all the things to take into consideration. If there is a long delay, I must find a payphone and call the bus parking. The driver must be informed as he is only allocated half an hour of free parking outside arrivals. In summer, the phones are so busy that it's quicker to walk."

"Fingers crossed then."

"Everything crossed," said Ann, grimacing.

"This is worse than Southend on Sea in winter," said a smartly dressed middle-aged couple approaching. "We're the Brayshaws. It didn't mention monsoons in the brochure."

Ann ticked them off without comment. I led them over to the marshalling point, explained the routine and returned for the next.

Half an hour later, I walked them to the bus and waved goodbye. It was still raining, so heaven knows when I will see them again. If they were grumpy now, I couldn't imagine how they would be after a ten-hour bus ride to Nerja.

Eventually, the diverted flight from Seville landed at Málaga, and I greeted my friends, who were as white as a sheet and the children exhausted.

"I thought it was always sunny in Spain," they exclaimed. They had never travelled abroad before.

"It usually is for over 320 days a year. Unfortunately, your timing is a bit out," I said.

I called the hostel to inquire about the state of the bridge. La Rubia confirmed it had sunk in the middle and was closed.

We drove from Málaga to Granada, down to Motril, and turned right along the coast road through Almuñecar, La Herradura, eventually arriving in Nerja at five in the morning. By this time, the car looked like it had been in the East African Safari Rally. Despite continual floods, detours and traffic queues, my friends slept most of the way. On the other hand, I loved racing along inland roads covered with brown torrents of flood water, landslides and fallen trees.

As I entered Nerja, I drove straight to the bridge to check if I hadn't driven halfway around Andalucía for nothing.

It was indeed down, and despite the time of the day, there were still long traffic queues on both sides, including our Wings coach on the wrong side.

The local council hadn't wasted time. JCBs and earth-moving equipment were carving a path down from each side of the road leading to the bridge to create a drivable passageway for the traffic to pass. This included dumping lorry loads of earth to build up a surface above the still-raging river.

By mid-morning, traffic started to pass in both directions. The Wings coach eventually got across and made its way to the Fontainebleau. I hadn't slept and was there to greet and console the weary guests.

"Welcome to the Fontainebleau," I said. "Where the sun always shines."

"A wide range of expletives was the reply."

We issued room keys quickly and carried their luggage to their room. Within minutes, they were asleep.

As a result of the bridge collapse, Nerja Council accelerated its plans to build a new bridge. However, it still took months, so the makeshift track engineered to circumnavigate the sunken bridge remained for quite a while.

CHAPTER 47

GIVE ME THE FINGER

An ear-splitting scream reverberated around the Fontainebleau patio. Vicky dropped the glass she was drying in the sink behind the bar and rushed out with me to see who the perpetrator was.

It was Syreeta, our dearest daughter, who was only three years old.

She was lying on the floor, a patio table on its side next to her, and holding her finger. A pool of blood spread slowly across the floor.

"I'll call the ambulance," I said.

"No," said Vicky, comforting our sobbing daughter. "It will take too long. She's lost the top of her finger and is bleeding out. Fetch the First Aid box. We must stop the blood flow, then drive her straight to the doctor."

Vicky bandaged up the finger as best she knew how. I carried a sobbing Syreeta out of the car, and we set off for the doctor's house on Calle Carabeo. We headed down Calle Pintada, using a white handkerchief to wave out the window to indicate we had an emergency and were in a hurry. This was customary in those days. However, despite my frantic arm movements, other vehicles couldn't get out of the way, given the narrow one-way street.

I double-parked outside the doctor's house. We rushed in yelling, *"Médico, médico, rápido"*. Doctor Don Carlos rushed out of his surgery, startled by the noise. He attended to us immediately and unwrapped Vicky's handiwork. He took one look and said, "I can do nothing here. She would be best in hospital. Take her to Urgencias in Málaga."

We set off along the busy coastal road with Vicky cuddling Syreeta and me waving furiously. The handkerchief had more effect on the main road, but it took two hours to reach the Carlos Haya Hospital in the city centre. I stopped outside the emergency entrance, and Vicky rushed in with Syreeta while I parked the car.

"Give me the finger?" said the doctor, who attended to them immediately. "I can sew it back on."

In the heat of the moment when Syreeta had cried out, it never occurred to us to look for the rest of the finger. We just had to get to a doctor. I called Antonio, our regular taxi driver in Nerja. I asked him to go to the Fontainebleau, pick up anything resembling a finger on the patio and drive like hell for Carlos Haya.

Antonio did not bat an eyelid at such an unusual request. He arrived with the tip wrapped in a bandage and presented it to the doctor.

He took it away, returning several minutes later, shaking his head.

"Sorry," he said. "It's too late. We'll have to make the best of what's left." He stitched the end of the finger and applied a bandage. We would need a local doctor to change it regularly.

We returned home several hours later with a sleepy daughter. When we returned to the Fontainebleau the next day, Syreeta held her hand high to everyone, pointing to her bandaged finger.

On the patio was a low, wooden outdoor coffee table with rounded legs, making it a little unstable and top-heavy. Syreeta had been playing with a doll on the table when she dropped it. On trying to retrieve it, she leaned down towards the floor, only for her weight to topple the table over. Instinctively, she spread her arms out to break her fall and hit the floor with them outspread simultaneously. The table edge landed on the index finger of her left hand and sliced the end off.

"Is she alright?" inquired a young dark-haired man in Spanish carrying a clipboard.

"Yes, thanks," I said. "Minus the end of a finger but recovering."

I nodded at his clipboard. "Can I help you with anything?"

"What, er... thanks, just coffee," said the clipboard man, smiling at Syreeta. "We are a film crew making a new TV series set in Nerja. I'm the assistant director, and we're filming the first scene up the street. She is so cute."

"Thanks, what's it about?" I asked.

"It's called Verano Azul. It's a fictional story of a group of children, Bea, Desi, Javi, Quique, Piraña, and Tito, who spend summer with their parents in Nerja. They meet Pancho, a local boy, a milk delivery man; Julia, a painter; and Chanquete, an old fisherman. Today, we're filming the first episode of many. It leads to friendships that make this summer the most important of their lives. We've been looking for locations throughout Spain and decided Nerja offers the perfect background for the story."

"When is it due for broadcasting?" I said.

"Sometime next year. It will go out all over Spain and probably South America.

"That'll put Nerja on the map," I said.

"We expect so," said the assistant director.

Indeed, it did. The series was a huge success and attracted Spanish-speaking tourists to seek out where the scenes were shot. The cast also regularly returned for reunions and holidays. The series was translated into other languages, further boosting foreign tourism. It is still regularly re-shown here in Spain today.

When the actor Antonio Ferrandis, who played the children's favourite fisherman, Chanquete, died, the whole town mourned, and flags flew at half-mast.

CHAPTER 48

WHY NERJA?

The number of Fontainebleau customers returning year after year was becoming increasingly evident. Most came for their regular fortnight, and while their first few visits were with Wings, many now booked directly. Having initially stayed with us, two of our regular families, O'Leary's and Harris's, were now well established in their properties within close walking distance of the hotel. Despite the growing number of new bars and restaurants, they preferred spending their evenings with us and had become friends rather than customers. I asked them to identify why the Fontainebleau drew them back so often.

"We like the ambience, music, pricing and familiar company," said George Harris, sitting at the bar one lunchtime. "You know what we drink and all about us, so we don't have to go through the getting-to-know-you routine."

"And the cottage pies aren't too shabby," added his wife, Cheryl. "But I think the bigger question is, why do we keep returning to Nerja? This is our fifth year on the trot."

"We do go to other destinations," said George. "For example, we were in Paris and Vienna earlier this year for weekend breaks. We love historical buildings and the food, but while they were fascinating places, nothing makes us relax more than a beach holiday. The combination of guaranteed sunshine, a gentle paddle and a leisurely fish lunch while wriggling our toes in the sand touches the spot. Like at the Fontainebleau, the beach restaurants are family-run; the staff don't change and have come to know us as old friends. We feel part of their family as they do ours."

"It's not just that," said Cheryl. "It combines many little things that make Nerja extra special. The charming, unspoiled, narrow streets are so clean and well-maintained. There are few high rises and a crime-free environment. Prices of everything are incredibly cheaper than back home, so we never have to worry about the cost of anything before ordering the finest champagne, lobster or a special gift to take back for Auntie Doris. Should we fancy it, there is an incredible range of day trips from the wonders of old Arab cities such as Granada and Córdoba to the magnificent cathedral in Málaga. The gastronomic experience varies from a delicious free tapa with your drink to succulent acorn-fed Iberian ham or Manchego cheese, and the fresh fish is to die for. We could go hiking in the mountains if we were athletically minded."

"Or dance until dawn in one of the amazing nightclubs," said George. "And those spectacular festivals. I'll never forget when you and Vicky escorted us to watch the Easter processions, and San Isidro was the ultimate family day experience."

"Turkey, for example," said Cheryl. "Is also beautiful, friendly, inexpensive, and hot. Along with Greece, Cyprus, and Malta, they need much longer flights. While we enjoyed our holidays there, they can't compete with the warm welcome and familiarity of Nerja."

"I feel more at home here than back in London," said George. "When I walk down the street or commute to work, I never see a happy face or bump into anyone I know. In Nerja, even though I'm only here for six odd weeks a year, I can't move more than a few metres from the house without seeing a familiar smiling face saying good morning in many different languages."

"In Turkey, I feel I am just passing through," said Cheryl. "Yes, I'll have a wonderful time, but there isn't the emotional engagement. Here, I feel I've put down roots. Both of us would spend more time here if we could."

"But we can't abandon the jewellery business," said George. "Robert, perhaps you could give some thought about how we could earn money here using our facilities in the UK?"

"What do you know about Real Estate?" I asked.

"Not much, but we could learn," said George.

"Food for thought," I said, topping up their glasses.

CHAPTER 49

IN LOVE WITH A BEAUTIFUL WOMAN

The 1979 season was drawing to a close. Most rooms were vacant, but the bar was crowded with the usual locals enjoying an evening drink.

"Has anybody not bought a Lions Club Christmas Raffle ticket," I announced. "Vicky has purchased a few, all in charity's best interests. How many can I put you down for?"

"I'll take half a dozen," said Ian Anderson, sitting on a bar stool. He was a mid-height, slender man with mousy hair in his late fifties. After selling his newspaper chain of shops in the West Midlands, he had recently retired to Nerja and adopted The Fontainebleau as his favourite watering hole.

"So will we," said Charles. "What's the prize this year?"

"A 50cc moped," I said. "Perfect for solving parking problems. Jam it between the nearest cars and go about your business."

"Will I need a licence for it?" said Ian.

"Probably," said Charles. "But I wouldn't worry unduly. Nobody bothers with mere trifles such as moped legalities. I saw a guy driving one in the rain last week. He steered with one hand and held his brolly up with the other. His young daughter clung to his back, and he gripped a shopping bag between his thighs."

"Multipurpose vehicles, mopeds," I said. "It will make an excellent prize. We could use one for emergency grocery purchases or to pop into the liquor store when Rowcroft has drunk all the vodka. By the way, you are all invited to our annual New Year's Eve Party. It's our way of thanking you for your custom. Everything is provided, including party hats, streamers, and ghastly noisemakers."

"Thanks," said Charles. "When is the draw?"

"New Year's Day," I said. "On the Balcón at midday."

"Should have recovered by then," said Rowcroft.

"To kick off the Festive Season," I said. "Here is your first musical treat. I changed the disc from, *When You're in Love with a Beautiful Woman* by Dr Hook to *Merry Christmas* by Slade.

After initial jeers and mock vomiting, they were soon singing along.

As the record ended, I spotted a familiar figure entering the bar. Our eyes met, and she waved at me. For a moment, I couldn't figure out who it was. Then it clicked.

"My God," I said, pouring a pint.

"Not like you to express religious sentiments," said Vicky, drying glasses.

"See the beautiful woman by the door with Michel, the flamboyant French estate agent you fancy," I said. "It's my first girlfriend, Alison."

"You never mentioned her."

"Nothing to say. We were fourteen, maybe fifteen. I haven't seen her for over ten years."

"Where did you meet?"

"During the sixties, my parents and I cruised on 'RMS Andes,' a luxury liner out of Southampton. We visited ports from Vigo to Gibraltar and on into the Mediterranean. For three years, we reunited with other regulars we met during the first year. After the final voyage, I tried to keep in touch and even visited her once at her home in Broadstairs, Kent, but we lost touch. I never expected to see her again, especially here."

"Then you better say Hola. No kissing, and don't take long. We're inundated."

"You recognised me," I said after pushing through the crowd.

"You've hardly changed a bit, except for the beard. What are you doing in Nerja?"

"This is our family hotel. How about you?"

"I'm visiting Michel. We met in France during the summer."

"An incredible coincidence."

"Amazing."

"Why is the pretty lady behind the bar glaring at me?"

"That's Vicky, my wife and mother of my daughter Syreeta."

"Congratulations. I'm single. Imagine, things could have turned out different if you'd bothered to keep in touch."

"That goes for both of us."

"True."

"Never mind, nothing we can do about it. Now you have Michel. I'm sure he's a more than adequate replacement."

"Don't mind me," said Michel in his charming French accent. "Now she knows you are no longer available, perhaps. She will marry me?"

"In your dreams," said Alison.

"A man has to try," said Michel.

She's beckoning," said Alison.

"Sorry. I have to go; we're hectic. It was lovely to see you again. Come and see me when we are quieter for a catch-up."

We hugged briefly. I returned to work.

"I can see you still like her," said Vicky as I resumed filling beer glasses.

"Everyone fondly remembers their first kiss. Don't you?"

"Mmm," said Vicky. "When are you taking me on a cruise?"

Alison never came back. With the buildup to Christmas and the New Year's Eve party, I was too busy to dwell on how much I had loved her as a teenager.

This was our third *Noche Viejo* celebration. We still didn't have any guests at Christmas, but a growing number of property owners flew out for the week, so we were frantically busy.

We provided a buffet meal with party bags for all. Without exception, all the customers were sporting silly hats and streamers and blowing their paper trumpets.

Most paced themselves well, but one of Ted Bartlett's group, who fancied himself as a Spanish wine connoisseur, had somewhat overdone it. Ted had a quiet word in my ear.

"No more wine for my friend; serve him water; he's had so much he won't notice the difference.

"What if he does?"

"Tell him it was a joke, but he won't."

Strangely, I was sure he appeared even more drunk. How the mind plays tricks, I thought. When it was time to depart, Ted asked his friend how the wine was. He looked slightly bemused at Ted's question. Ted laughed aloud and told him he'd been drinking water for the last three hours. The friend said it was impossible; he'd know the difference. So, Ted asked me to confirm it. When I did, the guy's face was a picture.

I turned off the taps at eleven thirty. We joined everyone at the Balcón for the Final Countdown and munched our twelve grapes as the clock struck.

We gathered on the Balcón at noon on New Year's Day under a clear blue sky. Graham Maynard, the current President of the Lions Club, stood outside the cinema holding a bucket packed with ticket stubs next to Mayor Antonio Jiménez Gálvez and various dignitaries.

Syreeta was invited to select the winning ticket. She pulled one out and shouted the winning number.

"*Madre mia*," screamed Vicky. "I've won."

Whoops, I thought, looking around in total shock. I'd sold her the ticket, and my daughter had drawn it. Several surprised and suspicious-looking faces were looking accusingly in my direction. Some comments suggested a stitch-up, but I deemed them unworthy of defending. They'd never believe me anyway, even though it is genuine.

The moped lasted for years.

CHAPTER 50

WISH YOU WERE HERE

The future of Spain was starting to feel rosy. It had been four long years since Franco died. Spain was emerging from decades of economic and mental depression under his dictatorship, and Democracy was slowly evolving. We had survived family turmoil and several disasters. Our relationship with tour operators was well established, and during high season, we generated enough to see us through the winter. However, I never forgot how many times we thought we'd made it, only for there to be another setback or unforeseen drama.

We had practically reformed every room because the original builder had been incompetent. On the other hand, if we hadn't met Emilio de Miguel, we wouldn't have discovered the half-built hostel and the Fontainebleau wouldn't have existed. It was easy to criticise our mistakes and lack of experience, but somehow, we'd managed this far with perseverance, stubborn doggedness, and a touch of luck. Despite all this, I could never stop worrying about what might be around the corner.

It was one of those rare occasions when all our family members were in Nerja simultaneously. It was hardly surprising because there were so many of us and we needed many valuable rooms. I was conscious that I'd become my father.

We were gathered around the bar dressed in shorts and t-shirts, sitting on stools with children on various laps. My eldest sister, Gloria, her husband, Fred, and daughters, Tracy, Nicky, and Natalie. My other sister, Diane, is with her husband Colin, and their children are Julie, Brian, Leslie, and Carol. Jim returned after building a successful removal company with his wife Jenny, Jim Junior, Samantha, and Steven, their latest addition. Vicky is holding Syreeta, myself, Mum, and Dad behind the bar. It was a huge Edwards occasion to treasure, yet we were discussing the never-ending problem of how to attract visitors in the low season.

We were interrupted by a man with long hair. He resembled a hippy, minus the flowers and bells.

"Excuse me," he said in BBC English, confident. "I need to talk with the manager."

"Concerning?" said Vicky.

"My name is Nigel. I'm the assistant producer for an English TV consumer series. We'd like to include your hostel in our next program about the Costa del Sol."

"I'm the owner," I said, feeling astounded. Was this my luck running again? "What do you need us to do?"

"Oh, er... cool. Are you happy if I return the day after tomorrow with our film crew?"

"Of course. Should we prepare anything special?"

"Could you summarise key points such as contact

details for the hostel and your UK Tour Operator, distance from the airport, a bit about Nerja, beaches, highlights, and prices for a week or fortnight's stay? While our narrator describes all that. We'll be filming your bar and restaurant. Can you provide some people pretending to enjoy themselves? Then we'll shoot one of the bedrooms with a presentable chambermaid cleaning it."

"Anything we should avoid?" I said.

"No drunks in the bar, but otherwise, go about your business as usual."

"What's the name of the series," said Gloria.

"Oh, didn't I say? It's for ITV and is called Wish You Were Here. The narrator is Judith Chalmers, and it's one of our most popular programs. You should be prepared for a massive influx of Brits almost immediately after the show is broadcast."

"I see," said Vicky. "When does it go out?"

"In a month."

"How long will the filming take?" I said. "We don't want to disturb our guests."

"It doesn't take long, but setting up the lighting and equipment does. Have you somewhere we could park our truck?"

"There is a cul de sac to the side of the hostel. We'll make sure there is a space available."

"Great, thanks. Here is my card should you have any further questions."

"Wonderful," I said. "Here is our card. See you on Tuesday. What time will you be arriving?"

"Around midday, and please don't change any timings. We're on a tight schedule and must be out of here by four p.m. to arrive at the next hotel while there is plenty of light."

"See you on Tuesday," I said.

We remained calmly looking at each other with silly grins, watching Nigel leave. As soon as we judged him out of earshot, we leapt into a family hug, jumping up and down with glee. For the Edwards to express any outward emotion was an extremely rare moment, even for Jim.

"Ok, ok," I said. "Enough. Any ideas about how we prepare?"

"Pick an available room to film and decide who will be the chambermaid," said Mum. "And we need people to be enjoying themselves in the bar."

"I'll ask Irena to clean the place top to bottom until it gleams," said Vicky.

"And you can be the pretty chambermaid," I said. "See if you fit in one of the uniforms."

"Cheeky bugger."

"And the whole family can be the beautiful people in the bar," said Dad. "We won't have to pretend anything."

"When are they coming?" I said.

"Tuesday, midday," said Vicky. "They need to park their truck in the cul de sac."

"Then we have a serious problem."

"What?"

"Tuesday is market day; access will be impossible until after three pm."

"They have to depart by four," said Vicky. "What can we do?"

"Don't worry," I said. "I'll deal with the market traders."

By Tuesday morning, the hostel gleamed inside and out.

It cost me dear, but for the first and only occasion,

the market stalls usually set up at the entrance to our street were moved to the far end of Calle Cristo. I expected they would make more money from me than their usual sales turnover, so everyone was happy.

The TV truck arrived bang on time, and the local police directed them straight into the cul-de-sac. The producer loved the market, and while the technicians set up the lighting in the bar and bedroom, the cameraman and sound engineer recorded some typical market scenes before shooting the hostel exterior.

Finally, they were all set.

The family enjoyed being themselves, sitting at the bar while I served drinks. When the producer was happy with the footage, Vicky dashed to the first floor and changed into the maid's uniform. Unfortunately, we didn't meet Judith Chalmers. Her narration, describing the delights and costs of staying at Fontainebleau, was to be recorded in the UK studios.

They sent us a video of the final cut. It was fantastic, and we waited nervously until it was due to be shown on live TV.

Which was a problem.

There was still no British TV in Spain. How could we watch it? Gloria suggested we phone her when the episode was showing, and we could listen in, which is what we did. Only when I heard The Fontainebleau on air did I believe it had happened.

The response was almost instant. The phone never stopped ringing.

The postman delivered letters to 'The Fontainebleau, Spain'; somehow, they found us.

Bookings did indeed go through the roof, but others would reap the long-term success.

CHAPTER 51

A NEW DIRECTION

The euphoria of fame didn't linger. After all the excitement, returning to behind the bar and the usual routine of pouring drinks while listening to sob stories left a sour taste in my mouth. The increase in trade eased the pain, especially when reservations started pouring in for winter. But only half of me was delighted; the rest cringed about the prospect of year-round drunken maudlin. What a price to pay for building a successful business. It spurred me to consider my conversations with George and Cheryl Harris.

If I could earn a million pesetas by introducing two buyers to Paco Rico, imagine how much more I could do working full-time at it. To put that in perspective. One million pesetas covered the mortgage for two years, including a lavish lifestyle. I could pay a large deposit on a luxury car, and all those dreams I had as a twenty-year-old driving down to start work at the Fontainebleau would have come true. I shook my head; surely there must be a more fulfilling way to earn money than wiping these glasses.

Not for the first time, I considered the strengths and weaknesses of the existing real estate businesses in town. Capistrano were by far the most successful, but they had to be. With an enormous team of builders to pay, they needed weekly sales to generate enough cash flow; to do so, their UK advertising spending was considerable. I wasn't going to be a developer. Yes, there were large rewards but enormous risks. What if the market turned halfway through a project? Another weakness of their business is that not all attending weekend inspection flights purchased anything. They declined for various reasons but mainly because it was a long way from the beach and the attractions of the town centre. Buyers had many dreams, but not all wanted to holiday in an urbanisation full of English-speaking people. They preferred a more genuine Spanish environment.

I ran down the list of other property sales organisations in the town, which were mainly Spanish and struggled to communicate in English. The only real competitor was Charles, but he relied on passing trade. I decided the best way forward was to start a traditional estate agency and promote a personalised property-finding service to UK buyers in their home market. Miguel, the fisherman, would then track down what they wanted.

I tossed and turned in my bed that night. As the idea grew, I became more convinced that this was what I wanted to do. I had the money to set it up; it was just a matter of convincing George and Cheryl to handle the UK activities. They would do the marketing and send clients. Occasionally, they could accompany them and spend longer in their beloved Nerja. I found the properties that matched the client's requirements, and we divided the commissions.

I only had to wait a few weeks to discuss my idea with George and Cheryl. Rather than meet in the bar, I took them to dinner at Udo Heimer's restaurant. They were easily convinced and agreed to establish the London office next to George's brother John's printing business and advertise in the national press.

With Miguel, the fisherman's help, George and I opened our first office in Nerja on Calle Pintada opposite Kronox.

All I had to do was find a buyer for the Fontainebleau.

EPILOGUE

FIFTY YEARS ON

By the middle of 1980, our hostel was fully booked all year. Our objective had been achieved, and the thriving business had a value worth selling. My family sold the Fontainebleau in 1980 to Ian Anderson, a regular customer in the bar who had been a close observer of our success.

I established a property business with George Harris, which went from strength to strength as Nerja rapidly expanded.

Ian owned the hostel until the 1990s when, much to the concern of his two children who ran the place, he went completely off the rails with alcoholism and spiralled downhill. He went bankrupt in 1996 when Andy Pryor, a businessman from Inverness, took it over. He ran out of money before his plan to upgrade the hostel to a boutique establishment could be completed. Due to the collaboration of Spanish bureaucracy and nobody around to pay lawyers to resolve the mess, the half-finished building sat abandoned, with the upstairs open to the elements. Years later, a Spanish hotel company bought the ruin from the bank, demolished it, and started from scratch. It is now a luxury Aparthotel known as Toboso Plaza.

The Fontainebleau was basic by comparison, but for just over twenty years, the old wreck of a building had played a massive role in kick-starting Nerja tourism from zero to over 176,000 annual visitors, with 40,000 coming in August alone, almost doubling the standing population. Today, it is rated among the top ten Spanish resorts.

Many years later, we repurchased my father's Rolls Royce. Well, sort of. My daughter, Syreeta, raised the subject, wondering where it might have ended its days. I told her it had been sold to someone in America. She suggested we could search for it on the Internet, which was still in its infancy. Within four hours, I tracked down the car via various Rolls Royce Clubs and talked to its third owner in the States over the phone. My brother showed interest, so I negotiated a price. Eventually, he bought the car and imported it back to the UK. He re-registered the vehicle with its original number plate, AFC 27. Sadly, my parents weren't around to see it.

Thousands of people had enjoyed their first night in Spain at the Fontainebleau. They returned year after year with their kids and then grandchildren. It was where I learned Spanish, met my wife and brought up our first child. A little later, two more would come along, Scott and Tanya.

Each time I walk past the elegant façade of the Aparthotel, I pause outside the unchanged Bar Bilbainos, still going strong after fifty years, and take a trip down memory lane.

Occasionally, a tear dampens my cheek when my ageing brain flashes back to our happy times there. We belted out great sounds until the early morning, such as Abba, Pink Floyd, Stones, Beatles, Motown, and more.

The initial Irish invasion swelled to thousands. Today, there is at least one Irish wedding a week in the church, with photos taken on the Balcón from the exact locations we did.

The money we raised through treasure hunts for the Lions Club enabled us to donate an ambulance to the town. I could go on, but enough now. Memories of the Fontainebleau will remain with me forever. For many, it was the place where their love affair with Spain began. It is as much a part of me as I am of it.

ACKNOWLEDGEMENTS

Thanks to our editor Gary Smailes, cover designer Simon Thompson, Fran Poelman, La Rubia, Edwards family members and the good people of Nerja for their encouragement.

PAUL S BRADLEY - AUTHOR

The Bradley family has resided in Spain since 1974. Initially in Menorca, then relocated to Nerja in 1987. Paul ran a marketing agency from home, publishing guidebooks and lifestyle magazines in German, Spanish, and English. On retirement, he started the first of five novels in his Andalusian Mystery Series. His mother, Edna Bradley, arranged the flowers in the Fontainebleau during Ian Anderson's time. Bat Carrott, his brother-in-law, managed the refurbishment project during Andy Pryor's tenure, and his niece, Daisy, used to distribute leaflets.

ROBERT H EDWARDS - AUTHOR

Robert initially ran the Fontainebleau bar and restaurant but took over the management when his parents retired. After forty years in Real Estate and other businesses in and around Nerja and Málaga, Robert, now retired, continues a lifelong hobby of providing real estate photography services. He now lives in the neighbouring town of Torrox.

Printed in Great Britain
by Amazon